Ethics in Econometrics

Applied econometrics uses the tools of theoretical econometrics and real-word data to develop predictive models and assess economic theories. Owing to the complex nature of such analysis, various assumptions are often not understood by those people who rely on it. The danger of this is that economic policies can be assessed favorably to suit a particular political agenda and forecasts can be generated to match the needs of a particular customer. *Ethics in Econometrics* argues that econometricians need to be aware of potential ethical pitfalls when carrying out their analysis and that they need to be encouraged to avoid them. Using a range of empirical examples and detailed discussions of real cases, this book provides a guide for research practices in econometrics, illustrating why it is imperative that econometricians act ethically in terms of the way they conduct their analysis and treat their data.

PHILIP HANS FRANSES is Professor of Applied Econometrics at the Erasmus University Rotterdam. He is a fellow of the *Journal of Econometrics*, the *Journal of Applied Econometrics*, the *International Journal of Forecasting*, and the Royal Netherlands Academy of Arts and Sciences. He has published monographs and textbooks with Cambridge University Press.

Ethics in Econometrics

A Guide to Research Practice

PHILIP HANS FRANSES

Erasmus University Rotterdam

CAMBRIDGE
UNIVERSITY PRESS

CAMBRIDGE
UNIVERSITY PRESS

Shaftesbury Road, Cambridge CB2 8EA, United Kingdom

One Liberty Plaza, 20th Floor, New York, NY 10006, USA

477 Williamstown Road, Port Melbourne, VIC 3207, Australia

314–321, 3rd Floor, Plot 3, Splendor Forum, Jasola District Centre, New Delhi – 110025, India

103 Penang Road, #05–06/07, Visioncrest Commercial, Singapore 238467

Cambridge University Press is part of Cambridge University Press & Assessment, a department of the University of Cambridge.

We share the University's mission to contribute to society through the pursuit of education, learning and research at the highest international levels of excellence.

www.cambridge.org
Information on this title: www.cambridge.org/9781009428040

DOI: 10.1017/9781009428033

© Philip Hans Franses 2025

First published 2025

A catalogue record for this publication is available from the British Library

Library of Congress Cataloging-in-Publication Data
Names: Franses, Philip Hans, 1963– author.
Title: Ethics in econometrics : a guide to research practice / Philip Hans Franses, Erasmus University.
Description: Cambridge, United Kingdom ; New York, NY : Cambridge University Press, 2025. | Includes bibliographical references and index.
Identifiers: LCCN 2023047193 | ISBN 9781009428040 (hardback) | ISBN 9781009428033 (ebook)
Subjects: LCSH: Econometrics – Methodology – Moral and ethical aspects.
Classification: LCC HB139 .F7225 2025 | DDC 330.01/5195–dc23/eng/20231110
LC record available at https://lccn.loc.gov/2023047193

ISBN 978-1-009-42804-0 Hardback
ISBN 978-1-009-42807-1 Paperback

Contents

Figures

Tables

Preface

This book provides various guidelines for proper econometric research practice. There are some general ethical issues that hold for any research practice, but for econometricians there are various additional ones. This is because those who receive our advice most often are not econometricians, and the associated knowledge gap can be large. We therefore need their trust. This can be achieved by obeying various ethical guidelines such as making data and code available, and at the same time making explicit which choices were made. Econometricians make choices concerning data, samples, methods, models, estimation routines, and more. Using a range of empirical examples, and sometimes simulated data, this book shows that there can be many choices to make, that results are path dependent, and that such knowledge is important in research practice.

The running thread throughout this book is that the application of econometric methods and techniques requires us to make choices, and that ethics in econometrics involves that these choices are well articulated and well documented.

The topics in this book in part draw on my own academic work and experience but most often from my experience with supervision of students. Master students at the Econometric Institute in Rotterdam frequently embark on internships with companies or institutions. These internships concern questions that these parties have, and these questions can address macroeconomics, finance, marketing, charity, transport and much more. During these internships, the students become acquainted with practical questions, asked by people who are not familiar with econometrics, and they encounter databases and real report writing. Rarely if ever are the databases complete and fully free from measurement error, or are the questions precisely articulated, and sometimes the results are not what management would have hoped for. Yet the advisees are always happy with the new insights when the student outlines step by step how the results were obtained.

This book is not a standalone textbook: The reader is expected to have knowledge of basic statistical and econometric methods and techniques. There are many good textbooks around, and at times this book suggests further reading and consultation of such books. There is no econometric theory in this book and there are no proofs of the usefulness of methods. In fact, the book draws on the empirical analysis of actual data. The data are either presented in print in the book or are available from www.enjoyable-econometrics.com in Excel format. Many computations in this book were done using EViews version 12, but these could just as well have been done using any other similar computing package or by using R or Python code. The choice of the empirical cases is of course made by me, but no doubt there are many other cases with similar issues and there are also possible other issues than those dealt with in this book. Hence, this is a collection of guidelines, and it is certainly not the final collection.

At times, this book discusses cases of willful deception and of accidentally misleading behavior. All are based on publicly available information, either on the internet or otherwise in articles and books.

This book will be useful for applied researchers who want to learn what we can encounter in the real world outside textbooks. It will be useful for academics who use econometric methods for specific research questions. And it will be useful for students at masters and PhD level who want to gain awareness of aspects of proper research practice.

Acknowledgments

First, I want to thank the hundreds of students who chose me to be their internship and thesis supervisor over the last thirty or so years. I am also grateful to students Sean Gilbert and Carlijn Smeets for alerting me to a range of errors (textual and numerical) in previous versions of this manuscript. All remaining errors are of course mine.

I had great conversations with Richard Paap, Dick van Dijk, Robin Lumsdaine, and the late Alex Koning that shaped my thinking, writing, and presentation. Philip Good of Cambridge University Press and three anonymous reviewers provided helpful feedback on the first draft of the book. Finally, I thank Christiaan Heij, my book and MOOC colleague, who meticulously read all chapters and gave especially useful feedback on an initial version of the book.

Recommended Reading

The current book is not meant to be a standalone textbook but as a valuable addition once an introductory econometrics course has been completed. Useful textbooks that use specific econometric software are:

Baum, Christopher F. (2006), *An Introduction to Modern Econometrics Using Stata*, College Station, TX: Stata Corporation, Stata Press.

González-Rivera, Gloria (2012), *Forecasting for Economics and Business*, Abingdon: Routledge.

Vogelvang, Ben (2005), *Econometrics: Theory and Applications with E-Views*, Harlow: FT Prentice Hall.

Useful introductory textbooks on specific areas, such as time series or macroeconomics, are:

Favero, Carlo (2000), *Applied Macroeconometrics*, Oxford: Oxford University Press.

Lütkepohl, Helmut and Markus Krätzig (2004), *Applied Time Series Econometrics*, Cambridge: Cambridge University Press.

Patterson, Kerry (2000), *An Introduction to Applied Econometrics: A Time Series Approach*, Basingstoke: Macmillan Press.

And there is also some interesting further reading on ethics in:

Cave, Jonathan (2016), The ethics of data and data science: An economist's perspective, *Philosophical Transactions of the Royal Society, A*, 374, 20160117.

Dolfsma, Wilfred and Ioana Negru (2019, editors), *The Ethical Formation of Economists*, Abingdon: Routledge.

Franks, Bill (2020), *97 Things About Ethics Everyone in Data Science Should Know: Collective Wisdom from the Experts*, Sebastopol, CA: O'Reilly Media.

Levy, David M. and Sandra J. Peart (2008), Inducing greater transparency: Towards the establishment of ethical rules for econometrics, *Eastern Economic Journal*, 34 (1), 103–114.

Introduction

Econometricians develop and use methods and techniques to model economic behavior, create forecasts, do policy evaluation, and develop scenarios. Often, this ends up in some advice. This can be a prediction for the future or for another sector or country; it can be a judgment on whether a policy measure was successful or not; or it can offer a possible range of futures.

A recent example of a range of futures is provided by the econometricians of the Netherlands Bureau for Economic Policy Analysis (CPB) in March 2020, who sketch four scenarios, based on four types of contact restrictions (owing to COVID-19):[1]

Scenario 1: First signs of recovery in 2020. Production capacity retained, partly owing to government support package. Economic growth –1.2 in 2020 and 3.5 in 2021.

Scenario 2: Industry affected more severely. World trade declines further. Economic growth –5.0 in 2020 and 3.8 in 2021.

Scenario 3: Economic downturn lasts longer owing to more problems in global economy and financial sector. Economic growth –7.7 in 2020 and 2.0 in 2021.

Scenario 4: Recession lasts for one and a half years, partly owing to increased problems in the financial sector and abroad. Economic growth –7.3 in 2020 and –2.7 in 2021.

The actual figures for economic growth, known at the beginning of 2022, are –3.7 for 2020, and 4.8 for 2021, respectively. So, it seems that scenario 2 came closest, but that is of course with hindsight.

Like the four scenarios of the CPB, which were discussed in those days on mainstream media and social media, the advice of an

---

[1] www.cpb.nl/sites/default/files/omnidownload/CPB-Scenarios-March-2020-Scenarios-economic-consequences-corona-crisis.pdf.

econometrician is usually given to people who are not econometricians. Therefore, the advisees must trust the quality of the advice. Such trust can be gained by making data available, by allowing access to the programming code, by writing and presenting in a nontechnical manner, but then, still, there remains to be a gap as noneconometricians cannot check all this.

Econometricians (must) make choices that can only be understood by fellow econometricians. A key claim in this book is that it is important to be clear on those choices.

This book is about choices. More precisely, it will show how substantial their consequences can be, even though they might seem harmless in the beginning. Indeed, models can be useful and informative, but sometimes they are not. For example, forecasts can be made upon demand of the customer, and it is sometimes not difficult to make them look very reasonable or to make them align with the wishes of that (paying) customer. If a client wants to hear that profits go up next year, it is not too difficult to create a model and an associated forecast, even using actual data, that meets those wishes. If someone wants to show that a policy measure was unsuccessful, there are ways to make that happen, at least on paper.

If you know how to play around with your data and models, you can also recognize when someone else did something wrong (by accident or on purpose) and then you can ask the proper questions. So, one might think that the motto of this book benefits from the following quote:

> Think like a criminal to beat them at their own game.
> *Frank Abagnale Jr*[2]

Or how about this one?

> To catch the bad guys, you've got to think like a bad guy – and that's why all the best detectives have a dark side...
> *David Videcette, The Theseus Paradox*[3]

---

[2] www.information-age.com/criminal-frank-abagnale-jr-14183/.
[3] www.goodreads.com/quotes/8037583-to-catch-the-bad-guys-you-ve-got-to-think-like.

Indeed, in Chapter 2 we will encounter cases of scientific misconduct that could have gone unnoticed if the misconduct were conducted much better. Indeed, we will see that some by now classic misconduct cases were obviously geared by a shortage of knowledge on basic statistics by the deceivers. In fact, we will learn how to cheat better (so that of course in the end we learn not to do so).

And this leads to the key feature of ethical behavior in econometrics, and sound research practice, that you report all the choices you have made. Choices on the data, on the methods, on the methodology, and on the configurations in certain methods: One should report all the choices. For a regular MSc or PhD thesis or academic paper or business advice, this may make the number of pages unduly large, but then, the internet can store massive numbers of background appendices. This material should be well structured so that others can check and then redo the analysis. To report everything constitutes Ethics in Econometrics. In this book we shall see that this is not as trivial as it may sound, partly because there are so many choices to make.

This book has thirteen chapters (after the current one), with the last chapter summarizing what we have learned. Each chapter can be considered independently of what is presented in other chapters. Most chapters contain various empirical exercises to illustrate the main points. These empirical exercises are based on my own work, either academically or while consulting for companies and institutions. This also implies that many econometric methods and techniques will not be considered in this edition.[4] References to more theoretical background are given when relevant. Sometimes we rely on simulated data, where it is indicated how the simulations can be replicated. All chapters contain detailed discussions of real cases, with the data made available in Excel format. This allows for replication by the reader. Most computations were made using the

---

[4] To take just a few examples, the topics do not cover Bayesian analysis, panel data, vector autoregressions, and the interpretation of the coefficient of determination.

statistical package EViews, version 12. Some chapters additionally contain exercises to be done by the reader, which may be helpful in making the material more understandable. Each chapter contains some suggestions for further reading and/or presents the background material that was used to compile the main text.

A brief outline of each of the chapters follows. There is no strict order to the chapters, as each deals with different issues that can be relevant in research practice. In Chapter 1 we encounter what is commonly viewed as good practice. There are various guidelines available for research and advice, both in general as well as for focusing on the application of statistical methods. Note that the statistical approach here is the so-called classical (or frequentist) approach and not the Bayesian approach. Much of what holds for the classical approach in terms of ethics also holds for the Bayesian approach, but there are some differences too.

Chapter 2 gives some examples of bad practice or, better said, of scientific misconduct, which here amounts to creating fake data, fake tables with "results," and fake statistical summaries of data. This chapter thus deals with willful deception. We will learn that in various cases the bad practice was obvious and not at all difficult to detect. All cases are publicly available via the internet. We see in this chapter that simple methods can detect misconduct. We will also learn how apparent scientific misconduct could have been done "better" in the sense that the chances of discovery would have been smaller.

From Chapter 2 onwards, we encounter various situations that can be (accidentally) misleading but are not necessarily the result of willful deception. In Chapter 3 we learn that econometric analysis can be seriously distorted by (highly) influential observations. And there do not have to be many of them. They are influential in small samples and in large samples. Nonexistent results can appear owing to influential observations, while existent results can be made to disappear. In Chapter 3 we present methods that are used to discover such influential data points.

Chapter 4 deals with model selection. In practice it turns out that there is always more than one model that matches the data or gives decent forecasts. The question is whether we should try to end up with one final model to include in our advice, or whether we can better combine the models. It is quite common to combine forecasts, so perhaps combining the inference from different models would be better too. Indeed, if two individuals start with the same database, they will usually not end up with the same outcome.[5]

In Chapter 5 we encounter the situation in which a first designed model may suffer from some shortcomings. For example, one or more of the explanatory variables can be endogenous, which means that the error term in the model is correlated with these variables. This is not something that can be seen from the results, as the residuals are unknown and are usually one of the outcomes of the analysis. Endogenous variables require estimation via a method called Instrumental Variables. The next question is what are good instruments? This is not easy to define in practice, and inappropriate choices have devastating effects. Next to endogeneity, it can happen that variables are observed with measurement errors. Such errors can be ignored ("and also introduced" says the econometrician with a dark side), but it seems wise to take care of such measurement error. Another feature is so-called multicollinearity, which means that some explanatory variables are extremely correlated. What to do with such multicollinearity, and how to detect it?

In Chapter 6 we look at what happens if data are missing. There are several reasons why this can be the case. Some are problematic, others not so much. There are several ways to deal with missing data, and these have consequences for analysis and subsequent results. We

---

[5] In a recent interesting study by Albert J. Menkveld, Anna Dreber, Felix Holzmeister, Juergen Huber, Magnus Johannesson, Michael Kirchler, Sebastian Neusüss, Michael Razen, Utz Weitzel, and many others (2021), Non-standard errors, Tinbergen Institute Discussion Paper, TI 2021-102/IV, https://papers.ssrn.com/sol3/papers.cfm?abstract_id=3981597, the authors state: "Our working definition of non-standard errors is the standard deviation across researchers for the results they report when independently testing the same hypotheses on the same sample."

will see that interpolation impacts parameter estimates. The econometrician with a dark side can also choose to make certain data disappear, for example by choosing only the most recent observations when making forecasts.

In Chapter 7 we address spurious relations. Such relations are all too often found in practice, and they lead to distorted inference and inappropriate forecasts. We will see that this is due to, for example, ignoring dynamics, which leads to spurious results. Ignoring variables can also be the culprit. Cohort studies and panel studies are very vulnerable to spurious outcomes when dynamics are ignored. In fact, significant statistical results are easily found if one considers the wrong model.

The material in Chapter 8 may require the most practical econometric expertise for the reader to grasp the key issues. In this chapter we often resort to simulated data or an empirical analysis of real data and refer to theoretical studies at the end. Many economic variables have one or more of the following features. They can have a trend, show seasonality, have outlying observations, have periods where forecasts are easier to make than in other periods (alternating levels of volatility), or they may experience regime shifts (nonlinearity). It can happen, however, that ignoring outliers erroneously suggests nonlinearity or changing volatility. And ignoring structural breaks, can suggest the presence of a trend.

This makes the connection with Chapter 9, where we discuss the limits to predictability. That is, how far ahead can we predict? Weather forecasters often consider the next five days, but long-run forecasts sometimes concern decades. We will see that the accuracy of forecasts can depend on the chosen sample, and that the choice of the sample impacts confidence intervals around forecasts. If you do not want a potential outcome to lie within an interval, you can have a choice (which of course you should report and defend). These are not necessarily very new insights, but it is useful to reiterate here that reporting confidence intervals is a wise thing to do.

Often, forecasts from econometric models are manually adjusted. This can be for good reasons or for bad reasons. In Chapter 10 we look at the proper ways to do such manual adjustment. What are the effects on forecast intervals? What to do if manual adjustment is not reported? What if people did not use a model at all, but do not tell?

Since 2000, we have heard about a phenomenon called Big Data, which is indeed written with capital letters. Chapter 11 focuses on the situation when data become plentiful, and it is argued that choices now become even more important. Do we aggregate the data? Do we select observations from the data to make analysis easier? Do we cluster the data first before we consider a regression model? Are we doing all our computations using classical model-based statistics, or are we relying on the help of so-called machine learning algorithms? It turns out that Big Data entails many more choices, for example, the choice of parameter configurations for various machine learning methods. It might help to open the black box for some of these methods, and an illustration of an artificial neural network shows how this can be done.

The penultimate chapter, Chapter 12, zooms in on the question of what algorithms can do. Can outcomes from algorithms be trusted? Are they the way forward for much empirical analysis in the future? What is and will be the contribution of humans? And when racial or gender discrimination is at stake, is that to be blamed on the program code or on the programmer?[6] There is also the worrying issue that we sometimes see people using methods and techniques that they, themselves, barely seem to understand. Many applications of machine learning methods just use some R code that is available on the internet, and not everybody knows what the code does.

Chapter 13 reviews the lessons learned in this book. It shows that Ethics in Econometrics involves the explicit documentation of choices you have made. There may be many, but it must still be done.

---

[6] Have a look at this story: www.reuters.com/article/us-amazon-com-jobs-automation-insight-idUSKCN1MK08G, and see how algorithms can discriminate.

EPILOGUE

What rarely happens is that scientific misconduct is immediately obvious. Although, here is an example of obvious misconduct! In 1996, in the *Journal of Forecasting*, I published a paper with the then MSc student at our Econometric Institute, Dick van Dijk (who now is a full professor), with the title "Forecasting stock market volatility using (non-linear) GARCH models."[7] The abstract of this paper reads:

In this paper we study the performance of the GARCH model and two of its non-linear modifications to forecast weekly stock market volatility. The models are the Quadratic GARCH (Engle and Ng, 1993) and the Glosten, Jagannathan and Runkle (1992) models which have been proposed to describe, for example, the often-observed negative skewness in stock market indices. We find that the QGARCH model is best when the estimation sample does not contain extreme observations such as the 1987 stock market crash and that the GJR model cannot be recommended for forecasting.[8]

Google Scholar (consulted October 31, 2022) indicates that this paper has been cited 507 times.

In one of the early years of the 2000s, we were approached by a US-based PhD student who was looking at all studies on nonlinear GARCH models, and who indicated to us that there was another paper with strong similarities to ours. This is the study from Weixian Wei of Xiamen University, with the title "Forecasting stock market volatility with non-linear GARCH models: a case for China." The abstract of this paper reads:

---

[7] Key references to GARCH models are Robert F. Engle (1982), Autoregressive conditional heteroskedasticity with estimates of the variance of United Kingdom inflation, *Econometrica*, 50 (4), 987–1007 and Tim Bollerslev (1986), Generalized autoregressive conditional heteroskedasticity, *Journal of Econometrics*, 31 (3), 307–327.

[8] Philip Hans Franses and Dick J. C. van Dijk (1996), Forecasting stock market volatility using (non-linear) GARCH models, *Journal of Forecasting*, 15 (3), 229–235.

This paper studies the performance of the GARCH model and two of its non-linear modifications to forecast China's weekly stock market volatility. The models are the Quadratic GARCH and the Glosten, Jagannathan and Runkle models which have been proposed to describe the often-observed negative skewness in stock market indices. It is found that the QGARCH model is best when the estimation sample does not contain extreme observations such as the stock market crash, and that the GJR model cannot be recommended for forecasting.[9]

Google Scholar (consulted October 31, 2022) indicates that this paper has been cited 44 (!) times. And, even more interesting, the 1996 *Journal of Forecasting* article is not cited in this 2002 paper!

Let us have a look at the first paragraph of the original 1996 paper:

A stylized fact of financial time series is that aberrant observations seem to cluster in the sense that there are periods where volatility is larger than in other periods. Typically, these volatile periods correspond to major (economic) events such as stock market crashes and oil crises. Although most evidence in empirical finance indicates that returns on financial assets seem unforecastable at short horizons (see e.g., Granger, 1992, for a recent survey), the current consensus is that the variance of returns can be predicted using particular time series models. Within this class of models, the Generalized Autoregressive Conditional Heteroscedasticity (GARCH) model proposed by Engle (1982) and Bollerslev (1986) seems to be the most successful (see Bollerslev, Chou and Kroner, 1992, for a survey of GARCH applications). Roughly speaking, in a GARCH process the error variances can be modelled by an Autoregressive Moving Average (ARMA) type process. A useful feature of the GARCH model is that it can effectively remove the excess kurtosis in returns.

---

[9] Weixian Wei (2002), Forecasting stock market volatility with non-linear GARCH models: a case for China, *Applied Economics Letters*, 9 (3), 163–166.

The underlined part is the only difference from the first paragraph of the 2002 paper:

> A stylized fact of financial time series is that aberrant observations seem to cluster in the sense that there are periods where volatility is larger than in other periods. Typically, these volatile periods correspond to major (economic) events. Although most evidence in empirical finance indicates that returns on financial assets seem unforecastable at short horizons (see Granger, 1992, for a survey), the current consensus is that the variance of returns can be predicted using particular time series models. Within this class of models, the Generalized <u>Autogressive</u> Conditional Heteroscedasticity (GARCH) model proposed by Engle (1982) and Bollerslev (1986) seems to be the most successful (see Bollerslev et al., 1992, for a survey of GARCH applications). Roughly speaking, in a GARCH process the error variances can be modelled by an <u>Autogressive</u> Moving Average (ARMA) type process. A useful feature of the GARCH model is that it can effectively remove the excess kurtosis in returns.

Note that the second paragraph contains the same typo twice: *Autogressive* instead of *Autoregressive*. Well, this match is too obvious, but later in this book we will see that there are refined ways in which to cheat or to play around. Obvious plagiarism such as the above is perhaps increasingly rare, and with modern search and matching methods it is also much easier to find.

I   Ethical Guidelines

We start with an overview of what is accepted as good practice. We will review several general ethical guidelines. These guidelines can be used to appreciate good research and to indicate where and how research does not adhere to these guidelines. Good practice is "what we all say we (should) adhere to." In the second part of this chapter, the focus is more on specific ethical guidelines for statistical analysis. Of course, there is overlap with the more general guidelines, but there are also a few specifically relevant for statistics. In that case one can think of misinterpreting p values, malpractice such as p hacking and harking.

I.I   WHAT IS GOOD PRACTICE?

Before we can learn something about bad practice and how to recognize it, we must establish what good practice is. Good practice is what we hope happens most of the time. However, interviews, literature studies, and individual cases tell us that various degrees of sloppy science happen frequently and that questionable research practices (QRPs) are around.[1] Before we turn to general ethical guidelines, consider the following principles:[2]

Respect
People who participate in research, as informants or otherwise, shall be treated with respect.

---

[1] See, for example, Gowri Gopalakrishna, Gerben ter Riet, Gerko Vink, Ineke Stoop, Jelte M. Wicherts, and Lex M. Bouter (2022), Prevalence of questionable research practices, research misconduct and their potential explanatory factors: A survey among academic researchers in the Netherlands, *PLoS ONE* 17(2), e0263023.

[2] www.forskningsetikk.no/en/guidelines/general-guidelines.

Good Consequences

Researchers shall seek to ensure that their activities produce good consequences and that any adverse consequences are within the limits of acceptability.

Fairness

All research projects shall be designed and implemented fairly.

Integrity

Researchers shall comply with recognized norms and behave responsibly, openly, and honestly towards their colleagues and the public.

These four principles translate into fourteen guidelines:[3]

1 Quest for truth:
   Being honest, open, and systematic, and documenting clearly
2 Academic freedom:
   Choice of topic and methodology, implementation of research, and publication of results.
3 Quality:
   Possessing the necessary competence, designing relevant research questions, undertaking suitable choices of methodology, and ensuring sound and appropriate project implementation in terms of data collection, data processing, and safekeeping/storage of the material.
4 Voluntary informed consent:[4]
   Explicit, voluntary, and documentable.
5 Confidentiality:
   No damage to individuals who are the subjects of research.
6 Impartiality:
   No conflicts of interest. Openness to colleagues, research participants, sources of finance, and other relevant parties.
7 Integrity:
   Trustworthiness of research. No fabrication, falsification, or (self-) plagiarism.[5]

---

[3] www.forskningsetikk.no/en/guidelines/general-guidelines.

[4] This is relevant when people participate in experiments or surveys.

[5] Self-plagiarism has received much attention in recent years. See Serge P. J. M. Horbach and Willem Halffman (2019), The extent and causes of academic text recycling of "self-plagiarism," *Research Policy*, 48 (2), 492–502.

We need a few more insights here.

Self-plagiarism is well defined. Indeed, "Self-plagiarism is defined as a type of plagiarism in which the writer republishes a work in its entirety or reuses portions of a previously written text while authoring a new work."[6] Some people believe that self-plagiarism is a consequence of what is called the "publish or perish" culture at academic institutions. Wikipedia says:

> "Publish or perish" is an aphorism describing the pressure to publish academic work in order to succeed in an academic career. Such institutional pressure is generally strongest at research universities. Some researchers have identified the publish or perish environment as a contributing factor to the replication crisis.[7]

When people are pushed to produce many publications, it can be tempting to incorporate, for example, parts of previous papers into a new paper, without telling the reader. Quoting one's own work is not a problem, however, at least if one tells the reader that it occurs.[8]

So far, we have reviewed seven guidelines, but there are seven more.[9]

8 Good reference practice:[10]

Verifiability (meaning that one should be able to find the references).

9 Collegiality:

Data ownership and sharing, authorship, publication, peer review, and cooperation.

---

[6] www.gla.ac.uk/research/ourresearchenvironment/prs/pgrcodeofpractice/self-plagiarism/definingselfplagiarism/.

[7] https://en.wikipedia.org/wiki/Publish_or_perish.

[8] Where self-plagiarism is about one's own work, plagiarism refers to someone else's work. More than two decades ago, the following happened. In 1998, a book was published with Cambridge University Press under the title *Time Series Models for Business and Economic Forecasting*. We used the book to teach time series analysis to our second-year undergraduate students at our Econometric Institute. While trying to find updates of data for a second edition of the book (which would eventually appear in 2014), this time with Dick van Dijk and Anne Opschoor as coauthors, we came across a set of proceedings for the Proceedings of Algoritmy conferences, for 2000 and other years, conferences on scientific computing, where we made a remarkable discovery. Various chapters of the book we were using were presented as separate papers, with different authors!

[9] www.forskningsetikk.no/en/guidelines/general-guidelines.

[10] An interesting phenomenon, which is in stark contrast to correct citations, is Stigler's law of eponymy, which says that "no scientific discovery is named after its original discoverer." A nice illustration of this phenomenon is presented in Stephen M. Stigler (1983), Who discovered Bayes's theorem? *The American Statistician*, 37 (4), 290–296.

Indeed, these days, various journals include statements such as:

Conceptualization, P.H.F. and M.W.; methodology, P.H.F.; software, M.W.; validation, P.H.F. and M.W.; formal analysis, P.H.F. and M.W.; investigation, P.H.F. and M.W.; resources, P.H.F.; data curation, P.H.F.; writing – original draft preparation, P.H.F. and M.W.; writing – review and editing, P.H.F.; visualization, P.H.F. and M.W.; supervision, P.H.F.; project administration, P.H.F. and M.W. All authors have read and agreed to the published version of the manuscript.[11]

10 Institutional responsibilities:
Ensure compliance with good academic practice and with establishing mechanisms that can address cases of suspected violations of ethical research norms.

11 Availability of results:[12]
Openness, verifiability, returning benefit to research participants and society in general.

12 Social responsibility:
Research will benefit research participants, relevant groups, or society in general, and prevent from causing harm. Distinction between being an expert and having an opinion. Refrain from abusing authority.

13 Global responsibilities:
Research should help counteract global injustice and preserve biological diversity.

14 Laws and regulations:[13]
To be abided by.

I.2   ETHICAL GUIDELINES FOR STATISTICAL PRACTICE

The American Statistical Association publishes a list of ethical guidelines for statistical practice.[14] The general guidelines address the following items:

- professional integrity and accountability
- integrity of data and methods

---

[11] From Philip Hans Franses and Max Welz (2022), Forecasting real GDP growth for Africa, *Econometrics*, 10 (1), 3, https://doi.org/10.3390/econometrics10010003.

[12] Sometimes we use FAIR, which is findable, accessible, interoperable, reusable.

[13] Laws and regulations can of course change over time.

[14] www.amstat.org/ASA/Your-Career/Ethical-Guidelines-for-Statistical-Practice.aspx.

- responsibilities to science/public/funder/client
- responsibilities to research subjects
- responsibilities to research team colleagues
- responsibilities to other statisticians or statistics practitioners
- responsibilities regarding allegations of misconduct
- responsibilities of employers, including organizations, individuals, attorneys, or other clients employing statistical practitioners

Each item is detailed on their website. There are guidelines for statistical practice that go beyond the more general guidelines noted here. There is a knowledge asymmetry between the statistical practitioner and, for example, a client or funder. Clients receive statistical advice and may not be able to reproduce how the statistician created the advice. This requires "extra" ethical behavior from statisticians.

Let us zoom in on even more specific features that hold for statistics, and as such also for econometrics. There are a few concepts in statistics that are commonly used, but it may happen that people misunderstand these. We will see in Chapter 2 that simple statistical tools can highlight fabricated data, for example because the results are simply too good to be true.

In the remainder of this chapter, we will address asking for the source of the data, the notion to abstain from drawing suggestive graphs, what p values mean,[15] why p hacking is malpractice, why harking (after defining it) is even worse, and we present some basic insights concerning multiple testing. The last issue concerns the notion that when you run enough statistical tests, you will always find something.

1.3 WHERE DO THE DATA COME FROM? AND WHAT DO THEY LOOK LIKE?

A first question that one could ask is: What is the source of the data? Who compiled the data and for which purpose? Does the data provider have an interest in the outcomes?[16]

---

[15] See Ronald L. Wasserstein and Nicole A. Lazar (2016), The ASA statement on p-values: Context, process, and purpose, *The American Statistician*, 70 (2), 129–133.

[16] A recent case at Erasmus University Rotterdam concerned one of the university's companies, which engaged in making predictions of the future success of Maastricht Aachen

On page 95 of *Calling Bullshit*, we read:

> If you are looking at quantitative indicators that others have compiled, ask yourself: Are these numbers measuring what they are intended to measure? Or are people gaming the system and rendering this measure useless?[17]

This notion is particularly relevant in the case of bid books for large events or infrastructural projects. Think of the situation when the mayor of a city asks for insights into whether it could be beneficial to attract the Olympic Games to her city. The mayor does not want to hear that organizing such an event could be a financial disaster. So, most often bid books excel in providing tables and graphs where returns are exaggerated. Bid book compilers will always find sources that can support their enthusiastic projections in terms of income and their downward-sized cost projections. In the end, it is well known and widely documented that hosting the Olympic Games rarely leads to profits.[18]

An interesting recent case study on closely looking at data is a beautifully written paper that has been cited hundreds of times; it is on a fascinating topic: surveys.[19] People are sometimes asked to complete a survey in which one of the last items asks them to indicate whether they filled in the questionnaire honestly. The authors of this paper decided to discover if not *ending* the survey with this statement but *beginning* with it would lead to more honest behavior. To do this, they decided to study the miles that people report they drive when they are asked this by an insurance company.

The study has been summarized as follows:

airport. Some of the data delivered on certain projected success were provided by the airport itself. www.erasmusmagazine.nl/en/2021/07/23/integrity-review-committee-eur-study-on-maastricht-airport-constitutes-questionable-behaviour/.

[17] Carl T. Bergstrom and Jevin D. West (2020), *Calling Bullshit*, New York: Random House.

[18] https://towardsdatascience.com/how-big-is-cost-overrun-for-the-olympics-46e803cbf7d5.

[19] Lisa L. Shu, Nina Mazar, Francesca Gino, Dan Ariely, and Max H. Bazerman 2012), Signing at the beginning makes ethics salient and decreases dishonest self-reports in

Our focus here is on Study 3 in the 2012 paper, a field experiment (N = 13,488) conducted by an auto insurance company in the southeastern United States under the supervision of the fourth author. Customers were asked to report the current odometer reading of up to four cars covered by their policy. They were randomly assigned to sign a statement indicating, "I promise that the information I am providing is true" either at the top or bottom of the form. Customers assigned to the "sign-at-the-top" condition reported driving 2,400 more miles (10.3%) than those assigned to the "sign-at-the-bottom" condition.

It continues:

Let's first think about what the distribution of miles driven *should* look like. If there were about a year separating the Time 1 and Time 2 mileages, we might expect something like the figure below, taken from the UK Department of Transportation based on similar data (two consecutive odometer readings) collected in 2010.[20]

Now before the reader turns to Figure 1.1, what would we think a histogram of mileages would look like? Some people drive frequently, some drive rarely, and a large group will report mileages around some mean or median value. The data would not reflect a Gaussian distribution, as there might be some skewness to the right where there are people who really drive many miles for their work. Indeed, one could imagine that the data would look like those in Figure 1.1.

Indeed, the histogram in Figure 1.1 mimics a nonsymmetric right-skewed distribution with a few large outlying observations in the right tail. However, when we look at the data that were analyzed in the study of Shu et al.,[21] we have the data as in Figure 1.2. These data look like data from a uniform distribution, where all mileages

comparison to signing at the end, *Proceedings of the National Academy of Sciences of the United States of America*, 109 (38), 15197–15200, https://doi.org/10.1073/pnas.1209746109.

[20] http://datacolada.org/98.

[21] Shu et al., Signing at the beginning makes ethics salient.

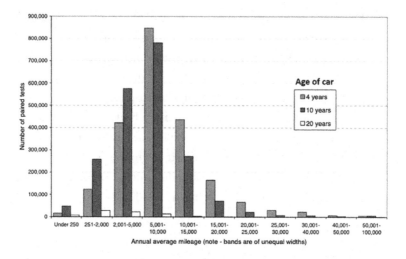

FIGURE 1.1   Annual average mileage.
Source: http://datacolada.org/98

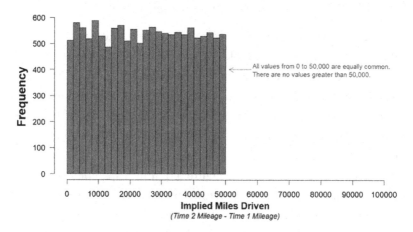

FIGURE 1.2   Data analyzed in Shu et al.
Lisa L. Shu, Nina Mazar, Francesca Gino, Dan Ariely, and Max H.
Bazerman 2012), Signing at the beginning makes ethics salient and
decreases dishonest self-reports in comparison to signing at the end,
*Proceedings of the National Academy of Sciences of the United
States of America*, 109 (38), 15197–15200; https://doi.org/10.1073/
pnas.1209746109
Source: http://datacolada.org/98

have an equal probability of being observed. And that is not the only thing. Beyond 50,000 miles there are no observations. There seems to be a cut-off point. This case provides an example where it pays off to first imagine how the data could look before you analyze any data. You would never have imagined a uniform distribution in the first place, given the type of variable that you are considering.

1.4 NO SUGGESTIVE GRAPHS

Statistical data analysis may start with visualizations of the data. This can be done via histograms, as mentioned earlier, but also line graphs and pie charts, and there are various other ways to visually present or summarize data. Making useful graphs is an art,[22] and the graphs should be informative. Look at Figure 1.3, which puts the number of flat stages in the Tour de France and the number of mass sprints at the finish, over the years, in one graph. The headline of the associated article in a Dutch newspaper was "Do more flat stages in the Tour de France lead to more mass sprints at the finish?" with, of course, the emphasis being on the word "lead." If you casually looked at the graph, given that you had seen the headline, you would be tempted to answer the question with a "no," even though no formal analysis has been conducted.

As another example, Figure 1.4 depicts the number of unfree countries in the world, when observed over a thirteen-year period. Indeed, if you look at the graph, you would be tempted to fully agree with the title of the report, that "democracy is under siege." Obviously, the line goes up, and from 2008 to 2020 the number of unfree countries increases from forty-two to fifty-four. We shall not

---

[22] See Darrell Huff (1985), *How to Lie with Statistics*, Harmondsworth: Penguin Books (this introduction to statistics was first published in 1954); and Sanne Blauw (2020), *The Number Bias: How Numbers Lead and Mislead Us*, London: Sceptre (a very readable book by one of our former students at the Econometric Institute). A nice reference to visualization of data is Howard Wainer (1997), *Visual Revelations: Graphical Tales of Fate and Deception from Napoleon Bonaparte to Ross Perot*, New York: Copernicus.

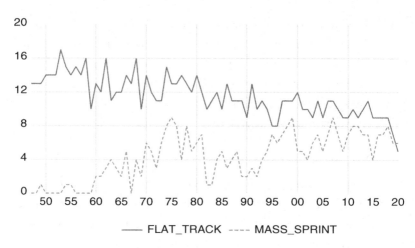

FIGURE 1.3 The number of flat stages in the Tour de France and the number of mass sprints at the finish, 1947–2020.
Source: NRC Handelsblad

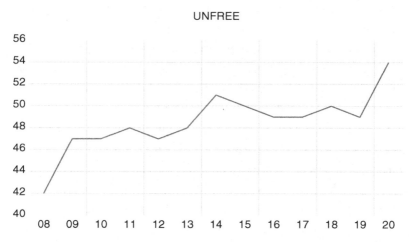

FIGURE 1.4 Number of unfree countries in the world, 2008–2020.
Source: https://freedomhouse.org/report/freedom-world/2021/democracy-under-siege

doubt that there is an increase in the number of unfree countries, nor shall we question how "democracy" is measured, but it is insightful to consider a longer period of data, as is done in Figure 1.5.

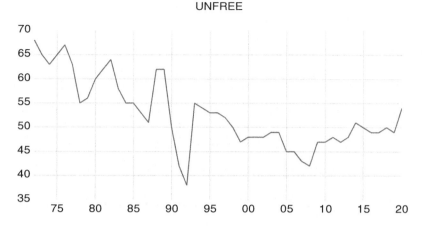

FIGURE 1.5 Number of unfree countries in the world, 1972–2020.
Source: https://freedomhouse.org/report/freedom-world/2021/
democracy-under-siege

When we look at the same variable since 1972, we see that the year 2008 is the lowest point in the graph since 1993, and thus to start the graph in 2008 as in Figure 1.4 makes the steepness of the line the greatest. Overall, from 1972, the number of unfree countries shows a downward trend, with, admittedly, a recent increase. As the number of countries in the world is not fixed, with new countries in Eastern Europe, in former Yugoslavia, and in Africa, we can also illustrate the fraction of countries that can be labeled as unfree, as is done in Figure 1.6.

From this, we see that the downward trend that was visible in Figure 1.5 is now even steeper when we look at the fraction of unfree countries. Again, there is no doubt that in recent years there has been an increase in unfree countries, but the extent of this increase can be visualized in diverse ways.[23]

---

[23] Visually presenting choice options in experiments can also impact the results. See Christoph Huber and Jürgen Huber (2019), Scale matters: Risk perception, return expectations, and investment propensity under different scalings, *Experimental Economics*, 22 (1), 76–100.

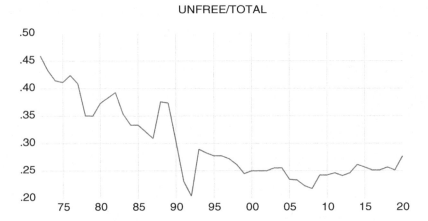

FIGURE 1.6 Fraction of unfree countries in the world, 1972–2020.
Source: https://freedomhouse.org/report/freedom-world/2021/
democracy-under-siege

1.5   p VALUE

The most often used metric in (classical) statistical analysis is the
so-called p value. Looking at assorted studies,[24] it is also the most
misunderstood metric or even the most misused.

Wikipedia says:

> In null hypothesis significance testing, the p-value is the
> probability of obtaining test results at least as extreme as the
> results actually observed, under the assumption that the null
> hypothesis is correct. A very small p-value means that such an
> extreme observed outcome would be very unlikely under the null
> hypothesis.[25]

The p value is associated with the Type 1 error (α) in hypothesis testing. This is defined as the case when you reject the null hypothesis
H_0 if H_0 is true. You preferably want this error to be small. Note

---

[24] A recent comprehensive study is Daniel Lakens et al. (2018), Justify your alpha,
Nature Human Behaviour, 2 (March), 168–171.
[25] https://en.wikipedia.org/wiki/P-value.

that the Type 1 error will never be exactly equal to zero. There is always some risk that a wrong decision will be made.[26]

Now, in much research we see that a small p value is interpreted as that the alternative hypothesis H_1 is correct.[27] We see that researchers claim to have found "an effect" when they reject the null hypothesis. We also see studies where people have made the decision for you, that is, which p value is relevant.[28] You then find tables with labels such as ***, which means a p value smaller than 0.01, **, meaning a p value smaller than 0.05, and *, meaning the p value is smaller than 0.10, or something like that. Often, these cut-off points are arbitrary choices, where 0.05 is often conveniently chosen as 0.05 matches with t values larger than 2 or more negative than –2, for a standard normal distribution. A t value measures the number of standard deviations that a number or estimate is away from the mean, where this mean is often equal to 0 in case of hypothesis testing.

In contrast to using asterisks, we would recommend allowing readers of a study to make their own choice of which value they deem large or small, and hence one should better just report the obtained p value itself. Some argue that a small p value, suggesting the rejection of a null hypothesis, could be seen as meaning that more research is needed.[29]

[26] There is always a risk of having false positives, and it is recommended to have more tools in the statistical toolbox than just p values; see, for example, Jae H. Kim (2019), Tackling false positives in business research: A statistical toolbox with applications, *Journal of Economic Surveys*, 33 (3), 862–895.

[27] Some go even as far as stating that the use of p values and the proposition of a null hypothesis amounts to "mindless statistics." See Gerd Gigerenzer (2004), Mindless statistics, *The Journal of Socio-Economics*, 33 (5), 587–606.

[28] Note that p values get smaller when the sample size increases, see for some consequences if this is ignored. For example, see James A. Ohlson (2022), Researchers' data analysis choices: An excess of false positives, *Review of Accounting Studies*, 27 (2), 649–667.

[29] John Quiggin (2019), The replication crisis as market failure, *Econometrics*, 7, 44, https://doi.org/10.3390/econometrics7040044. When the null hypothesis is rejected, there is a need for more research instead of stopping there. It can also be argued that statistical nonsignificance can be more informative than statistical significance. See Alberto Abadie (2020), Statistical nonsignificance in empirical economics, *AER: Insights*, 2 (2), 193–208.

1.6 p HACKING

The misuse of p values on purpose is called p hacking, and indeed, it is something we should not do.

Wikipedia says:

> Data dredging (also known as data snooping or *p* hacking), is the misuse of data analysis to find patterns in data that can be presented as statistically significant, thus dramatically increasing and understating the risk of false positives. This is done by performing many statistical tests on the data and only reporting those that come back with significant results.[30]

If you read this quote, you would immediately feel that p hacking is malpractice. p hacking is also associated with false positives, which can occur if you run many tests, as we will see in Section 1.8.[31]

1.7 HARKING

Another "do not do this" in statistics is called harking.

Wikipedia says:

> HARKing is an acronym coined by social psychologist Norbert Kerr that refers to the questionable research practice of Hypothesizing After the Results are Known. Kerr defined HARKing as "presenting a post hoc hypothesis in the introduction of a research report as if it were an a priori hypothesis."[32] HARKing may occur when a researcher tests an a priori hypothesis but then omits that hypothesis from their research report after they find out the results of their

---

[30] https://en.wikipedia.org/wiki/Data_dredging.

[31] One way to avoid p hacking is to make the researcher to prepare a research plan in advance, where it is specified how the data will be collected and how they will be analyzed. See Guido W. Imbens (2012), Statistical significance, p-values, and the reporting of uncertainty, *Journal of Economic Perspectives*, 35 (3), 157–174.

[32] Norbert L. Kerr (1998), HARKing: Hypothesizing after the results are known, *Personality and Social Psychology Review*, 2 (3), 196–217.

test; inappropriate forms of post hoc analysis and/or post hoc theorizing then may lead to a post hoc hypothesis.[33]

This behavior goes against a main principle in statistics, which is that you first formulate a hypothesis and then collect data to see if there is evidence against or in favor of that hypothesis. Pretending that you already knew the outcome in advance by shifting the order of actions leads to no sound addition to the knowledge base. Harking does not bring science any further, and in fact may even obstruct progress.

Obviously, when you read about the misuse of p values, p hacking, and harking, you would think that nobody would do this. But still, there are plenty of examples around, and therefore it is important that you are clear about your research design, your hypothesis, and your data collection before you begin.[34]

1.8 SIZE AND POWER

To see what happens when multiple tests are conducted, and how false inference can occur, consider again three basic aspects of statistical testing. We have already mentioned the Type 1 error (α), which is that you reject H_0 if H_0 is true (which is preferably small but will never be exactly zero). There is also a Type 2 error (β), which is that you do not reject H_0 if H_0 is not true (and this is also preferably small), and its mirror concept called the power of a test $(1-\beta)$, which is that you reject H_0 if H_0 is false indeed (which is preferably large, and is of course never exactly equal to 1). Even though α and β can be small, they will never be exactly zero as there is always a positive chance of making a wrong decision. If you run just a single test, then the chance of making a wrong decision is of the size of α and β. However, if you run a test many times, then the size of the overall chance can become quite large. Here are two illustrations of this phenomenon.

---

[33] https://en.wikipedia.org/wiki/HARKing.

[34] A very readable book on practical statistics is Paul Goodwin (2021), *Something Doesn't Add Up: Surviving Statistics in a Number-Mad World*, London: Profile Books.

Suppose there is a test on fraud with power 0.80, so the test finds fraud in 80 percent of the cases when fraud occurs. The same test incorrectly indicates fraud in 0.02 of the cases when people do *not* commit fraud. Hence, 0.02 is probability of the Type 1 error. In a two-by-two table, this hypothetical situation looks like

		True fraud	
		yes	no
Test says	yes	80	2
	No	20	98

Suppose now that 1 percent of the people truly do commit fraud. And suppose further that you examine 10,000 individuals, which thus means that 100 of those commit fraud. The test finds 80 of the 100 individuals. But what happens to the others? Of the 9,900 individuals who do not commit fraud, 2 percent (Type 1 error) will be marked as committing fraud, which gives 198 additional hits. Taking the 80 and 198 together, we thus have the percentage of innocent individuals over all individuals for which the test gives a signal as

$$\frac{198}{80+198} = 71\%$$

The probability went from 0.02 (α) and 0.20 (β) to 0.71.

Here is another example that shows the impact of multiple testing. At a crime scene, a DNA sample is taken. The sample is compared with DNA profiles of 20,000 men. Suppose the DNA test erroneously gives a match in 1 of any 10,000 comparisons. This means there is a small error of type 1, namely 0.0001. Suppose that there is a match found for one man. Is the man guilty because the test makes no mistakes in 9,999 of the 10,000 cases? Well, not really!

Suppose that in reality no one of the 20,000 men in the database has ever been at the crime scene. What is now the probability of still finding at least one match?

The probability of a match by pure chance is

$$\frac{1}{10,000}$$

The probability of no match by pure chance is therefore

$$1 - \frac{1}{10,000}$$

The probability of no match when trying 20,000 times (independent cases) is

$$\left(1 - \frac{1}{10,000}\right)^{20,000}$$

The probability of at least one match by pure chance after trying 20,000 times is then

$$1 - \left(1 - \frac{1}{10,000}\right)^{20,000} = 0.865$$

You will see that the probability of making an incorrect judgment has increased from 0.01 percent to 86.5 percent. This is called a false positive, and this frequently happens in statistical practice. If you run enough tests, there is virtually always a test result with a hit.

In these examples, the 10,000 and 20,000 cases could be viewed as independent cases. But in many settings, cases are not independent, and then the chance of getting false positives becomes even larger. Indeed, you do not need so many cases then, as with a small number of cases you will already obtain false inference. Similarly, searching many variables to see which ones have significant parameters in a regression model will virtually always lead to significant results, at least if you keep the p value cut off point constant as you proceed. We return to this in Chapter 4.

I.9 CORRELATION AND CAUSALITY

Correlation and causality do not mean the same thing. When there is causality, there is likely correlation, but when there is correlation

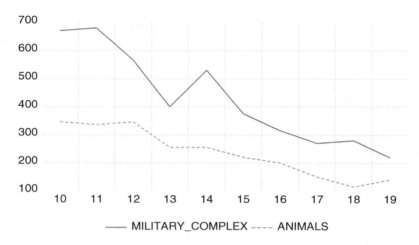

FIGURE 1.7 Thefts from a military complex and thefts of animals, the Netherlands, yearly data for 2010–2019.
Source: Statistics Netherlands

there does not need to be a causal link. Yet it is tempting to mix the two concepts – even more so when graphs show suggestive common features and when there is an underlying variable that drives the variables.

Look at the two lines in Figure 1.7, which correspond with the number of thefts from a military complex and the number of thefts of animals, both on an annual basis.[35] To make it even more suggestive, look at the scatter plot in Figure 1.8.

By plotting one variable against the other and by making the choice of putting one variable on the x axis and the other on the y axis, one could be framed to believe that the variable on the x axis is causing (or leading) the variable on the y axis. When a graph as in Figure 1.8 is presented, you could be inclined to consider the regression model:

Thefts of animals$_t$ = α + β Thefts from a military complex$_t$ + ε_t

---

[35] Central Bureau of Statistics Netherlands, and reprinted in Philip Hans Franses (2021), *Quantitative Insights for Lawyers*, The Hague: Eleven International Publishing.

FIGURE 1.8 Thefts of animals against thefts from a military complex, the Netherlands, yearly data for 2010–2019. Source: Statistics Netherlands

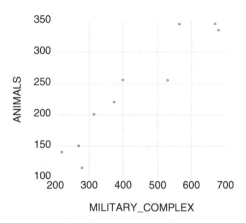

where $t = 2010, 2011, \ldots, 2019$, and where ε_t is an error term. Application of Ordinary Least Squares (OLS) to estimate α and β results in

$$a = 28.755(27.450)$$
$$b = 0.481(0.060)$$

where standard errors are presented in parentheses. The t value for the hypothesis $\beta = 0$ is 8.049, and this is beyond the 5 percent critical value of 2. The R^2 of this regression is 0.890, which is quite close to 1. Hence, one could be tempted to believe that there is a strong link between the two variables, and even that thefts from a military complex is leading or causing the thefts of animals.

Looking back at Figure 1.7, we see that both variables show a downward trending. pattern. Could it be that behind the two patterns there is a downward trend because of better precautionary measures or more surveillance? If the latter effects are proxied by a variable $Trend_t$, which takes the values 0, 1, 2, ..., 9, and when we consider the regression model

$$Thefts\ of\ animals_t = \alpha + \beta\ Thefts\ from\ a\ military\ complex_t$$
$$+ \gamma\ Trend_t + \varepsilon_t$$

then the following OLS based estimates are obtained:

$$a = 275.87(94.197)$$
$$b = 0.126(0.141)$$
$$c = -20.947(7.853)$$

We can see now that the t value for the null hypothesis $\beta = 0$ is 0.894, and hence the suggestive relation between the two variables is just driven by a previously omitted variable, where the trend can also measure an increase in precautionary rules. The correlation between the two variables is a spurious correlation. In Chapter 7, we return to the phenomenon of spurious correlations.[36]

1.10 WHAT TO DO?

A good starting point for your own research is to try to replicate earlier studies.[37] You contact the original authors, ask for the data that they used, or retrieve the data from a publicly available database, then you use the same methods of analysis and the same estimation methods. In the case of data obtained from experiments, you can run a similar experiment to see if you end up with the same conclusions.

This is nicely put by Aarts et al.: "Innovation points out paths that are possible; replication points out paths that are likely; progress relies on both."[38]

---

[36] An interesting case where causation is suggested is described in Ernst-Jan de Bruijn and Gerrit Antonides (2022), Poverty and economic decision making: A review of the scarcity theory, *Theory and Decision*, 92 (1), 5–37. The authors show that the study in Anandi Madi, Sendhil Mullainathan, Eldar Shafir, and Jiaying Zhao (2013), Poverty impedes cognitive function, *Science*, 341 (6149), 976–980 does not suggest that poverty reduces IQ, as is commonly believed. This common belief is brought about because the authors used as a measure of cognitive functioning the same measure that people use to measure IQ. So new causality is suggested by using the same measurement tool.

[37] When we were PhD students, we published Lourens Broersma and Philip Hans Franses (1990), The use of dummy variables in consumption models, *Econometric Reviews*, 9 (1), 109–116, with the following abstract: "In this paper the consumption model in Winder and Palm [1989] is subjected to a sensitivity analysis. Small and reasonable changes in several dummy variables provide that the original model with a moving planning horizon becomes observationally equivalent with a random walk specification."

[38] Alexander A. Aarts et al. (2015), Estimating the reproducibility of psychological science, *Science*, 349 (6251), aac4716.

I.II   WHAT MAKES US DEVIATE FROM ETHICAL GUIDELINES?

Even though the various guidelines in this chapter make sense and have obvious face value, as we will also see in Chapter 2, it does happen that these guidelines are not met. What could be the reason that this happens?[39]

One reason can be ignorance. If you are not aware of multiple testing problems, then you may just run many tests or regressions without being aware that the results are most likely flawed. Hence, solid knowledge of the ins and outs of the methods and techniques that you use is important.

Some people claim that the editors of journals make people misbehave. Journals like to publish significant results,[40] results that attract readership and citations. Journals with more citations have more impact; they climb up the ladder and gain high esteem. Editors of top journals at the same time increase their recognition.[41]

Not following ethical guidelines can be motivated by the fact that many universities want academics to have impact. This can be

---

[39] Several reasons are presented in a survey discussed in Gowri Gopalakrishna, Gerben ter Riet, Gerko Vink, Ineke Stoop, Jelte M. Wicherts, and Lex M. Bouter (2022), Prevalence of questionable research practices, research misconduct and their potential explanatory factors: A survey among academic researchers in The Netherlands, *PLoS ONE*, 17(2), e0263023.

[40] Interesting studies on publication bias where models are presented that can correct for publication bias are Isaiah Andrews and Maximilian Kasy (2019), Identification of and correction for publication bias, *American Economic Review* 109 (8), 2766–2794; Justin McCrary, Garret Christensen, and Daniele Fanelli (2016), Conservative tests under satisficing models of publication bias, *PLoS ONE* 11 (2), e0149590; and John P. A. Ioannidis, Why most discovered true associations are inflated, *Epidemiology*, 19 (5), 640–648.

[41] A widely read and cited study (more than 380 citations in Thomson Reuters, November 2022) on "evidence of precognition" was published in such a top journal: it is Daryl J. Bem (2011), Feeling the future: Experimental evidence for anomalous retroactive influences on cognition and effect, *Journal of Personality and Social Psychology*, 100 (3), 407–425. Attempts to replicate the results all failed; see, for example, D. Samuel Schwarzkopf (2014), We should have seen this coming, *Frontiers in Human Neuroscience*, 8, article 332; and Thomas Rabeyron (2020), Why most research findings about psi are false: The replicability crisis, the psi paradox and the myth of Sisyphus, *Frontiers in Psychology*, 11; www.frontiersin.org/articles/10.3389/fpsyg.2020.562992/full.

obtained if mainstream or social media pick up research results, and they like results that attract attention and sell. Some academics have become media stars, and some sell thousands of copies of popularized versions of their academic work.

It may also be that university boards follow the "publish or perish" rule, mentioned earlier, which can make people hastily draft many papers, thereby perhaps falling into the self-plagiarism trap.

Finally, clients of econometricians' advice may wish to hear certain outcomes that are convenient to them and suit their managerial purposes.

Anyway, whatever the reasons are, it is mandatory for valid science to follow the ethical guidelines. Be aware that there is judgment at all stages of the model building and forecasting process. There is always something to decide. The ethics part comes in when you know what the consequences of the choices are and when you do not know these. And one simple strategy, to make sure that others can be convinced that you are indeed behaving ethically, is to write everything down. Report all choices that you have made.[42] In the next chapters, we will see that this may be easier said than done.

FURTHER READING

Bergstrom, Carl T. and Jevin D. West (2020), *Calling Bullshit*, New York: Random House.

A highly informative and well-written book on how numbers and graphs can fool us.

Jerven, Morten (2013), *Poor Numbers: How We Are Misled by African Development Statistics and What to Do about It*, Ithaca, NY: Cornell University Press.

Kennedy, Peter E. (2002), Sinning in the basement: What are the rules? The ten commandments of applied econometrics, *Journal of Economic Surveys*, 16 (4), 569–589.

To gain some impression of parts of the forthcoming chapters.

---

[42] A claim that fraud can be detected by just presenting all data and results is for example made in Uri Simonsohn (2013), Just post it: The lesson from two cases of fabricated data detected by statistics alone, *Psychological Science*, 24 (10), 1875–1888.

Simmons, Joseph P., Leif D. Nelson, and Uri Simonsohn (2011), False-positive psychology: Undisclosed flexibility in data collection and analysis allows presenting anything as significant, *Psychological Science*, 22 (11), 1359–1366.

A key publication addressing the shortcomings of much research in social psychology.

ON REPLICATIONS

Dewald, William G., Jerry G. Thursby, and Richard G. Anderson (1986), Replication in empirical economics: The journal of money, credit and banking project, *American Economic Review*, 76 (4), 587–603.

An early attempt to replicate results, with difficult to obtain original data and computer programs.

Harvey, Campbell R. (2019), Editorial: Replication in financial economics, *Critical Finance Review*, 8 (1–2), 1–9.

Serra-Garcia, Marta and Uri Gneezy (2021), Nonreplicable publications are cited more than replicable ones, *Science Advances*, 7, eabd1705.

INTERESTING READING ABOUT WHY ETHICAL GUIDELINES ARE NOT FOLLOWED

Brodeur, Abel, Nikolai Cook, and Anthony Heyes (2020), Methods matter: p-hacking and publication bias in causal analysis in economics, *American Economic Review*, 110 (11), 3634–3660.

Camerer, Colin F. et al. (2016), Evaluating replicability of laboratory experiments in economics, *Science*, 351 (6286), 1433–1436.

Cox, Adam, Russell Craig, and Dennis Tourish (2018), Retraction statements and research malpractice in economics, *Research Policy*, 47 (5), 924–935.

McCloskey, Donald N. (1985), The loss function has been mislaid: The rhetoric of significance tests, *American Economic Review*, 75 (2), 201–205.

Necker, Sarah (2014), Scientific misbehavior in economics, *Research Policy*, 43 (10), 1747–1759.

Vivalt, Eva (2019), Specification searching and significance inflation across time, methods and disciplines, *Oxford Bulletin of Economics and Statistics*, 81 (4), 797–816.

RECOMMENDED READING

www.amstat.org/ASA/Your-Career/Ethical-Guidelines-for-Statistical-Practice.aspx.

Vardeman, Stephen B. and Max D. Morris (2003), Statistics and ethics, *The American Statistician*, 57 (1), 21–26.

2   Scientific Misconduct

In this chapter we will discuss a few cases of scientific misconduct that turned out to be easy to spot, given some basic knowledge of statistics. We will learn that it is always important to begin with a close look at the data that you are going to analyze. What is the source of the data, how were they collected, and who collected the data and for what purpose? Next, we will discuss various specific cases where the misconduct was obvious. We will see that it is not difficult to create tables with fake regression outcomes, and that it is also not difficult to generate artificial data that match with those tables. Sometimes results are too good to be true. Patterns in outcomes can be unbelievable. We will also see that it is not difficult to make the data fit better to a model.[1] These are of course all unethical approaches and should not be replicated, but it is good to know that these can happen and how they work.

Let us go back to the study that we introduced in Chapter 1, which was "Signing at the beginning makes ethics salient and decreases dishonest self-reports in comparison to signing at the end."[2] A histogram of the data in Figure 1.4 indicated that there was something strange about the data, and there is more to say about this.[3] We go back to http://datacolada.org/98, where it is written that "These data are consistent with the hypothesis that a random

---

[1] Or to make data disappear, see https://nltimes.nl/2022/01/27/fmr-leiden-university-researcher-accused-fraud-15-studies.

[2] https://doi.org/10.1073/pnas.1209746109. Lisa L. Shu, Nina Mazar, Francesca Gino, Dan Ariely, and Max H. Bazerman, and which has been published in *Proceedings of the National Academy of Sciences of the United States of America*, September 18, 2012, 109 (38) 15197–15200.

[3] www.sciencemag.org/news/2021/08/fraudulent-data-set-raise-questions-about-superstar-honesty-researcher.

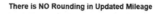
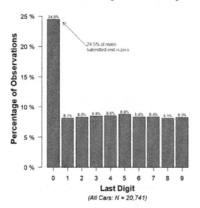
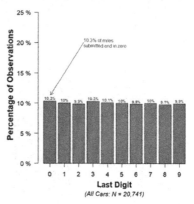

FIGURE 2.1 Features of the data in Shu et al.
Lisa L. Shu, Nina Mazar, Francesca Gino, Dan Ariely, and Max
H. Bazerman, and which has been published in *Proceedings of the
National Academy of Sciences of the United States of America*,
September 18, 2012, 109 (38) 15197–15200
Source: Figure 4 in http://datacolada.org/98

number generator was used to create the Time 2 data." In fact, if we
look at the histograms in Figure 2.1, we see that the last digits of the
mileages that were quoted by the survey participants also seem to
follow a uniform distribution.

And there is more: see Figure 2.2. The text at http://datacolada
.org/98 continues:

> Perhaps the most peculiar feature of the dataset is the fact that
> the baseline data for Car #1 in the posted Excel file appears in
> two different fonts. Specifically, half of the data in that column
> are printed in Calibri, and half are printed in Cambria. Here's
> a screenshot of the file again, now with a variable we added
> indicating which font appeared in that column. The different
> fonts are easier to spot if you focus on the font size, because
> Cambria appears larger than Calibri. For example, notice that
> Customers 4 and 5 both have a 5-digit number in "baseline_car1,"
> but that the numbers are of different sizes:

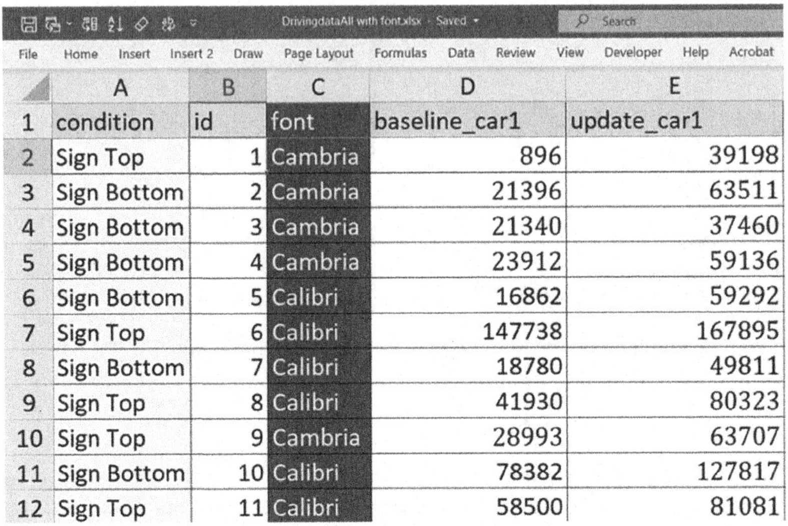

	A	B	C	D	E
1	condition	id	font	baseline_car1	update_car1
2	Sign Top	1	Cambria	896	39198
3	Sign Bottom	2	Cambria	21396	63511
4	Sign Bottom	3	Cambria	21340	37460
5	Sign Bottom	4	Cambria	23912	59136
6	Sign Bottom	5	Calibri	16862	59292
7	Sign Top	6	Calibri	147738	167895
8	Sign Bottom	7	Calibri	18780	49811
9	Sign Top	8	Calibri	41930	80323
10	Sign Top	9	Cambria	28993	63707
11	Sign Bottom	10	Calibri	78382	127817
12	Sign Top	11	Calibri	58500	81081

FIGURE 2.2 Features of the data in Shu et al.
Lisa L. Shu, Nina Mazar, Francesca Gino, Dan Ariely, and Max
H. Bazerman, and which has been published in *Proceedings of the
National Academy of Sciences of the United States of America*,
September 18, 2012, 109 (38) 15197–15200
Source: http://datacolada.org/98

At first sight, it seems a bit odd to have an Excel database in which
the fonts differ. This is therefore another aspect you may want to
look at when someone delivers a database for you to analyze.

And, finally, Figure 2.3 shows another interesting but confusing feature of the data, unveiled at http://datacolada.org/98, which
continues with "To understand what we mean by 'match' look at
these two customers":

> The top customer has a "baseline_car1" mileage written in
> Calibri, whereas the bottom's is written in Cambria. For all
> four cars, these two customers have *extremely* similar baseline
> mileages. Indeed, in all four cases, the Cambria's baseline mileage
> is (1) greater than the Calibri mileage, and (2) within 1,000
> miles of the Calibri mileage. Before the experiment, these two
> customers were like driving twins.

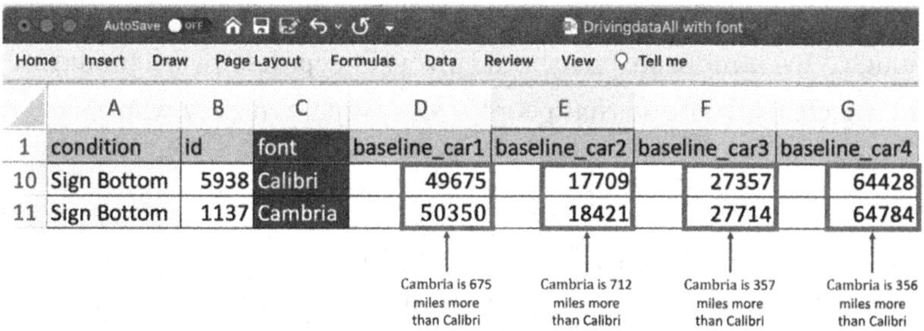

	A	B	C	D	E	F	G
1	condition	id	font	baseline_car1	baseline_car2	baseline_car3	baseline_car4
10	Sign Bottom	5938	Calibri	49675	17709	27357	64428
11	Sign Bottom	1137	Cambria	50350	18421	27714	64784

Cambria is 675 miles more than Calibri | Cambria is 712 miles more than Calibri | Cambria is 357 miles more than Calibri | Cambria is 356 miles more than Calibri

FIGURE 2.3 Features of the data in Shu et al.
Lisa L. Shu, Nina Mazar, Francesca Gino, Dan Ariely, and Max H. Bazerman, and which has been published in *Proceedings of the National Academy of Sciences of the United States of America*, September 18, 2012, 109 (38) 15197–15200
Source: http://datacolada.org/98

The point is clear by now. It is always important to take a close look at the data that are provided. This closer look does not just involve the histograms but can also involve the last digits and even the fonts in which the data are reported.

It may occur that you need to clean the data before analysis. It can be that a datafile reports prices in hundreds of dollars, and after a while it moves on to prices in thousands of dollars. It can also be that respondents have filled in specific values in case data were missing. It may happen that the N/A (Not Available) data were replaced by a strange number such as –9999. If you erroneously treat these –9999 observations as genuine, your results will look odd. In fact, you may end up with very skewed histograms of the residuals (of a regression model).

It is of course no problem to clean the data and prepare them for analysis. It is our experience with supervising students who take an internship at a company or institution that they always spend a few weeks cleaning and preparing data before they can analyze them. It rarely happens that the data provided appear in a ready-to-analyze format. But when you clean the data, you should document exactly what you have done. Deleting all –9999 observations seems perfectly fine. But just simply stating that you have cleaned the data is not enough.[4] Even more so, one should always keep the raw original data and the cleaned data so that people can compare, if they want.

2.1 TABLES BASED ON NON-EXISTENT DATA

We now turn to a case where both the raw original data and the cleaned data were not kept. In fact, it turned out there were no data at all. There were papers with tables with outcomes, reportedly obtained by applying regression or using some other models and methods. In reality. there were no data at all.

What happened? Diederik Stapel created tables like Table 2.1 (the title of the table is by the author).[5]

Next, he asked (PhD) students or colleagues to interpret the results and write a theory that would match with the estimation results. They were told not to worry about the data collection and regression analysis, as he "would have done all that." He claimed to have collected complete questionnaires and that the data in these questionnaires were used to obtain the estimation results. What he did not say was that the questionnaires did not exist at all.

Before we continue with Table 2.1 and show how such estimation results can be created, let us first have a look at the numbers in the work of Stapel. We do so by considering Benford's law.[6] It is well known that individuals have difficulties creating random numbers. If we ask you to create a sequence of numbers drawn from 1 to 9, then

---

[4] An exceptional bad way of cleaning the data is by simply deleting the data of some test subjects; see, for example, https://nltimes.nl/2022/01/27/fmr-leiden-university-researcher-accused-fraud-15-studies.

[5] https://en.wikipedia.org/wiki/Diederik_Stapel. He authored a book in which he explained in detail what he did and how: see Diederik Stapel (2002), *Ontsporing* (Derailment) (in Dutch), Amsterdam: Prometheus.

[6] Interesting articles on Benford's law are Frank Benford (1938), The law of anomalous numbers, *Proceedings of the American Philosophical Society*, 78 (4), 551–572; Simon Newcomb (1881), Note on the frequency of use of the different digits in natural numbers, *American Journal of Mathematics*, 4 (1), 39–40; Mark J. Nigrini (1999), I've got your number, *Journal of Accountancy*, 187 (5), 79–83; and Theodore P. Hill (1995), A statistical derivation of the significant-digit law, *Statistical Science*, 10 (4), 354–363.

Table 2.1 *Artificially created linear regression results of output variable y on an intercept and scores on two variables x_1 and x_2, that is, $y_i = \alpha + \beta_1 x_{1,i} + \beta_2 x_{2,i} + \varepsilon_i$*

Variable	Estimated parameter	p-value
Constant	4.567	(0.022)
x_1	0.234	(0.013)
x_2	−0.567	(0.046)

Table 2.2 *Benford's law of first digits in numbers*

First digit	1	2	3	4	5	6	7	8	9
Frequency	30.1	17.6	12.5	9.7	7.9	6.7	5.8	5.1	4.6

after some time patterns will emerge. For example, each time you quote 3, after some time you will start quoting 6. This is not the case for the first twenty or forty numbers, but after a while it will happen. This means that you have an (unconscious) preference for (sequences of) certain numbers. One way to diagnose that, and one that is useful in case of t values or p values with 3 decimals) is to consider Benford's law. This law implies that the probability of observing a first digit d obeys the following distribution:

$$P(d) = \log_{10}\left(1 + \frac{1}{d}\right) \text{ with } d = 1, 2, \ldots, 9$$

where $\log_{10}$ denotes the logarithmic transformation with base 10. In Table 2.2 the frequency is given for each of the 9 digits.

Let us now have a look at articles published in the same issue of a journal in which a retracted paper of Stapel and coauthors appeared. More precisely, we look at eleven retracted Stapel papers and 125 nonretracted articles in the same issues of a range of journals.

In Figure 2.4 we report the frequency of the first digits of all numbers reported in 125 nonretracted articles. We see that the shape

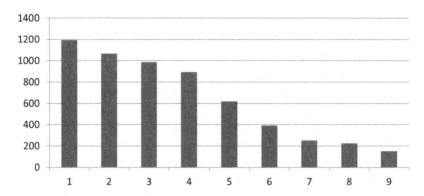

FIGURE 2.4 Frequency of first digits (out of 5,774 numbers), 125 non-retracted articles.
Source: Author's calculations (Thanks to Robbert Mens)

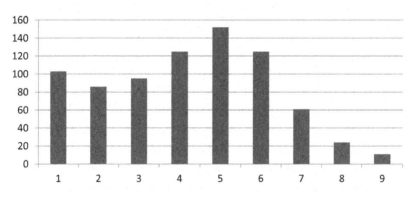

FIGURE 2.5 Frequency of first digits (out of 782 numbers), eleven retracted articles.

of the distribution of the 5,774 numbers mimics the pattern of the Benford distribution. In Figure 2.5 the frequencies of the digits are presented for the eleven retracted Stapel articles.

It is clear from Figure 2.5 that the shape of the distribution of these digits is far from that of a Benford distribution. In fact, Stapel had a preference to begin his fake results with a 5, and next with a 4 and a 6. This is another indication that the reported results in these retracted studies were made up.

2.2 CREATING DATA FROM ESTIMATION RESULTS

Now let us go back to Table 2.1. If the estimates there are supposed to originate from a linear regression model where the parameters are estimated using OLS, then it is not difficult to create artificial data for a sample of, say, thirty hypothetical respondents that approximately match the reported estimation results. The associated final data look like real data, as we will see. This provides an additional motivation to store actual filled-in surveys on paper or in web-files. Analysts can compare these stored files of raw data with the data that are used in the papers (Figures 2.6 and 2.7).

To create (a table like) Table 2.1 we start with creating thirty hypothetical observations, such as

$$x_{1,i} \sim N(0,1)$$
$$x_{2,i} \sim N(0,1)$$
$$\varepsilon_i \sim N(0,1)$$

and

$$y_i = 5 + 2x_{i,1} - 6x_{2,i} + \varepsilon_i$$

Scatterplots of y versus x_1 and versus x_2 look like Figures 2.6 and 2.7

FIGURE 2.6 Artificial y_i against artificial $x_{1,i}$.

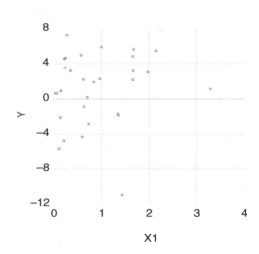

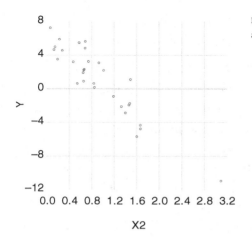

FIGURE 2.7 Artificial y_i against artificial $x_{2,i}$.

The properties of these artificial data (for this specific attempt) are

	y	x_1	x_2
Mean	1.089	0.902	0.916
Median	2.047	0.672	0.718
Maximum	7.236	3.297	3.099
Minimum	-10.989	0.023	0.069

Making the observations look more like real survey responses, for example on a scale of 1 to 4, the next step is to create

$$x_1^* = Round(x_1) + 1$$
$$x_2^* = Round(x_2) + 1$$

This gives the following statistics:

	x_1^*	x_2^*
Mean	1.900	1.933
Median	2	2
Maximum	4	4
Minimum	1	1

For the dependent variable, we can do something similar, that is,

Table 2.3 *Artificially created linear regression results of output variable* y^* *on an intercept and scores on two variables* x_1^* *and* x_2^*, *that is* $y_i^* = \alpha + \beta_1 x_{1,i}^* + \beta_2 x_{2,i}^* + \varepsilon_i$

Variable	Estimated parameter	p-value
Constant	8.481	(0.000)
x_1^*	0.771	(0.125)
x_2^*	−2.627	(0.000)

$$y^* = Round(y) + 3$$

This gives (again for this specific attempt) for the dependent variable a mean 4.067, median 5, maximum 10, and a minimum of −8. To make the y to look like a variable with scores 0 to 10, we place the four negative numbers (obtained here by chance because it is just one run) by 1, 2, 3, and 4 (from most negative to least negative). This new y^* has now mean 4.867, median 5, maximum 10, and minimum 0. The OLS-based regression results for these newly created variables with thirty observations are in Table 2.3.

Where the R^2 is found equal to 0.429. Note that this is just one attempt, and with this attempt the parameter b_1 does not seem significantly different from zero at the 5 percent level. Hence, in the practice of misconduct, one could redo this a couple of times and pick the one that looks best. Excessively small p values for moderately sized samples, as we will see, make the results look too good to be true.

Here is an exercise that you can do using the approach just outlined. Create thirty hypothetical data points that match with the following linear regression results of output score y on scores on x_1 and x_2.

Variable	Estimated parameter	p-value
Constant	10.567	(0.021)
x_1	1.324	(0.043)
x_2	−2.567	(0.042)

And you can also try the following exercise. Create thirty hypothetical data points that match with the following linear regression results of output score y on scores on x_1, x_2 and x_3,

Variable	Estimated parameter	p-value
Constant	10.567	(0.021)
x_1	1.324	(0.043)
x_2	−2.567	(0.042)
x_3	1.256	(0.831)

You will see that after a while you will become quite "good" at this.

2.3   TOO GOOD TO BE TRUE

When people create fake results, they might be tempted to create results that look too good to be true.[7] This happens in the following case study. Table 2.4 is taken from Geraerts et al. (2008).

We see that the mean scores are similar, with the clear exception of the outcome for Group 1 and Event 1. One may now wonder how likely this italicized outcome (italics are the author's) is in the left-hand column. Otherwise put, how different are the scores 1.27 (0.98) from the scores for Event 1 and Groups 2, 3, and 4 jointly?

Let us have a look at a statistical test for the hypothesis that the scores are all from the same distribution. There are four experimental groups. Three have the same mean and variance, call these μ_1 and σ_1^2. One has possibly a different mean μ_2 and variance σ_2^2.

The null hypothesis H_0 is $\mu_1 = \mu_2$. The alternative hypothesis H_1 is $\mu_1 \neq \mu_2$. To test the null hypothesis, we can rely on the test statistic

$$t = \frac{\overline{y}_2 - \overline{y}_1}{\sqrt{\dfrac{s_2^2}{n_2} + \dfrac{s_1^2}{n_1}}}$$

[7] This next empirical example is taken from Elke Geraerts, Richard J. McNally, Marko Jelici, Harald Merckelbach, and Linsey Raymaekers (2008), Linking thought suppression, and recovered memories of childhood sexual abuse, Memory, 16 (1), 22–28. This paper has been retracted: see https://psycnet.apa.org/record/2013-40347-012.

Table 2.4 *Mean (standard deviation)*
(group sizes 30)

	Event 1	Event 2
Group 1	*1.27 (0.98)*	3.17 (5.05)
Group 2	3.97 (3.14)	3.57 (2.75)
Group 3	3.10 (4.09)	3.77 (4.89)
Group 4	3.50 (3.04)	4.13 (4.61)

where $\bar{y}_1, \bar{y}_2, s_1^2$ and s_2^2 are estimators for μ_1, μ_2, σ_1^2 and σ_2^2, respectively.
We know from Table 2.4 that

$$\bar{y}_2 = 1.27$$
$$s_2^2 = 0.98^2 = 0.960$$
$$n_2 = 30.$$

What we need to compute are

$$n_1 = a_1 + a_2 + a_3 = 30 + 30 + 30 = 90$$
$$\bar{y}_1 = \frac{a_1 m_1 + a_2 m_2 + a_3 m_3}{a_1 + a_2 + a_3} = \frac{30(3.97 + 3.10 + 3.50)}{90} = 3.52$$

and finally

$$s_1^2 = \frac{1}{n_1 - 1} \sum_{j=1}^{3} \sum_{i=1}^{a_j} \left(y_{ij} - \bar{y}_1 \right)^2 = \frac{1}{n_1 - 1} Total\ Sum\ of\ Squares\ (TSS)$$

We know

$$\hat{\sigma}_j^2 = \frac{1}{a_j - 1} \sum_{i=1}^{a_j} \left(y_{ij} - m_j \right)^2$$

And hence we know

$$TSS_j = \left(a_j - 1 \right) \hat{\sigma}_j^2$$

which for the data in Table 2.4 are equal to

$$TSS_1 = 29 * 3.14^2 = 285.93$$

$$TSS_2 = 29 * 4.09^2 = 485.11$$
$$TSS_3 = 29 * 3.04^2 = 268.01$$

It can be derived (see the appendix to this chapter) that

$$TSS = \sum_{j=1}^{3} TSS_j + \sum_{j=1}^{3} a_j \left(m_j - \overline{y}_1 \right)^2$$

In this case, this is

$$285.93 + 485.11 + 268.01 + 30(3.97 - 3.52)^2 + 30(3.10 - 3.52)^2$$
$$+ 30(3.50 - 3.52)^2 = 1050.43$$

This gives

$$s_1^2 = \frac{1}{90-1} 1050.43 = 11.803$$

and the test statistic value thus becomes

$$t = \frac{\overline{y}_2 - \overline{y}_1}{\sqrt{\dfrac{s_2^2}{n_2} + \dfrac{s_1^2}{n_1}}} = \frac{1.27 - 3.52}{\sqrt{\dfrac{0.960}{30} + \dfrac{11.803}{90}}} = -5.571$$

The p value is now calculated as < 0.00001.[8] This is a very small p value, and this immediately attracts attention as it may be too good to be true. If the authors had wanted to avoid attracting such attention, they could have chosen to take other values than 1.27 and (0.98). Using the same tools as used here, if you change 1.27 (0.98) into 2.27 (0.98) the t test statistic would be −3.095, and when you change it into 2.57 (0.98), then the t test statistic value is −2.352. You can also opt for another standard deviation. Indeed, 2.27 (3.98) gives a t test value of −2.812, while 2.57 (3.98) gives a test value of −2.137 (which has p value of 0.035).

2.4   UNBELIEVABLE PATTERNS IN THE RESULTS

Unbelievable superior results are presented in Figure 2.8.[9] It does not matter here what the experiments were, but there were

[8] www.socscistatistics.com/pvalues/tdistribution.aspx.
[9] https://retractionwatch.files.wordpress.com/2014/04/report_foerster.pdf.

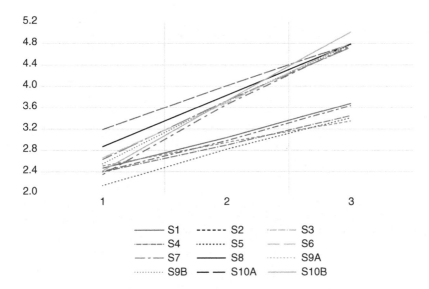

FIGURE 2.8 Scores on twelve experiments (S1 to S10B) when there are three treatments (Low, Medium, High).

twelve of them, with average scores across three treatments. Each line connects three points, which associate with three levels of treatments.

The lines in Figure 2.8 all look like straight lines, in fact perfectly straight.[10] To elicit the straightness of the lines, consider the following regression analyses. Denote Low as 1, Medium as 2 and High as 3, and then run OLS on a regression of the scores on an intercept and $T = 1, 2$, and 3. This gives the following t test values for the variable T for each of the experiments.

Experiments	t test value
S1	29.940
S2	36.373
S3	36.373

---

[10] The data can be found in https://retractionwatch.files.wordpress.com/2014/04/report_foerster.pdf.

(cont.)

Experiments	t test value
S4	23.671
S5	24.441
S6	69.282
S7	36.373
S8	Not available (Standard error = 0)
S9A	19.877
S9B	35.113
S10A	41.377
S10B	225.167

As there are three observations, and two parameters, there is just one degree of freedom. The 5 percent critical value according to the t distribution with one degree of freedom is 12.71. We see three times a t test value of 36.373, which is remarkable, given that there are only three data points. For experiment S8 the data perfectly fit a straight line and a standard error cannot computed. Finally, the t test score on experiment S10B is exceptionally high. These results could not do otherwise than to attract much attention by statisticians, and it is unsure whether the researchers involved were keen on having that attention. Anyway, t values of this size, given this sample size, say that there is something wrong.

2.5   MAKING DATA FIT BETTER TO THE MODEL

Another way to make the results look better is simply to manipulate the data.[11] This does not have to be done in an incredibly involved way, as we will see next.

Let us have a look. In the same fashion as before, create thirty observations with

---

[11] Omitting data to obtain significant effects seems to be present in the case of Dirk Smeesters: see www.jennifervonk.com/uploads/7/7/3/2/7732985/smeesterscase.pdf and www.science.org/content/article/rotterdam-marketing-psychologist-resigns-after-university-investigates-his-data.

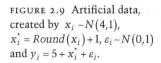

FIGURE 2.9 Artificial data, created by $x_i \sim N(4,1)$, $x_i^* = Round(x_i) + 1$, $\varepsilon_i \sim N(0,1)$ and $y_i = 5 + x_i^* + \varepsilon_i$.

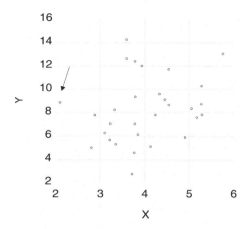

$$x_i \sim N(4,1)$$
$$x_i^* = Round(x_i) + 1$$

Then this x_i^* has mean 3.033, median 3, maximum 5, and minimum 1, at least for this first try.

Next, create an y with a small effect of x as follows

$$\varepsilon_i \sim N(0,1)$$
$$y_i = 5 + x_i^* + \varepsilon_i$$

For thirty observations, a regression of y on an intercept and x^* gives a coefficient 1.040 for x^* with a standard error of 0.562, and hence a t test value of 1.849 with associated p value 0.075. The R^2 is 0.109. Suppose now that one is not that happy with this result and wants to improve the regression outcomes. This can be achieved by modifying just a single observation.

The first created data are in Figure 2.9. The point on the left-hand side of the graph for which x is 1 and the y value is close to 9 can now be moved towards x is 1 and a y value with 5. This new point will then match better with a regression line with a slightly steeper slope and a smaller standard error around that slope. The new data are in Figure 2.10.

When we now run a regression of y on an intercept and this modified x variable, we get using OLS a coefficient 1.382 for x^*

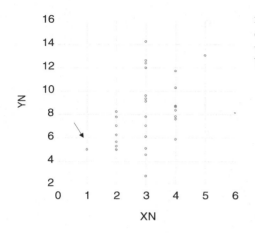

FIGURE 2.10 The same observations as in Figure 2.9, where one observation has been moved downwards.

with a standard error of 0.550, and hence a t test value of 2.514 with associated p value 0.018. The R^2 is now 0.184. So, by just moving one observation towards a regression line we will improve the results.

So far, we considered a few specific and publicly available cases, but engagement in questionable research practice is much more widespread than just by a few individuals.[12] In the following list we see statements and after that a report of the percentages of "yes" to the question whether an individual had engaged in any of the four questionable research practices:[13]

"In a paper, failing to report all of a study's dependent measures"	63.4%
"Deciding whether to collect more data after looking to see whether the results were significant"	55.9%
"In a paper, selectively reporting studies that 'worked'"	45.8%
"Deciding whether to exclude data after looking at the impact of doing so on the results"	38.2%

---

[12] Leslie K. John, George Loewenstein, and Drazen Prelec (2012), Measuring the prevalence of questionable research practices with incentives for truth telling, *Psychological Science*, 23 (5), 524–532.

[13] Source: Leslie K. John, George Loewenstein, and Drazen Prelec (2012), Measuring the prevalence of questionable research practices with incentives for truth telling, *Psychological Science*, 23 (5), 524–532, specifically Table 1, page 525.

What is evident is that in (social) psychology it seems common to engage in questionable research practice.

2.6 WHAT DID WE LEARN?

In this chapter we have learned that it is not difficult to create fake data from fake tables. To detect such fake results, we should hope that people overdo it. We also saw that it is easy to "improve" results even by just changing a single observation. Of course, and this should be clear by now, these insights all entail scientific misconduct.

In the cases studied, we noticed that sometimes people make mistakes because they do not fully understand statistical methods and techniques. To create data that associate with t test values larger than 200 is of course ridiculous even for very small samples. To have p values in small samples that are so much smaller than, for example, 0.001 does not indicate an understanding of statistics.

It is certainly not the case that the detected fraud cases described here are the only ones around. What is clear, though, is that when an academic researcher is found guilty of scientific misconduct, papers get retracted and, quite often, an academic career ends.

How can we prevent such scientific misconduct from happening? The simple lesson is that one should report everything that one has done. How do the raw data look like, how did you clean the data, which data did you decide to change and for what reasons? Can we replicate your analysis, starting from the original data?

2.7 APPENDIX

The total sum of squares is

$$TSS = \sum_{i=1}^{a_1}\left(y_{i1} - \overline{y}_1\right)^2 + \sum_{i=1}^{a_2}\left(y_{i2} - \overline{y}_1\right)^2 + \sum_{i=1}^{a_3}\left(y_{i3} - \overline{y}_1\right)^2$$

This can be written as

$$TSS = \sum_{i=1}^{a_1}\left(y_{i1} - m_1 + m_1 - \overline{y}_1\right)^2 + \sum_{i=1}^{a_2}\left(y_{i2} - m_2 + m_2 - \overline{y}_1\right)^2$$
$$+ \sum_{i=1}^{a_3}\left(y_{i3} - m_3 + m_3 - \overline{y}_1\right)^2$$

When we focus only on

$$\sum_{i=1}^{a_1}\left(y_{i1}-m_1+m_1-\overline{y}_1\right)^2$$

then we can write it is

$$\sum_{i=1}^{a_1}\left(y_{i1}-m_1+m_1-\overline{y}_1\right)^2 = \sum_{i=1}^{a_1}(y_{i1}-m_1)^2 + a_1\left(m_1-\overline{y}_1\right)^2$$

$$+2\sum_{i=1}^{a_1}(y_{i1}-m_1)\left(m_1-\overline{y}_1\right) = \sum_{i=1}^{a_1}(y_{i1}-m_1)^2 + a_1\left(m_1-\overline{y}_1\right)^2$$

Parts 2 and 3 can be written in the same format. This gives for the total sum of squares

$$TSS = \sum_{i=1}^{a_1}(y_{i1}-m_1)^2 + a_1\left(m_1-\overline{y}_1\right)^2$$

$$+ \sum_{i=1}^{a_2}(y_{i2}-m_2)^2 + a_2\left(m_2-\overline{y}_1\right)^2$$

$$+ \sum_{i=1}^{a_3}(y_{i3}-m_3)^2 + a_3\left(m_3-\overline{y}_1\right)^2$$

And hence

$$TSS = \sum_{j=1}^{3}TSS_j + \sum_{j=1}^{3}a_j\left(m_j-\overline{y}_1\right)^2$$

2.8 EPILOGUE

Not all retracted papers are signals of scientific misconduct. A good example is Thurik et al.[14] The authors found out that there was something wrong with their data. They wished to retract their study: see Stephan.[15] A revised version of the retracted paper with the correct data analyzed was published by Wismans et al.[16]

---

[14] Roy Thurik, Anis Khedhauoria, Olivier Torrès, and Ingrid Verheul (2016), ADHD symptoms and entrepreneurial orientation of small firm owners, *Applied Psychology*, 65 (3), 568–586.

[15] Ute Stephan (2020), Retractions are difficult – Perhaps they shouldn't be, *Applied Psychology*, 69 (3), 1113.

[16] Annelot Wismans, Roy Thurik, Ingrid Verheul, Olivier Torrès, and Katsuyuki Kamei (2020), ADHD symptoms and entrepreneurial orientation: A replication note, *Applied Psychology*, 69 (3), 1093–1112.

FURTHER READING

Joanne Horton, Dhanya Krishna Kumar, and Anthony Wood (2020), Detecting academic fraud using Benford law: The case of Professor James Hunton, *Research Policy*, 49 (8), 104084.

Lee Harvey (2020), Research fraud: A long-term problem exacerbated by the glamour for research grants, *Quality in Higher Education*, 26 (3), 243–261.

Nicola Lacetera and Lorenzo Zirulia (2011), The economics of scientific misconduct, *Journal of Law, Economics & Organization*, 27 (3), 568–603, with the quote:

> ... a strong "publish or perish" pressure may reduce, and not increase, scientific misconduct because it motivates more scrutiny.

Serge P. J. M. Horbach, Eric Breit, and Svenn-Erik Mamelund (2019), Organisational responses to alleged scientific misconduct: Sensemaking, sensegiving, and sensehiding, *Science and Public Policy*, 46 (3), 415–429.

Lori L. Murray and John G. Wilson (2021), Generating data sets for teaching the importance of regression analysis, *Decision Sciences Journal of Innovative Education*, 19 (2), 157–166.

Graham Elliott, Nikolay Kudrin, and Kaspar Wüthrich (2022), Detecting p hacking, *Econometrica*, 90 (2), 887–906.

Fang, Ferrie C., R. Grant Steen, and Arturo Casadevall (2012), Misconduct accounts for the majority of retracted scientific publications, *PNAS*, 109 (42), 17028–17033.

Abel Brodeur, Nikolai Cook, and Carina Neisser (2022), P-hacking, data type and data-sharing policy, IZA Discussion paper Series No. 15586.

The latter authors report that "we find a well-estimated null effect that requiring authors to share their data at the time of publication does not alter the presence of p-hacking."

3   Influential Observations

In Chapter 2 we saw that insufficient understanding of statistical methods and techniques can lead to (detectable) scientific misconduct. Reporting test results that are "too good to be true" makes alarm bells ring. Reporting test results that show you prefer certain numbers makes you vulnerable to easy detection of fraud. When test results all lie on the same perfectly straight line, then the apparent absence of noise makes people wonder about the trustworthiness of the outcomes.

In this chapter, we will move towards more subtle aspects of econometric analysis, where it is not immediately obvious from the numbers or the graphs that something is wrong. We will see that so-called influential observations may not be visible from graphs but will become apparent after creating a model. This is immediately one of the key takeaways from this chapter, and that is that we do not throw away data prior to econometric analysis. That is, we incorporate all observations in our models, and based on specific diagnostic measures, we can decide which observations are harmful.

3.1   WARMING UP

Before we start with the main content of this chapter, let us warm up a little with a few hypothetical cases. The reader can create the relevant data. Of course, we will all use different random number generators, so you will not find the same results, although they should look like it.

Let us begin with a data point, an observation, that we could call a "good" influential observation. Generate one hundred observations using the following scheme:

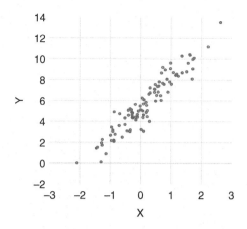

$$x_i \sim N(0,1)$$
$$v_i \sim N(0,1)$$
$$y_i = 5 + 3x_i + v_i$$

This results in a scatter diagram of y versus x as in Figure 3.1.

If we run the regression (meaning we estimate the parameters of the following model using OLS), that is,

$$y_i = \alpha + \beta x_i + \varepsilon_i$$

then we get something like (with standard errors in parentheses)

$$a = 5.072\,(0.108)$$
$$b = 2.851\,(0.108)$$

with an $R^2 = 0.877$. This is a good fit, and this is of course mainly owing to the small error v_i relative to three times x_i in the Data Generating Process (DGP). When we randomly replace just one of the points by the point (5, 20), we get the data as in Figure 3.2.

The regression results now become

$$a = 5.083\,(0.108)$$
$$b = 2.869\,(0.097)$$

with an $R^2 = 0.899$. We see that the standard error for b has decreased and that the R^2 has increased.

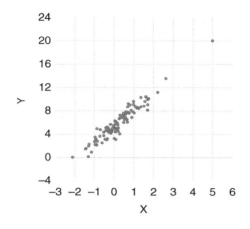

FIGURE 3.2 A scatterplot of artificially created data on y and x, where one observation is replaced by (5, 20). Source: Author's calculations

One can also create "too good" an influential observation. Consider, for example, 100 observations from independent standard normal distributions:

$$x_i \sim N(0,1)$$
$$y_i \sim N(0,1)$$

and put these in a scatter plot as in Figure 3.3.

As expected from Figure 3.3 there is no visual evidence of a relevant correlation among the two variables. This is established in a regression model, where the OLS estimates are

$$a = -0.113(0.098)$$
$$b = 0.116(0.088)$$

with an $R^2 = 0.017$. Now, suppose we replace one observation by (10,10) as in Figure 3.4. The effect of replacing just a single observation gives OLS-based output

$$a = -0.179(0.120)$$
$$b = 0.529(0.081)$$

with an $R^2 = 0.304$. Just replacing one observation with another one can create statistically significant estimation results for β. Note that the t ratio for b is larger than 6, which is large.

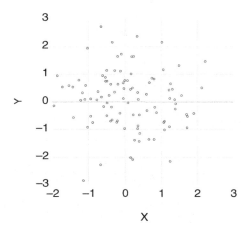

FIGURE 3.3 A scatterplot of artificially created y and x, with correlation close to zero. Source: Author's calculations

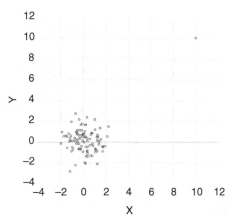

FIGURE 3.4 A scatterplot of artificially created y and x, when one randomly selected observation is replaced by $(10,10)$. Source: Author's calculations

Moving to a time series setting, and to see the impact of a harmful influential observation, consider the creation of data from a first order autoregression where the autoregressive parameter is equal to 1. Such a model is a random walk. So, create data such as

$$y_1 = 0$$
$$v_t \sim N(0,1)$$
$$y_t = y_{t-1} + v_t, \quad t = 2, 3, \ldots, 100$$

A graph of the data appears in Figure 3.5. Visual support for a random walk is that the data cross only twice the approximate average value. There is no evident mean reversion.

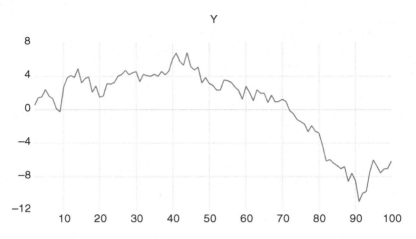

FIGURE 3.5 A random walk.
Source: Author's calculations

To verify if the data indeed have random walk properties, one can use the so-called Dickey–Fuller regression.[1] This is a regression of the first differences on lagged levels, like this one:

$$y_t - y_{t-1} = \alpha + \beta y_{t-1} + \varepsilon_t$$

When the null hypothesis $\beta = 0$ is not rejected, and y_{t-1} drops from the right-hand side of the model, we end up with a model for the first differences. OLS gives

$$a = -0.288(0.172)$$
$$b = -0.020(0.015)$$

and the t test statistic for $\beta = 0$ is –1.405. The critical values of this one-sided t test are not from the standard t distribution but follow from a distribution that is shifted to the left. For this case, with an intercept in the regression, the 5 percent critical value is –2.89, and hence indeed, the null hypothesis $\beta = 0$ is not rejected.

---

[1] David A. Dickey and Wayne A. Fuller (1979), Distribution of the estimators for autoregressive time series with a unit root, *Journal of the American Statistical Association*, 74 (366), 427–431.

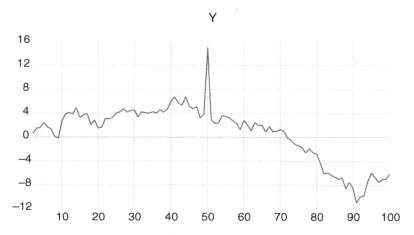

FIGURE 3.6 A random walk with a typographical error at $t = 50$.
Source: Author's calculations

FIGURE 3.7 A scatterplot of y_t
against y_{t-1} for a random walk
with an additive outlier at $t = 50$.
Source: Author's calculations

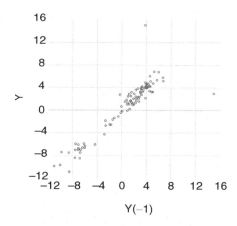

Suppose now that the data are not those as in Figure 3.5 but are those in Figure 3.6. The observation at $t = 50$ is replaced by 15, which amounts to having a so-called additive outlier that moment. Literally "additive," as we added a value to the observation to make it 15. The source of such an additive outlier in practice may be a typing error.

When we look at the scatter plot in Figure 3.7, depicting y_t against y_{t-1}, we see that the additive outlier appears twice. When we apply OLS to a regression of y_t on y_{t-1}, these two points will attract the regression line towards zero, that is, away from 1. In other words, the evidence of a unit root disappears.[2] This can be seen from applying OLS to

$$y_t - y_{t-1} = \alpha + \beta y_{t-1} + \varepsilon_t$$

for the data with the additive outlier, which now gives

$$a = -1.602\,(0.638)$$
$$b = -0.161\,(0.054)$$

Now, the one-sided t test on $\beta = 0$ is -3.002, which is to the left of the 5 percent critical value of -2.89. So, just a single typing error makes evidence for a random walk disappear.

3.2 EXERCISES

Here are exercises that you can do yourself to see what happens if you have an additive outlier at $t = 100$ where there are 200 observations from the DGP:

$$\Delta_1 y_t = 0.6\Delta_1 y_{t-1} + v_t$$

with $v_t \sim N(0,1)$, where $\Delta_1 y_t = y_t - y_{t-1}$, with $y_2 = y_1 = 0$, and you consider the so-called Augmented Dickey–Fuller test based on the augmentation with lagged differences, that is,

$$\Delta_1 y_t = \alpha + \beta y_{t-1} + \gamma\Delta_1 y_{t-1} + \varepsilon_t$$

where the 5 percent critical value is again -2.89. And next, suppose you consider the DGP:

$$\Delta_4 y_t = \varepsilon_t$$

where $\Delta_4 y_t = y_t - y_{t-4}$ with $y_4 = y_3 = y_2 = y_1 = 0$, and you consider the test regression

---

[2] Philip Hans Franses and Niels Haldrup (1994), The effects of additive outliers on tests for unit roots and cointegration, *Journal of Business and Economic Statistics*, 12 (4) 471–478.

$$\Delta_4 y_t = \alpha + \beta(y_{t-1} + y_{t-2} + y_{t-3} + y_{t-4}) + \varepsilon_t$$

where again the 5 percent critical value is –2.89. Note that the term on the right-hand side follows from the fact that

$$\Delta_4 y_t = \Delta_1(y_t + y_{t-1} + y_{t-2} + y_{t-3})$$

3.3 WHAT IS NEXT IN THIS CHAPTER?

Now we have seen to what extent and how single observations can be influential, let us move to the main content of this chapter. We start with methods to detect influential observations, and we will see that only looking at data plots will not help.

Wikipedia says:

> In statistics, an influential observation is an observation for a statistical calculation whose deletion from the dataset *would noticeably change the result of the calculation* [emphasis added]. In particular, in regression analysis an influential observation is one whose deletion has a large effect on the parameter estimates.[3]

Note that this definition starts with a model and then focuses on the effects of deleting an observation. It is not the other way around. We will see how we can counter influential observations; how seemingly satisfactory results can disappear when we properly deal with such influential observations, and how results can change, and what we can do when there is an influential observation at the end of the sample, that is, at the forecast origin. We will see that judgment can be necessary. If we exercise such judgment, we should report it.

3.4 ANSCOMBE'S QUARTET

Let us first begin with a famous set of data called Anscombe's quartet.[4] The data on four pairs of eleven observations on a y and an x are presented in Table 3.1.

---

[3] https://en.wikipedia.org/wiki/Influential_observations.

[4] Francis Anscombe (1973), Graphs in statistical analysis, *American Statistician*, 27 (1), 17–21, https://en.wikipedia.org/wiki/Anscombe%27s_quartet.

Table 3.1 *Four hypothetical pairs of variables*

y_1	x_1	y_2	x_2	y_3	x_3	y_4	x_4
8.04	10	9.14	10	7.46	10	6.58	8
6.95	8	8.14	8	6.77	8	5.76	8
7.58	13	8,74	13	12.74	13	7.71	8
8.81	9	8.77	9	7.11	9	8.84	8
8.33	11	9.26	11	7.81	11	8.47	8
9.96	14	8.1	14	8.84	14	7.04	8
7.24	6	6.13	6	6.08	6	5.25	8
4.26	4	3.1	4	5.39	4	12.5	19
10.84	12	9.13	12	8.15	12	5.56	8
4.82	7	7.26	7	6.42	7	7.91	8
5.68	5	4.74	5	5.73	5	6.89	8

Source: Anscombe (1973)

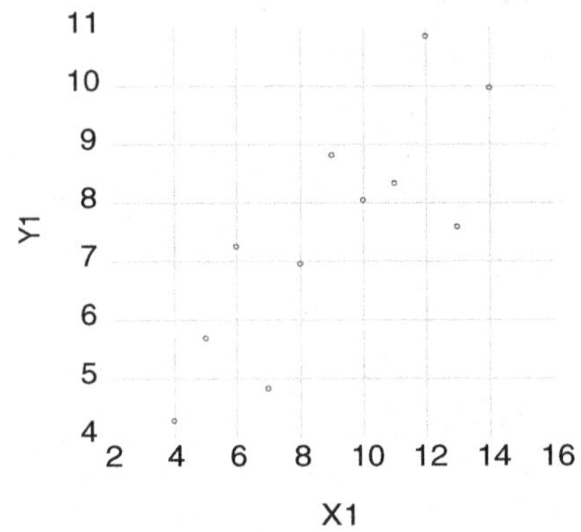

FIGURE 3.8 Data set 1.

Scatter plots of the four sets appear in Figures 3.8 to 3.11.

You can see from these graphs that the data sets all look quite different. Data set 1 seems to associate with a reasonable regression line. For data set 2, we could consider a linear regression perhaps with x^2 as regressor. Data set 3 has a single outlier in the top of the graph, whereas data set 4 has no fewer than ten observations with the same x values. However, if we had not looked at the graphs, and computed some summary statistics, we would see that these data

FIGURE 3.9 Data set 2.

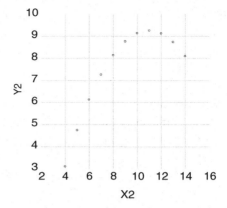

FIGURE 3.10 Data set 3.

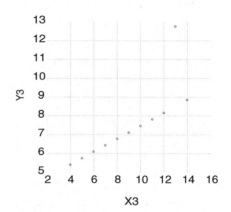

FIGURE 3.11 Data set 4.
Source: Author's calculations

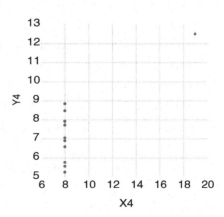

sets have much in common. Consider the following statistics for each of the four data sets:

Mean of each x	9
Sample variance of each x	11
Mean of each y	7.50
Sample variance of each y	4.125
Correlation between pairs y and x	0.816
Regression line	$y = 3.00 + 0.500\,x$
R^2 of regression line	0.67

These four data sets provide the same summary statistics, but the graphs tell us that the data are different. Here we have the first major lesson, which is that we should always visualize our data. There is no standard format that one should use, and one can think of line graphs and histograms. There is a range of possible visual tools.

If the raw summary statistics of the data are not informative, what could we then do? Here are helpful tools to detect influential observations in regression models. In Appendix 1 to this chapter we present formal expressions of these tools.

The so-called Rstudent values are based on creating 1/0 dummies for each observation, then including each time a dummy in the model, and finally looking at t test values of the parameters for that dummy variable.

Another useful tool considers the diagonal elements of the so-called hat-matrix $H = X(X'X)^{-1}X'$, in the regression model $y = X\beta + \varepsilon$, which measures the leverage of the observations. In a model with k regressors (including an intercept), the mean leverage is $\frac{k}{n}$, where n denotes the number of observations.

Next, DFFITS measures the difference in the fit with and without an observation. If |DFFITS| exceeds $2\sqrt{\frac{k}{n}}$ then it is significant at the 5 percent level.

Figure 3.12 presents these three measures for data set 3, when we consider a regression of $y_{3,i}$ on an intercept and $x_{3,i}$. The horizontal line in the graph for the hat-matrix is $\frac{k}{n}$.

Influence Statistics

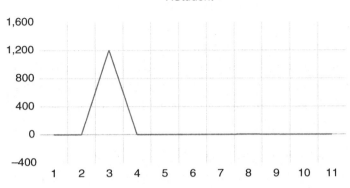

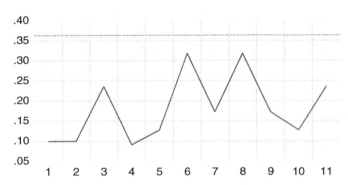

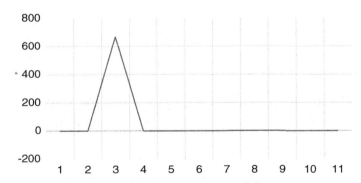

FIGURE 3.12 Regression diagnostics for data set 3.
Source: Author's calculations

Clearly, Rstudent and DFFITS tell us that there is something going on for the third observation. The hat matrix appears not to signal anything for the third observation. This, by the way, shows that you will not always find that all influence diagnostics point at the same observation, and hence it is good to look at more than one measure.

To continue, another useful diagnostic is DFBETAS, which measures the influence of an individual observation on the parameter estimates. The |DFBETAS| is significant at the 5 percent level when it exceeds $\frac{2}{\sqrt{n}}$.

For data set 3, the eleven DFBETAS values are

$$-0.004, \; -0.037, \; -357.91, \; -0.033, \; 0.049, \; 0.490, \; 0.027,$$
$$0.241, \; 0.137, \; -0.020, \; 0.105$$

where again the third observation stands out. This is confirmed by comparing the regression model with all eleven observations with that obtained after the third observation has been deleted. OLS applied to

$$y_{3,i} = \alpha + \beta x_{3,i} + \varepsilon_i$$

gives for all observations

$$a = 3.002(1.124)$$
$$b = 0.500(0.118)$$

with $R^2 = 0.666$. Without the third observation, we get for ten observations the OLS results

$$a = 4.006(0.003)$$
$$b = 0.345(0.0003)$$
$$R^2 = 0.999993$$

Note that the related t value for $\beta = 0$ and this last R^2 value once again show that there is something special about these data.

3.5 WHEN IT REALLY MATTERS

So far, all analyzed data have been artificially created. But now let us turn to a case where the outcomes could have had serious policy consequences.[5] Denote TFPG as Total Factor Productivity Growth (measured as the difference between averages of 1974–1976 and of 1969–1973), PRIV as R&D investments in private companies (1969–1973) and FED as research and development (R&D) investments by federal governments (again 1969–1973). There are observations on twenty-seven distinct industries in the United States. Suppose one considers the regression model

$$TFPG_i = \alpha + \beta_1 PRIV_i + \beta_2 FED_i + \varepsilon_i$$

Application of OLS gives

$$a = -0.579(0.295)$$
$$b_1 = 0.346(0.086)$$
$$b_2 = 0.010(0.023)$$

with an $R^2 = 0.443$. We see that $\beta_2 = 0$ is not rejected as the t test value is only 0.442. This may suggest an interpretation as being that the partial effects of R&D investments by federal governments are small.

Now, let us see if the results are influenced by one or two observations. Figure 3.13 displays the Rstudent, the diagonal entries of the hat matrix and the DFFITS for this model. Rstudent values do not ring a bell, while the hat matrix suggests that observations 2 and 18 are influential, and DFFITS seems to point at observation 2.

When we delete observations 2 (missiles and spacecraft) and 18 (office, computing, and accounting machines), OLS gives for the twenty-five remaining observations:

$$a = -0.455(0.297)$$
$$b_1 = 0.200(0.107)$$
$$b_2 = 0.188(0.089)$$

---

[5] Zvi Griliches and Frank Lichtenberg (1984), R&D and productivity growth at the industry level: Is there still a relationship? in Zvi Griliches (ed.), R&D, Patents, and Productivity, Chicago: Chicago University Press; Peter Reiss (1990), Detecting multiple outliers with an application to R&D productivity, Journal of Econometrics, 43 (3), 293–315. The data are from Griliches and Lichtenberg (1984, Table 21.A.2) and reproduced in Reiss (1990, page 311).

Influence Statistics

RStudent

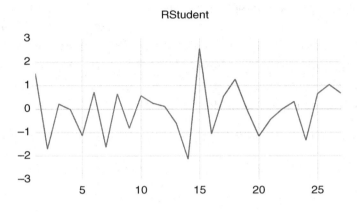

Hat Matrix

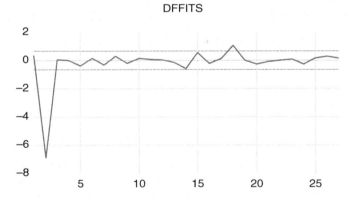

DFFITS

FIGURE 3.13 Diagnostics on influential observations.
Source: Author's calculations

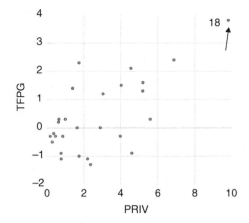

FIGURE 3.14 TFPG against R&D investments in private companies.

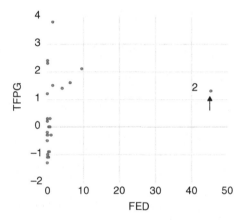

FIGURE 3.15 TFPG against R&D investments by federal governments.
Source: Author's calculations

The $R^2 = 0.363$, which is smaller than before. The two t values have become 1.876 and 2.110, respectively, and the parameter estimates are about equally large.

Could we have seen this from scatter plots? Figure 3.14 suggests that observation 18 would be one of those typical "good" influential observations, where Figure 3.15 suggests that observation 2 definitively needs attention.

When we only exclude observation 2, then OLS for twenty-six observations gives

Influence Statistics

RStudent

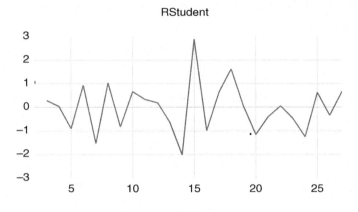

Hat Matrix

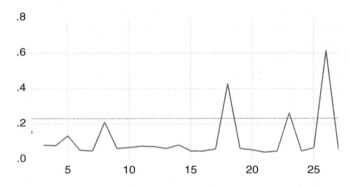

DFFITS

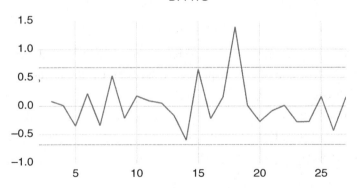

FIGURE 3.16 Diagnostics on influential observations, when observation 2 is deleted.
Source: Author's calculations

$$a = -0.632\,(0.286)$$
$$b_1 = 0.309\,(0.085)$$
$$b_2 = 0.159\,(0.090)$$

The $R^2 = 0.495$, and the two t values are 3.632 and 1.760, respectively. Note that now the value of b_1 is about twice the size of b_2. Figure 3.16 suggests that just deleting observation 2 gives no clear sign that anything is wrong in this respect.

3.6 HOW CAN SATISFACTORY RESULTS DISAPPEAR?

The following is based on my own personal experience: an experience that was helpful in shaping this chapter and formulating advice. This personal experience concerned carefully collected data on thirty-seven experts who could manually modify model-based forecasts (more on that in Chapter 10).[6] We could collect data on the average size of their adjustments. We also collected data on age, gender, and position within the company. Various hypotheses were formulated, all based on extant literature, and then we considered the following regression model for y_i, the average size of model adjustment, that is,

$$y_i = \alpha + \beta_1 x_{1,i} + \beta_2 x_{2,i} + \beta_3 x_{3,i} + \beta_4 x_{4,i} + \beta_5 x_{5,i} + \beta_6 x_{6,i} + \varepsilon_i$$

x_1 is Age
x_2 is $(Age - 39.5)^2$
x_3 is Position
x_4 is Gender (female = 1)
$x_5 = Gender \times Age$
$x_6 = Gender \times Position$

Note that we here subtract the average age (39.5) before squaring the variable, to reduce multicollinearity (more on that in Chapter 5). The estimation results are

---

[6] Rianne Legerstee and Philip Hans Franses (2007), Competence and confidence effects in experts' forecast adjustments, Econometric Institute Research Papers EI 2007-36, Erasmus University Rotterdam, Erasmus School of Economics, Econometric Institute. This unpublished paper contains results that are fully dependent on one single observation. We ourselves forgot to look at influential observations! The editor of the journal to which the paper was submitted analyzed the data that we had made available and found our mistake. We are very grateful that this was detected!

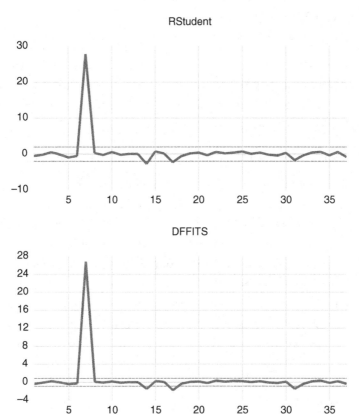

FIGURE 3.17 Influence of observation 7.
Source: Author's calculations

$$a = 3.570(3.846)$$
$$b_1 = -0.107(0.122)$$
$$b_2 = 0.016(0.005)$$
$$b_3 = 0.017(0.199)$$
$$b_4 = -12.668(5.218)$$
$$b_5 = 0.396(0.164)$$
$$b_6 = -0.230(0.287)$$

The $R^2 = 0.438$. As such, we thought we found support for part of our hypotheses, and we drafted the paper. One of the things we should

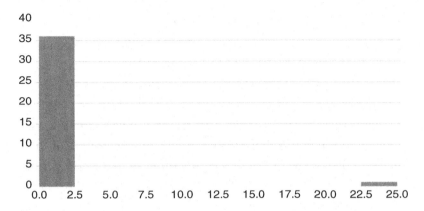

FIGURE 3.18 One obvious outlier (the seventh observation) in the dependent variable.
Source: Author's calculations

have done, however, was look at the influence statistics such as Rstudent and DFFITS. They appear in Figure 3.17, and indeed, the seventh observation stands out as a very influential observation.

When we look again at the regression, now for thirty-six experts and thus deleting the seventh observation, we obtain

$$a = 0.665(0.750)$$
$$b_1 = -0.006(0.024)$$
$$b_2 = -0.0004(0.001)$$
$$b_3 = 0.036(0.038)$$
$$b_4 = 1.028(1.120)$$
$$b_5 - -0.009(0.035)$$
$$b_6 = -0.054(0.056)$$

with an $R^2 = 0.136$. No single parameter is significant. Hence, we were misled by just a single observation. Well, it is even worse. If we had created the histogram as in Figure 3.18, we would have spotted the outlying observation immediately.

So, after experiencing this ourselves, we now recommend always visualizing the data.[7]

[7] Results without the seventh expert are now published in Philip Hans Franses (2014), *Expert Adjustments of Model Forecasts*, Cambridge: Cambridge University Press, page 66.

3.7 WHEN NEW GRAPHS SHOULD BE CREATED

We have just seen that making histograms of the data of a dependent variable is highly informative about potentially influential data. Sometimes we must make alternative and estimation-based graphs to see if there is something strange. Let us look at the annual data for Madagascar shown in Figure 3.19 relating to consumption and income (in millions of USD) and Figure 3.20 on growth rates of consumption and income.[8] Do you see something strange in the period around 1973–1974? Most likely not, and therefore we need to resort to other tools.

Denoting the natural log of consumption as y_t and the natural log of income as x_t, we can consider a simple so-called conditional error correction model,[9] which reads as

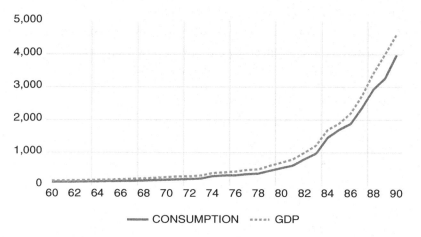

FIGURE 3.19 Consumption and income Madagascar, 1960–1990 (in millions of USD).

---

[8] In memory of Paul de Boer, who alerted us to this case and provided the data, and who passed away on September 19, 2021.

[9] Robert F. Engle and Clive W. J. Granger (1987), Co-integration and error correction: Representation, estimation and testing, *Econometrica*, 55 (2), 251–276, and H. Peter Boswijk (1994), Testing for an unstable root in conditional and structural error correction models, *Journal of Econometrics*, 63(1), 37–60.

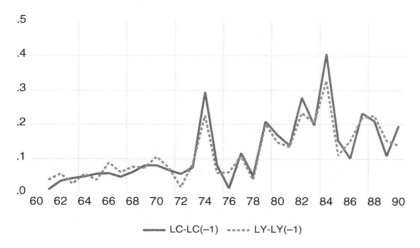

FIGURE 3.20 Growth rates of income and consumption Madagascar, 1961–1990.
Source: Author's calculations

$$\Delta_1 y_t = \alpha + \beta_1 \Delta_1 x_t + \beta_2 \left(y_{t-1} - x_{t-1} \right) + \varepsilon_t$$

For thirty observations, the OLS estimation results are

$$a = -0.071(0.030)$$
$$b_1 = 1.249(0.083)$$
$$b_2 = -0.165(0.082)$$

The $R^2 = 0.910$. This model seems to describe these annual data well. Now, let us estimate the model parameters recursively, that is for the samples 1961–1965, 1961–1966 until 1961–1990. The recursive residuals are the standardized one-step-ahead prediction errors (Figure 3.21).

The large recursive residual in 1974 stands out. So, something changed dramatically around that time.

When we compute the recursive coefficients (see Appendix 2 to this chapter for the relevant expressions), we get the results as presented in Figure 3.22. The expression c(1) stands for a, c(2) for b_1, and c(3) for b_2. What we would like to see is that the recursive coefficients

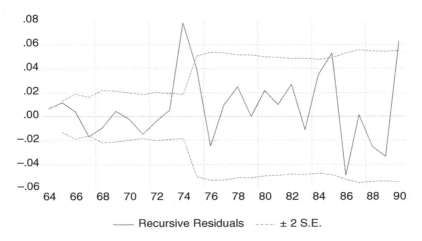

--- Recursive Residuals ---- ± 2 S.E.

FIGURE 3.21 Recursive residuals for the conditional error correction model and their 95 percent confidence intervals.
Source: Author's calculations

converge to a final fixed level, and that the confidence bounds around these get smaller and smaller as time proceeds. However, if we look at the middle panel of Figure 3.22, there is an obvious jump in the estimates of b_1, the short-run income multiplier.

When we next decide to estimate the parameters of the conditional error correction model for two different samples, we get for the sample 1961–1973

$$a = -0.105(0.028)$$
$$b_1 = 0.407(0.103)$$
$$b_2 = -0.396(0.083)$$

with an $R^2 = 0.816$, and for the sample 1974–1990 we get

$$a = -0.083(0.036)$$
$$b_1 = 1.247(0.112)$$
$$b_2 = -0.236(0.112)$$

Here the $R^2 = 0.899$. Notably, the estimate for β_1 shifts from 0.407 to 1.247. What happened around that time in Madagascar? In that

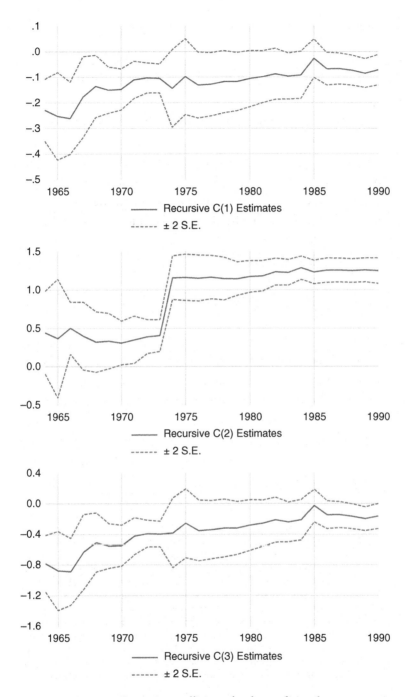

FIGURE 3.22 Recursive coefficients for the conditional error correction model.
Source: Author's calculations

period there is a move from the first to the second republic.[10] This transition occurred at the same time as there were changes in the national accounts.

The key takeaway from this econometric analysis of national accounts data is that the break in the parameter, even with this size, could not have been observed from the graphs of the raw data. Looking back again at Figures 3.19 and 3.20, we cannot see that something happens around 1974. So, again, detecting influential observations, or in this case even a structural break, can best be done by first designing a model, then estimating its parameters, and then looking at various influence statistics.

3.8   AN INFLUENTIAL OBSERVATION AT A FORECAST ORIGIN

The final topic in this chapter concerns the case where you have an influential observation right at the end of the sample, that is, the moment from which you are supposed to make a forecast: the forecast origin. Consider the artificially created data in Figure 3.23, which have this large observation at the end.

You can decide to just take on board the influential observation and assume that this could have been a regular observation. If you consider the autoregression

$$y_t = \alpha + \beta y_{t-1} + \varepsilon_t$$

---

[10] From https://en.wikipedia.org/wiki/Madagascar: "Since regaining independence, Madagascar has transitioned through four republics with corresponding revisions to its constitution. The First Republic (1960–72), under the leadership of French-appointed President Philibert Tsiranana, was characterized by a continuation of strong economic and political ties to France. Many high-level technical positions were filled by French expatriates, and French teachers, textbooks and curricula continued to be used in schools around the country. Popular resentment over Tsiranana's tolerance for this 'neo-colonial' arrangement inspired a series of farmer and student protests that overturned his administration in 1972. Gabriel Ramanantsoa, a major general in the army, was appointed interim president and prime minister that same year, but low public approval forced him to step down in 1975. Colonel Richard Ratsimandrava, appointed to succeed him, was assassinated six days into his tenure. General Gilles Andriamahazo ruled after Ratsimandrava for four months before being replaced by another military appointee: Vice Admiral Didier Ratsiraka, who ushered in the Socialist-Marxist Second Republic that ran under his tenure from 1975 to 1993."

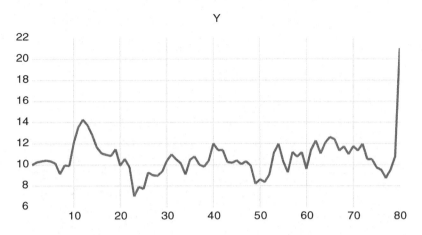

FIGURE 3.23 DGP is $y_t = 2 + 0.8y_{t-1} + v_t$, $v_t \sim N(0,1)$, $y_1 = 10$, and observation at $t = 80$ becomes $y_{80} = 21$.
Source: Author's calculations

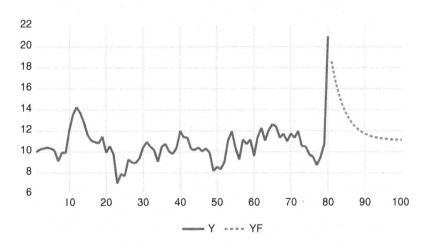

FIGURE 3.24 One-step-ahead to twenty-steps-ahead forecasts from a first order autoregression.
Source: Author's calculations

and estimate the parameters using OLS, the forecasts will then look like those in Figure 3.24. If you do so, you have treated the influential observation as a so-called innovation outlier.

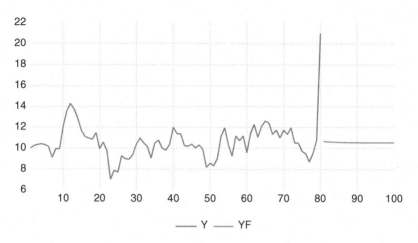

FIGURE 3.25 Forecasts when ignoring the last observation and start forecasting from $t = 79$.

You can also believe that this last observation is an additive outlier,[11] and then just delete the observation. You then take the observation at $t = 79$ as the new forecast origin and apply OLS for a first order autoregression. The subsequent multiple-steps-ahead forecasts are those in Figure 3.25.

It can also be that the large observation at $t = 80$ marks the beginning of a structural break, and hence that the level can stay high from that observation onwards. You can, for example, create forecasts from $y_t = 0.5 + a + by_{t-1}$, where you added 0.5 to a. The forecasts can then look like those in Figure 3.26.

In each case, we see that judgment comes in, and the choice options should be motivated. Such judgment can also be made a bit more formal. Suppose that the observation at time T, the forecast origin, is a one-off innovation outlier of size ω_T, that is,

$$y_T = \mu + \rho y_{T-1} + \varepsilon_T + \omega_T$$

---

[11] The effect of such an observation at the end on the OLS-based estimation results is minor: see Johannes Ledolter (1989), The effect of additive outliers on the forecasts from ARIMA models, *International Journal of Forecasting*, 5 (2), 231–240.

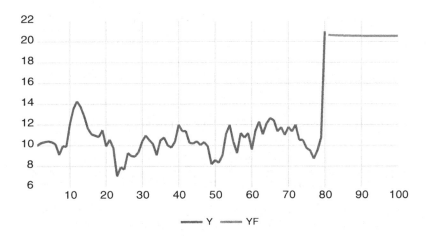

FIGURE 3.26 Forecasting with the assumption that $t = 80$ marks the beginning of a structural break.
Source: Author's calculations

then the observation at $T + 1$ is

$$y_{T+1} = \mu + \rho y_T + \varepsilon_{T+1}$$

and there is no need to (manually) modify the forecast. This is the first case noted earlier.

Now suppose there is an additive outlier at the forecast origin, that is,

$$y_T = \mu + \rho y_{T-1} + \varepsilon_T$$

But we observe

$$x_T = y_T + \omega_T$$

The forecast error at time $T + 1$, if you know ρ and μ becomes

$$\varepsilon_{T+1} + \rho \omega_T$$

Hence, a manually adjusted forecast for the observation at $T + 1$ given T could read as

$$\hat{y}^a_{T+1|T} = \hat{x}_{T+1|T} - \rho \hat{\omega}_T$$

Now, what is the value of $\hat{\omega}_T$? If $\hat{\omega}_T$ is set equal to the error at time T, then

$$\hat{y}_{T+1|T}^a = \hat{x}_{T+1} - \rho\left(\varepsilon_T + \omega_T\right) = \mu + \rho y_T - \rho\left(y_T - \rho y_{T-1} - \mu\right)$$
$$= \left(1 + \rho\right)\mu + \rho^2 y_{T-1} = \hat{y}_{T+1|T-1}$$

which is the two-steps-ahead forecast from origin $T - 1$.

3.9 WHAT DID WE LEARN?

First, we learned that anyone can make mistakes, and we have done so. Sometimes we learn the hard way.

Second, we learned that it is always wise to make graphs of the data or transformations of these data. Sometimes influential observations can then already be spotted. However, influential observations are not always visually obvious. We need diagnostic tests. These tests are based on the model estimation results. So, one should perform analysis on model estimation results and not remove data prior to model building.

Finally, and according to the main theme of this book, we learned that you should document precisely how you deal(t) with influential observations. Which observations did you delete and why? Which judgments did you make and based on what?

3.10 WHAT SHOULD WE BETTER NOT DO?

As an exercise, here is a strategy that is sometimes followed but does not seem wise. It deals with trimming or winsorizing the data before you start your analysis: "the vast majority of these studies winsorize the data or perform some sort of listwise deletion. Yet, this identification and treatment of outliers implicitly relies on outliers arising in a univariate context."[12]

Wikipedia says on winsorizing: "A typical strategy is to set all outliers to a specified percentile of the data; for example, a 90 percent

---

[12] From John Adams, Darren Hayunga, Sattar Mansi, David Reeb, and Vincenzo Verardi (2019), Identifying and treating outliers in finance, *Financial Management*, 48 (2), 345–384.

Table 3.2 *Two fictitious data sets with twenty observations*

y	x_1	x_2	y	x_1	x_2
4	10	2	4	10	2
5	7	3	5	7	3
6	4	7	6	4	7
7	15	1	7	15	1
7	3	12	7	3	12
7	3	10	7	3	10
11	10	9	11	10	9
11	7	12	11	7	12
11	20	3	11	20	3
11	16	4	11	16	4
11	12	8	11	12	8
12	3	12	12	3	12
12	19	2	12	19	2
12	19	10	12	19	10
13	20	5	13	20	5
15	19	9	15	19	9
16	15	10	16	15	10
17	16	17	17	5	2
18	19	19	5	19	19
21	17	20	21	17	20

Source: Adams et al. (2019)

winsorization would see all data below the 5th percentile set to the 5th percentile, and data above the 95th percentile set to the 95th percentile."[13] Wikipedia adds that "In a trimmed estimator, the extreme values are *discarded*; in a winsorized estimator, the extreme values are instead *replaced* by certain percentiles (the trimmed minimum and maximum)." So, there is the difference.

To see for yourself what can be the consequences of various strategies, consider the following two data sets each with twenty observations to be analyzed using a regression model in Table 3.2.

[13] https://en.wikipedia.org/wiki/Winsorizing.

The data sets with each a y and an x_1 and x_2 are the same except for the observations 18 and 19: Look at the italicized numbers.

As an exercise you can examine what happens to the OLS estimation results for data set 1 and for data set 2

- if you analyze all twenty data points;
- if you apply 90 percent winsorizing to the twenty data points;
- if you apply 90 percent trimming to the twenty data points;
- if you follow the DFFITS finding (applied to this data set 2) that the observations 18 and 19 are outliers and delete these observations.

You will see and can also see from Adams et al. that the estimation results are different. It provides yet additional support for the recommendation not to delete or modify any observations before you analyze a model.

3.11 APPENDIX I

This appendix provides formal expressions for the influence statistics, taken from Heij et al. (2004).[14] Consider the regression model

$$y = X\beta + \varepsilon$$

The diagonal elements of the hat matrix are

$$h_j = x_j' \left(X'X \right)^{-1} x_j$$

The studentized residual (Rstudent) is

$$e_i^* = \frac{e_i}{s_j \sqrt{1 - h_j}}$$

with s_j^2 is the OLS estimator of σ^2 in the regression

$$y_i = x_i'\beta + \gamma D_{ji} + \varepsilon_i$$

where D_{ji} is a 1/0 dummy variable for the j-th observation with $i = 1, 2, ..., n$.

---

[14] Source is Christiaan Heij, Paul de Boer, Philip Hans Franses, Teun Kloek, and Herman van Dijk (2004), *Econometric Methods with Applications in Business and Economics*, Oxford: Oxford University Press, pages 379–383.

DFBETAS$_{lj}$ is the difference in the l-th estimated parameter owing to the j-th observation

$$\text{DFBETAS}_{lj} = \frac{b_l - b_l(j)}{s_j\sqrt{a_{ll}}}$$

where $b_l(j)$ is the parameter estimate without the j-th observation, and with s_j^2 is the OLS estimator of σ^2 in the regression

$$y_i = x_i'\beta + \gamma D_{ji} + \varepsilon_i$$

where D_{ji} is a 1/0 dummy variable for the j-th observation, $i = 1, 2, ..., n$, and a_{ll} is the l-th diagonal element of $(X'X)^{-1}$.

The influence of the j-th observation on the fitted values $\hat{y} - \widehat{y(j)}$ is

$$\text{DFFITS}_j = e_i^* \sqrt{\frac{h_j}{1 - h_j}}$$

with $e_i^* = \dfrac{e_i}{s_j\sqrt{1 - h_j}}$, and with s_j^2 is the OLS estimator of σ^2 in the regression

$$y_i = x_i'\beta + \gamma D_{ji} + \varepsilon_i$$

where D_{ji} is a 1/0 dummy variable for the j-th observation with $i = 1, 2, ..., n$.

3.12 APPENDIX 2: RECURSIVE COEFFICIENTS IN TIME SERIES MODELS

Consider for illustrative purposes a first order autoregression

$$y_t = \alpha y_{t-1} + \varepsilon_t$$

Then, estimate α using OLS for the sample $t = 2, ..., n$ to obtain

$$y_t = a_n y_{t-1} + e_t$$

Change the sample into $t = 1, 2, ..., n + 1$, to get a_{n+1}, then move the sample to $t = 1, 2, ..., n + 2$ get a_{n+2}. The series a_n, a_{n+1}, a_{n+2}, are the recursive coefficients Around these, the recursively obtained standard errors can be presented.

3.13   EPILOGUE: TWO INTERESTING CASE STUDIES

We have already seen that seemingly interesting and relevant results could be driven just by a single observation. In this epilogue we present two relevant studies that also suffered from the impact of (neglected) influential observations.

3.13.1   Intersalt

> The INTERSALT Study was a 1988 international observational study which investigated the link between dietary salt, as measured by urinary excretion, and blood pressure. The study was based on a sample of 10,079 men and women aged 20–59 sampled from fifty-two populations around the world. The authors of the study attempted to provide a widespread international investigation of the correlation between dietary salt intake and blood pressure in a systematic and standardized way with regards for relevant confounding variables, beyond just age and sex.[15]

In sum, the large and very extensive study claimed to have found a significant causal relationship between dietary salt intake and blood pressure.[16]

However,

> In 2008, the statisticians David A. Freedman and Diana Pettiti published an article showing that the positive correlation between blood pressure and salt consumption observed in the InterSalt study was entirely driven by *four outlying data points* [emphasis added by the author] of the 52 total data points. These four communities had much lower salt consumption than the average community, as well as much lower blood pressure. When these four points were excluded, the correlation was in fact negative, contradicting the original interpretation of the data by the researchers. Freedman and Pettiti raised questions about why the researchers had failed to apply even basic robustness checks

---

[15] From: https://en.wikipedia.org/wiki/Intersalt_study.

[16] Source: Intersalt Cooperative Research Group (1988), Intersalt: an international study of electrolyte excretion and blood pressure. Results for 24 hour urinary sodium and potassium excretion, *British Medical Journal* 297 (6644), 319–328.

and criticised the overly simplistic view presented by medical researchers and policymakers of the role of salt in blood pressure outcomes.[17]

3.13.2 Return On Education

Vikesh Amin writes:

> In an article published in the *American Economic Review*, Dorothe Bonjour et al. (2003) used a dataset on female monozygotic twins and showed that the within-twin estimated return to one year of education was 7.7 percent and statistically significant at the 5 percent level. This comment illustrates that the point estimate conclusion is *driven by one twin pair* [emphasis added by the author], which is an outlier in the dataset. If one eliminates this twin pair, then the estimated return to education is 5.1 percent and statistically significant at the 10 percent level only.[18]

These two case studies show how disappointing it can be to find out that relevant and interesting results were driven by just a few observations, thus providing research results that do not add much to the scientific knowledge base.[19]

---

[17] Source: www.stat.berkeley.edu/~census/573.pdf.

[18] Vikesh Amin (2011), Returns to education: Evidence from UK twins: Comment, *American Economic Review* 101 (4), 1629–1635; Dorothe Bonjour, Lynn F. Cherkas, Jonathan E. Haskel, Denise D. Hawkes, and Tim D. Spector (2003), Returns to education: Evidence from UK twins, *American Economic Review*, 93 (5), 1799–1812.

[19] At the time of writing this chapter (January 2022) the Intersalt study has 2,283 citations on Google Scholar and Bonjour et al. (2003) have 150 citations.

4 Model Selection

Making choices is what econometricians must do in their empirical work. In Chapter 3 we dealt with influential observations and the diverse options of how to deal with these observations. In this chapter we focus on model selection.

There are two ends of the spectrum when we deal with model selection. At one end, one may wish to seek for a single final model, which is to be used to support an economic theory, or to evaluate the effects of a new policy, and/or to create out-of-sample forecasts. At the other end, one may keep a range of models and then somehow average the outcomes for inference or forecasting.

One may wonder why one would want to select a single final model in the first place.[1] This associates best with an idea of classical (frequentist) statistics, that is, that there is a DGP that can best be approached by one best (most suitable) model. When we think in terms of tossing a dice or a coin, it is easy to believe there is such a fixed DGP. The DGP is then a multinomial or binomial distribution with probabilities $\frac{1}{6}$ or $\frac{1}{2}$, respectively. Simply conducting a tossing experiment will show fractions that come closer to the true probabilities when the number of tosses increases. But do such constant probabilities exist for various economic settings? Is there a true money demand function or is there a true link between inflation and unemployment? And are these relations such that we can find these using econometric models?

---

[1] See, for example, Clive W. J. Granger and Yongil Jeon (2004), Thick modeling, *Economic Modelling*, 21 (2), 323–343. And in a recent study, Henrik Kleven (2022), The EITC and the extensive margin: A reappraisal, NBER Working Paper Series 26405, the author reports the results of all 432 different model specifications.

If one believes so, then such a model should be what is called congruent.

A congruent model has:

- homoscedastic, innovation errors
- weakly exogenous conditioning variables for the parameters of interest
- constant, invariant parameters of interest
- theory consistent, identifiable structures
- data admissible formulation on accurate observations.[2]

The instruments used to arrive at such a congruent model are diagnostic tests. There are diagnostic tests on each of these features, and one should also make choices about these. Choices for specific diagnostic tests can be facilitated by simulation studies to find out which of the available tests has the expected type 1 error and the largest power.

However, the road towards one single final model is bumpy. Not only do we need to run tests, and resulting test results can suggest conflicting outcomes, but we also need to decide which variables to include and which not. And we need to decide how the variables are measured. For example, if we talk about money demand,[3] does that concern M1, M2, or M3?

4.1 OUTLINE

That brings us to the outline of this chapter. We first discuss a phenomenon called data mining. This involves multiple tests on which variables or correlations are relevant. If used improperly, data mining may associate with scientific misconduct. Next, we discuss one way to arrive at a single final model, which involves stepwise methods. We will see with a simple illustration that various stepwise methods lead to different final models. Next, we will see that various

---

[2] David F. Hendry (1995), *Dynamic Econometrics*, Oxford: Oxford University Press. See also Christophe Bontemps and Graham E. Mizon (2003), Congruence and encompassing, Chapter 15 in Bernt P. Stigum (editor), *Econometrics and the Philosophy of Economics*, Princeton: Princeton University Press.

[3] https://en.wikipedia.org/wiki/Demand_for_money.

configurations in test situations, here illustrated for testing for cointegration, lead to different outcomes. It may be possible to see which configurations make most sense and will be used for empirical analysis. However, we suggest that it is better to keep various models and somehow combine inference. This will be illustrated for the analysis of the loss (of airline revenues in the United States) owing to 9/11. We will see that out of four different models, three will estimate a similar loss, while the fourth model suggests only 10 percent of that figure. Hence, choosing a single model does matter.

We start with an example of scientific misconduct that involves data mining. The following text is illustrative:[4]

> A PhD student from a Turkish university called to interview
> to be a visiting scholar for 6 months. Her dissertation was on a
> topic that was only indirectly related to our Lab's mission, but
> she really wanted to come, and we had the room, so I said "Yes."
> When she arrived, I gave her a data set of a self-funded, failed
> study which had null results (it was a one-month study in an
> all-you-can-eat Italian restaurant buffet where we had charged
> some people ½ as much as others). I said, "This cost us a lot of
> time and our own money to collect. *There's got to be something
> here* [emphasis added by author] we can salvage because it's a
> cool (rich & unique) data set." I had three ideas for potential Plan
> B, C, & D directions (since Plan A had failed). I told her what the
> analyses should be and what the tables should look like. I then
> asked her if she wanted to do them.
>
> Every day she came back with puzzling new results, and every
> day we would scratch our heads, ask "Why," and produce another
> way to reanalyze the data with yet another set of plausible
> hypotheses. Eventually we started discovering solutions that held
> up regardless of how we pressure-tested them. I outlined the first
> paper, and she wrote it up, and every day for a month I told her

---

[4] From: https://web.archive.org/web/20170312041524/www.brianwansink.com/phd-advice/the-grad-student-who-never-said-no.

how to rewrite it and she did. This happened with a second paper, and then a third paper (which was one that was based on her <u>own</u> discovery while digging through the data).[5]

This is clear example of the risk of data mining. If you run tests and calculate correlations long enough, there is always a result to find, which while you are harking can suggest an interesting hypothesis, with which you then begin the paper. Some of the quoted studies in footnote 5 are now retracted, but others are still around and get cited. This means that unfortunately these studies (appear to) add to the knowledge base and can blur more appropriate insights on the topic.

The concept of data mining was coined already in 1983 as we can read:

> When a data miner uncovers t-statistics that appear significant at the 0.05 level by running a large number of alternative regressions on the same body of data, the probability of a Type 1 error of rejecting the null hypothesis when it is true is much greater than the claimed 5%.[6]

So, simulation experiments show that significant parameters can be obtained when the true parameters are zero in the DGP. Hence, this amounts to finding spurious results. Two decades earlier, it had been discovered that "the distribution of correlation coefficients for pairs

---

[5] These are the studies that follow from this data mining exercise: Ozge Siğirci, Marc Rockmore, and Brian Wansink (2016), How traumatic violence permanently changes shopping behavior, *Frontiers in Psychology*, 7, 1298. RETRACTED; Ozge Siğirci and Brian Wansink (2015), Low prices and high regret: How pricing influences regret at all-you-can-eat buffets, *BMC Nutrition*, 1 (36), 1–5. RETRACTED; Kevin Kniffin, Ozge Siğirci and Brian Wansink (2016), Eating heavily: Men eat more in the company of women, *Evolutionary Psychological Science*, 2, 38–46; David R. Just, Ozge Siğirci, and Brian Wansink (2015), Peak-end pizza: Prices delay evaluations of quality, *Journal of Product & Brand Management*, 24 (7), 770–778; David R. Just, Ozge Siğirci, and Brian Wansink (2014), Lower buffet prices lead to less taste satisfaction, *Journal of Sensory Studies*, 29 (5), 362–370.

[6] Michael C. Lovell (1983), Data mining, *The Review of Economics and Statistics*, 65 (1), 1–12.

of variables randomly drawn from Historical Statistics for the United States shows that it is easy to find correlations larger than 0.5."[7]

That was back then, and in those days data mining indicated bad practice and a misunderstanding of sequential tests using fixed significance levels.[8] Data mining also occurs when many studies focus on the same research topic with similar data.[9]

4.2 HOW TO SELECT ONE FINAL MODEL

There are various strategies for selecting a single final model.[10] One option is to consider all possible useful and dependable models (which pass a range of diagnostic tests) and to use Akaike Information Criterion (AIC) or Bayesian Information Criterion (BIC) to make a final selection. This is particularly useful for nonlinear models, where the function that relates the explanatory variables with this dependent variable is not linear, as it is in the standard linear multiple regression model. In the latter case, one can use R^2. When there are many potential regressors, one can consider sequential (stepwise) estimation techniques. Stepwise forward is the method to each time add an additional regressor until a stop criterion (such as the p value of the parameter for the latest added variable is above 0.05). Stepwise backward is to start with including all regressors, and then delete until all parameters for the final regressors have p values smaller than 0.05 (or another value). Such a backward method can also involve intermediate reinclusion of variables. We should be aware though

---

[7] Edward Ames and Stanley Reiter (1961), Distributions of correlation coefficients in economic time series, *Journal of the American Statistical Association*, 56 (September), 637–656.

[8] Nowadays things seem to be different, which is evidenced by journals with titles such as *Data Mining and Knowledge Discovery* (www.springer.com/journal/10618) and *Statistical Analysis and Data Mining* (https://onlinelibrary.wiley.com/journal/19321872)

[9] An illuminating study is Campbell R. Harvey, Yan Liu, and Heqing Zhu (2016), ... and the cross-section of expected returns, *Review of Financial Studies*, 29 (1), 5–68, where the authors state "Hundreds of papers and hundreds of factors attempt to explain the cross-section of expected returns. Given this extensive data mining, it does not make any economic or statistical sense to use the usual significance criteria for a newly discovered factor, e.g., t-ratio greater than 2.0."

[10] https://en.wikipedia.org/wiki/Model_selection.

that these stepwise methods involve multiple tests, and that the final reported p values include all intermediate decisions. It is also likely that different stepwise methods end up with different models, as we will see in the following case study.

Consider growth rates in real Gross Domestic Product (GDP) for the years 1960–2016 for fifty-two African countries,[11] presented in Figure 4.1 Clearly, there is much variation in the data. Suppose

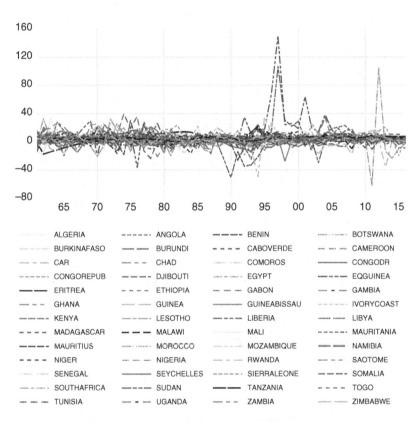

FIGURE 4.1 Annual growth rates in real GDP for fifty-two countries in Africa.
Source: Franses and Vasilev (2019)

[11] Data source: Philip Hans Franses and Simeon Vasilev (2019), Real GDP growth in Africa, 1963–2016, Econometric Institute Report EI2019-23, Erasmus School of Economics, the Netherlands.

that we aim to predict the growth rate of Algeria (just a random choice) for one year ahead, and suppose we consider fifty-two one-year-lagged growth rates as potentially explanatory variables to see if countries in Africa have predictive power for other countries. Let us start with a simple first order autoregression for the growth rate denoted as y_t, that is

$$y_t = \alpha + \beta y_{t-1} + \varepsilon_t$$

Application of OLS for the effective sample 1961 to 2016 gives

$$a = 4.788(1.079)$$
$$b = -0.165(0.128)$$

Hence, the hypothesis that $\beta = 0$ cannot be rejected.

If we include all fifty-two lagged growth rates, we learn (not reported to save space) that none of the parameters appears significant at the 5% level, even though the $R^2 = 0.944$. This is no surprise given the small degrees of freedom. Table 4.1 presents the results for the stepwise forward method. We see from Table 4.1 that there are seven predictors with parameters that have a t test value with a p value smaller than 0.05. The $R^2 = 0.678$.

Table 4.2 presents the outcome of a stepwise backwards method, where intermediate steps allow the inclusion of previously deleted variables. The $R^2 = 0.782$. Comparing the results in Tables 4.1 and 4.2, we see that the final models share the predictors $Algeria_{t-1}$, $Comoros_{t-1}$, and $Kenya_{t-1}$, but otherwise there is no overlap.

Table 4.3 reports on the final model when we rely on the stepwise backwards method, but now implemented as unidirectional. The $R^2 = 0.755$. Interestingly, there is more overlap between the two final models using the stepwise backwards methods.

Evaluating the results in Tables 4.1 to 4.3 shows that depending on the type of stepwise method,[12] different final models can be

---

[12] Perhaps one can also use Lasso or Elastic Net to reduce the number of variables (see Chapter 11) https://en.wikipedia.org/wiki/Lasso_(statistics); https://en.wikipedia.org/wiki/Elastic_net_regularization.

Table 4.1 *Regression results stepwise forward (stopping rule is a p value smaller than 0.05)*

Variable	Estimated parameter	p value
Intercept	−2.739	0.074
$Algeria_{t-1}$	−0.266	0.002
$Kenya_{t-1}$	0.792	0.000
$Morocco_{t-1}$	0.397	0.016
$Mauritania_{t-1}$	−0.386	0.001
$Sudan_{t-1}$	0.274	0.024
$Comoros_{t-1}$	0.443	0.020
$Sao Tome and Principe_{t-1}$	0.263	0.029

Source: Author's calculations

Table 4.2 *Stepwise regression backwards, not unidirectional (stopping rule is a p value smaller than 0.05)*

Variable	Estimated parameter	p value
Intercept	−7.042	0.002
$Algeria_{t-1}$	−0.159	0.037
$Kenya_{t-1}$	0.777	0.000
$Uganda_{t-1}$	0.374	0.018
$Eritrea_{t-1}$	−0.227	0.011
$Gambia_{t-1}$	0.638	0.001
$Comoros_{t-1}$	0.987	0.000
$Zambia_{t-1}$	−0.406	0.005
$Rwanda_{t-1}$	0.219	0.003
$Madagascar_{t-1}$	−0.643	0.000
$Congo Democratic Republic_{t-1}$	0.387	0.001
$Equatorial Guinea_{t-1}$	0.071	0.003
$Burkina Faso_{t-1}$	0.841	0.000

Source: Author's calculations

obtained. One idea might be to keep the three models and evaluate their out-of-sample forecasting performance on a hold-out sample. One could also combine the forecasts from the three models in a new

Table 4.3 *Stepwise backwards, unidirectional (stopping rule is a p value of 0.05)*

Variable	Estimated parameter	p value
Intercept	−2.579	0.204
$Algeria_{t-1}$	−0.159	0.042
$Kenya_{t-1}$	0.772	0.000
$Eritrea_{t-1}$	−0.194	0.024
$Gambia_{t-1}$	0.413	0.028
$Burkina\ Faso_{t-1}$	0.569	0.010
$Comoros_{t-1}$	0.844	0.000
$Benin_{t-1}$	−0.472	0.017
$Rwanda_{t-1}$	−0.212	0.005
$Madagascar_{t-1}$	−0.612	0.000
$Congo\ Democratic\ Republic_{t-1}$	0.385	0.002
$Equatorial\ Guinea_{t-1}$	0.089	0.000

Source: Author's calculations

forecast. It seems clear that just to focus on just one model cannot be justified.

A technique that is often used to evaluate the quality of models and forecasts is to consider the forecasts for a hold-out sample. This is called cross-validation.[13] Such cross-validation can prevent the same data being used twice, that is, for model design and for model evaluation.

Wikipedia says:

> Cross-validation, sometimes called rotation estimation or out-of-sample testing, is any of various similar model validation techniques for assessing how the results of a statistical analysis will generalize to an independent data set. It is mainly used in settings where the goal is prediction, and one wants to estimate how accurately a predictive model will perform in practice.[14]

---

[13] A beautifully written summary of cross-validation methods is Michael W. Browne (2000), Cross-validation methods, *Journal of Mathematical Psychology*, 44 (1), 108–132.

[14] https://en.wikipedia.org/wiki/Cross-validation_(statistics).

4.3 CONFIGURATIONS IN COINTEGRATION ANALYSIS

Variable selection techniques can lead to different finally selected models. Such a situation can also hold for model selection in case different deterministic terms are included in the model. In an earlier example we included an intercept, but sometimes we can also include a trend or even a quadratic trend. That the final conclusions can depend on the choice of these deterministic terms is illustrated next in the case of cointegration analysis.[15]

Suppose there are m time series $y_{i,t}$, $i = 1, 2, \ldots, m$, collected in the $(m \times 1)$ vector Y_t, and there are m error terms in the vector ε_t. Consider a vector autoregression or order 1 (for the moment without intercepts)

$$Y_t = \Lambda Y_{t-1} + \varepsilon_t$$

and write it in error correction format by subtracting Y_{t-1} from both sides:

$$\Delta_1 Y_t = \Pi Y_{t-1} + \varepsilon_t$$

We can always write

$$\Pi = \alpha \beta'$$

where α and β are $(m \times r)$ full rank matrices, where $r = \text{rank}(\Pi)$. When

$$0 < r < m$$

there are r cointegrating relations.[16] In a sense this amounts to a variable selection as previously seen as these cointegration relations become explanatory variables on the right-hand side for the first differenced dependent variables on the left-hand side. When $r = 0$, the model reduces to

$$\Delta_1 Y_t = \varepsilon_t$$

---

[15] Based on Philip Hans Franses (2001), How to deal with intercept and trend in practical cointegration analysis? *Applied Economics*, 33 (5), 577–579.

[16] Robert F. Engle and Clive W. J. Granger (1987), Cointegration and error-correction: Representation, estimation, and testing, *Econometrica*, 55 (2), 251–276; Søren Johansen (1995), *Likelihood-based Inference in Cointegrated Vector Autoregressive Models*, Oxford: Oxford University Press.

and hence there are no regressors to explain the growth rates. When $r = m$, the model is simply

$$Y_t = \Lambda Y_{t-1} + \varepsilon_t$$

and the m variables are stationary, as they do not have a stochastic trend. When $r = 1$, each equation of the error correction model has one explanatory variable to explain the elements of $\Delta_1 Y_t$. With the assumption that the parameter for $y_{1,t-1}$ is not zero, this explanatory variable (which is a cointegrating relation) can be scaled as

$$y_{1,t-1} - b_{1,2} y_{2,t-1} - b_{1,3} y_{3,t-1} - \ldots - b_{1,m} y_{m,t-1}$$

When $r = 2$, there are two such variables (and any linear combination of these), and so on.

To assess for the number of variables on the right-hand side, there is a test on the rank of the matrix Π. The most used tests are based on the eigenvalues and on the trace of this matrix.

A key question in practice is how to deal with an intercept and a deterministic trend, and what do they mean? This model

$$\Delta_1 Y_t = \Pi Y_{t-1} + \varepsilon_t$$

assumes that the m time series in Y_t, first, do not have a trend and, second, that the cointegrating relations, if there are any, have mean zero. This is quite exceptional in practice.

To illustrate that the inclusion of intercept and trend matters, consider the following case study. Figure 4.2 presents the natural logs of real GDP in three South American countries, Argentina, Bolivia, and Brazil. The data are indexed at 100 in 1950 and run until and including 2010. It may now be interesting to see if these three variables have one or two cointegration relations in common, which means that they share two or one stochastic trends.

In this illustration, we thus have $m = 3$, that is,

$$Y_t = \begin{pmatrix} \log Argentina_t \\ \log Bolivia_t \\ \log Brazil_t \end{pmatrix}$$

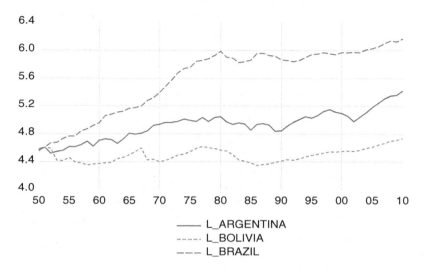

FIGURE 4.2 Natural logs of (1950 = 100) indexed Gross Domestic Product, Argentina, Bolivia, and Brazil.

Useful extensions of the model

$$\Delta_1 Y_t = \Pi Y_{t-1} + \varepsilon_t$$

involve assumptions about the type of trend. When none of the time series has a trending pattern but the cointegrating relations do not have mean zero, then we include the intercept with parameter μ as follows:

$$\Delta_1 Y_t = \alpha \left(\beta' Y_{t-1} - \mu \right) + \varepsilon_t$$

We can also allow that some or all the time series do have a trending pattern (hence the γ in the next equation) and the cointegrating relations do not have mean zero and may be trend-stationary (hence the $\mu + \delta t$). In that case the model is

$$\Delta_1 Y_t = \gamma + \alpha \left(\beta' Y_{t-1} - \mu - \delta t \right) + \varepsilon_t$$

To show that it matters which option you take, consider the outcome for the three South American countries:

Number of cointegrating relations, based on p value smaller than 0.05:

Trend	None	None	Linear	Linear
Intercept	None	Intercept	Intercept	Intercept
Trace[17]	2	1	1	1
Max. eigenvalue	2	2	0	0

We see that 0, 1, or 2 cointegrating relations can all be possible. Now suppose you continue with

$$\Delta_1 Y_t = \alpha \left(\beta' Y_{t-1} - \mu \right) + \varepsilon_t$$

then the test results (based on max eigenvalue) (and two lags of $\Delta_1 Y_t$ selected by AIC) suggest two cointegrating relations, and these are scaled to be equal to

$$b_1' = \left(1, 0, -0.567\right)$$
$$b_2' = \left(0, 1, -0.272\right)$$

Are these newly created series stationary? When we look at Figure 4.3, it seems doubtful that they both represent a stationary time series around a fixed mean. Indeed, the bottom variable looks a bit like the random walk data we created in Chapter 3.

When we next consider

$$\Delta_1 Y_t = \gamma + \alpha \left(\beta' Y_{t-1} - \mu - \delta t \right) + \varepsilon_t$$

and take the evidence from the trace seriously, then we obtain evidence for just a single cointegrating relation, which turns out to be

$$b_1 = \left(1, -0.542, -0.205, -0.006\right)$$

where -0.006 is the significant parameter for the linear trend. A graph of this cointegration variable appears in Figure 4.4, which seems stationary around a fixed mean at first sight.

Hence, in this setting there is only a single "variable" explaining the growth rates. The associated so-called error correction parameters α (with standard errors in parentheses) are estimated equal to

---

[17] See Søren Johansen (1995), *Likelihood-based Inference in Cointegrated Vector Autoregressive Models*, Oxford: Oxford University Press.

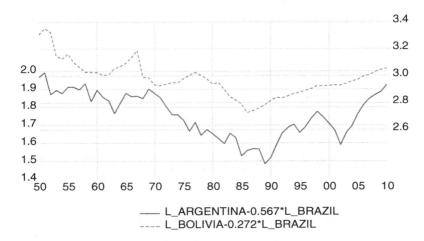

FIGURE 4.3 Estimated cointegration relations based on model
$\Delta_1 Y_t = \alpha \left(\beta' Y_{t-1} - \mu \right) + \varepsilon_t.$

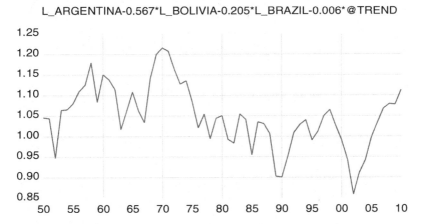

FIGURE 4.4 Estimated cointegration relation based on model
$\Delta_1 Y_t = \gamma + \alpha \left(\beta' Y_{t-1} - \mu - \delta t \right) + \varepsilon_t.$

$$a_1 = -0.248 (0.095)$$
$$a_2 = 0.046 (0.087)$$
$$a_3 = 0.236 (0.072)$$

where we can use the t distribution for the t values. This case study
shows that also the configurations for the deterministic regressors

such as a constant and a trend in a vector autoregression have an impact on the finally selected model.

4.4 IT CAN BE BETTER TO HAVE MORE THAN ONE MODEL

To provide an illustration that searching for only a single final model can lead to misleading inference, consider the following case study. Figure 4.5 provides a graph of monthly airline revenues (data are already in natural logs), ranging from 1993.01 to 2007.12. The impact of 9/11 in 2001 is immediately obvious. The line drops down, but then shortly afterwards it seems to pick up the trend again. The sample ends here in December 2007 to avoid confusion with the economic crisis of 2008/2009, because the goal here is to estimate the loss of airline revenues owing to 9/11 in the next few years.

To estimate such loss, one can consider the sample January 1993 to August 2001, which ends just the month before 9/11, and make predictions from August 2001 onwards, to see how the time series could have continued if 9/11 had not occurred.[18]

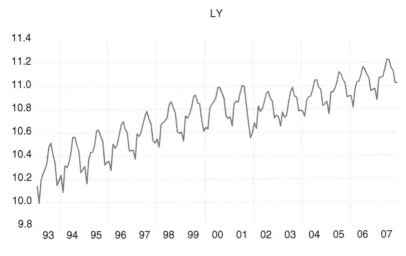

FIGURE 4.5 Monthly airline revenues (in natural logs).

[18] This can be called a counterfactual exercise; see, for example, Jurgen A. Doornik, Jennifer L. Castle, and David F. Hendry (2021), Modeling and forecasting the COVID-19 pandemic time-series data, *Social Science Quarterly*, 102 (5), 2070–2087.

There are four commonly used model options (where y_t represents log airline revenues) to describe the data as in Figure 4.5, and these are

1. $y_t = \mu + \sum_{s=2}^{12} \mu_s D_{s,t} + \delta t + \rho_1 y_{t-1} + \ldots + \rho_p y_{t-p} + \varepsilon_t + \theta_1 \varepsilon_{t-1} + \ldots + \theta_q \varepsilon_{t-q}$

2. $\Delta_1 y_t = \mu + \sum_{s=2}^{12} \mu_s D_{s,t} + \rho_1 \Delta_1 y_{t-1} + \ldots + \rho_p \Delta_1 y_{t-p} + \varepsilon_t + \theta_1 \varepsilon_{t-1} + \ldots + \theta_q \varepsilon_{t-q}$

3. $\Delta_{12} y_t = y_t - y_{t-12} = \mu + \rho_1 \Delta_{12} y_{t-1} + \ldots + \rho_p \Delta_{12} y_{t-p} + \varepsilon_t + \theta_1 \varepsilon_{t-1} + \ldots + \theta_q \varepsilon_{t-q}$

4. $\Delta_1 \Delta_{12} y_t = \Delta_{12} y_t - \Delta_{12} y_{t-1} = \mu + \rho_1 \Delta_1 \Delta_{12} y_{t-1} + \ldots + \rho_p \Delta_1 \Delta_{12} y_{t-p} + \varepsilon_t$
$+ \theta_1 \varepsilon_{t-1} + \ldots + \theta_q \varepsilon_{t-q}$

where p and q can vary across the models. These model options are autoregressive moving average models for various transformed y_t series. The $D_{s,t}$ are monthly dummy variables. Model (4) can reduce to

$$\Delta_1 \Delta_{12} y_t = \mu + \varepsilon_t + \theta_1 \varepsilon_{t-1} + \theta_{12} \varepsilon_{t-12} + \theta_{13} \varepsilon_{t-13}$$

which is called the airline model.[19]

Which one of the four models should be chosen? This decision can be based on so-called tests for (seasonal) unit roots.[20] This is because Δ_1 concerns one unit root and Δ_{12} involves one unit root with eleven so-called seasonal unit roots. The problem with these tests is that they have low power,[21] that it is not easy to explicitly incorporate moving average terms such as $\theta_1 \varepsilon_{t-1}, \ldots, \theta_q \varepsilon_{t-q}$, and that outliers and structural breaks, have a strong impact on the test results. Hence, one may wish to estimate parameters in all four models and combine the inference.

---

[19] George E. P. Box and Gwilym M. Jenkins (1970), *Time Series Analysis: Forecasting and Control*, San Francisco: Holden-Day.

[20] To evaluate model 3 versus models 2 and 1, one can use the test proposed in Svend Hylleberg, Robert F. Engle, Clive W. J. Granger, and Byung Sam Yoo (1990), Seasonal integration and cointegration, *Journal of Econometrics*, 44 (1–2), 215–238. To evaluate model 4 versus models 3 and 2, one can use the method in Denise R. Osborn, A. P. L. Chui, Jeremy P. Smith, and Chris R. Birchenhall (1988), Seasonality and the order of integration for consumption, *Oxford Bulletin of Economics and Statistics*, 50 (4), 361–377.

[21] Misspecification of the unit root property happens frequently, and hence to measure the size of average economic growth it may pay off to use robust methods, see, for example, H. Peter Boswijk, and Philip Hans Franses (2006), Robust inference on average economic growth, *Oxford Bulletin of Economics and Statistics*, 68 (3), 345–370.

Table 4.4 reports the estimation results for model 1 for the data until and including August 2001. Table 4.5 reports the estimation results for model 2 for $\Delta_1 y_t$. Table 4.6 presents the estimation results for model 3 for $\Delta_{12} y_t$ and Table 4.7 presents the estimation results for the airline model. The number of regressors is decided based on diagnostic tests for the absence of residual autocorrelation.

Figure 4.6 depicts the multiple-steps-ahead forecasts from 2001 September onwards, while keeping the models fixed. Three sets of forecasts look similar, and these are the forecasts from models 1, 2, and 3 (LF1, LF2, and LF3). The forecasts from model 4 (LF4) are markedly different. This is also evident from the forecast errors in Figure 4.7. In fact, model 4 turns out to be quite an accurate forecasting model

Finally, Table 4.8 presents the loss in thousands of USD, when we compare the forecasts with actual realizations (after transforming the logs back to the levels).

Table 4.4 *Estimation results for model (1) for* y_t

Variable	Estimated parameter	p value
Intercept	5.168	0.000
February	0.107	0.000
March	0.142	0.000
April	0.047	0.006
May	0.063	0.000
June	0.110	0.000
July	0.175	0.000
August	0.140	0.000
September	0.071	0.036
October	0.056	0.041
November	−0.095	0.000
December	−0.023	0.064
Trend	0.003	0.000
y_{t-1}	0.491	0.000

Table 4.5 *Estimation results for model (2) for $\Delta_1 y_t$*

Variable	Estimated parameter	p value
Intercept	0.022	0.103
February	−0.116	0.000
March	0.184	0.000
April	−0.013	0.419
May	0.001	0.939
June	0.040	0.050
July	0.077	0.000
August	−0.006	0.738
September	−0.080	0.000
October	−0.063	0.001
November	−0.191	0.000
December	−0.028	0.102
ε_{t-1}	−0.301	0.006
ε_{t-2}	−0.524	0.000

Table 4.6 *Model 3 for $\Delta_{12} y_t$*

Intercept	0.041	0.000
$\Delta_{12} y_{t-1}$	0.465	0.000
ε_{t-12}	−0.412	0.000

Table 4.7 *Model 4 for $\Delta_1 \Delta_{12} y_t$*

Intercept	−0.001	0.310
ε_{t-1}	−0.746	0.000
ε_{t-12}	−0.399	0.001
ε_{t-13}	0.331	0.006

We see that three models lead to approximate agreement, while model 4 provides a much lower estimate of loss. Which model should we now choose? If you want the estimated loss to be low, you just consider model 4. If you want the loss to be larger, then you consider

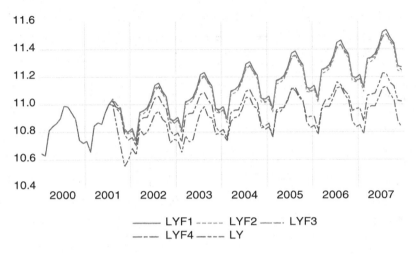

FIGURE 4.6 Four forecasts from September 2001 onwards.

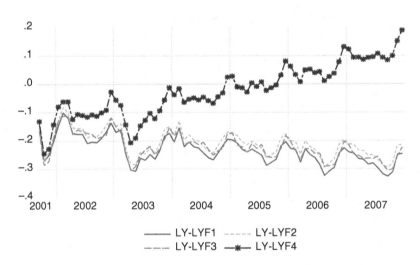

FIGURE 4.7 Multi-step-ahead forecast errors from the four different models.

models 1, 2, and 3, and take, for example, an average. But mind you, not saying which model you chose and why you made that choice is clearly unethical.

Table 4.8 *Loss owing to 9/11, averages over all months*

Model for	Mean loss	Median loss
y_t	15102	14684
$\Delta_1 y_t$	13334	13030
$\Delta_{12} y_t$	14153	14045
$\Delta_1 \Delta_{12} y_t$	1040	1421

4.5 BAYESIAN FORECAST COMBINATION

As already mentioned, the combination of models and/or the combination of forecasts from different models can be particularly useful.[22] Now, the next question is, what weight should be given to the various models and forecasts? The classic study on forecast combination derives the optimal weights for linear regression models and shows that simply taking unweighted averages can already be quite beneficial.[23] There are also other studies that derive optimal weights driven by the past performance of models or using linear regression techniques.

For linear regression models it may be simple to find suitable combinations, but when you have more complicated models, it may not be that easy to derive optimal weights. Let us have a look at the following case study to illustrate the point, and next describe a simple Bayesian averaging method.[24]

Suppose that you have data such as that in Figure 4.8, and you wish to make out-of-sample forecasts. The data run from February 27, 2020 (with the first case) to and including May 19, 2020. To have

---

[22] In case the forecasts concern probabilities, there is an option to average probabilities or quantiles, see Kenneth C. Lichtendahl Jr., Yael Grushka-Cockayne, and Robert L. Winkler (2013), Is it better to average probabilities or quantiles? *Management Science* 59 (7), 1594–1611, who document that averaging quantiles may be preferable.

[23] The classic study on the combination of forecasts is John M. Bates and Clive W. J. Granger (1969), The combination of forecasts, *Operations Research Quarterly*, 20 (4), 451–468.

[24] Based on Philip Hans Franses (2020), Simple Bayesian forecast combination, *Annals of Financial Economics*, 15 (4), 2050016.

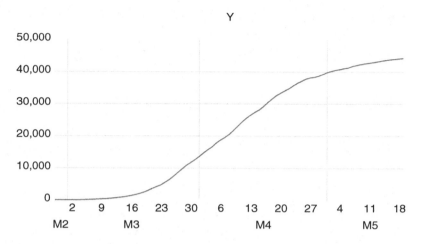

FIGURE 4.8 The cumulative daily COVID-19 cases in the Netherlands (end February to mid-May 2020).

a large enough sample to estimate the parameters, and to have a large enough sample to evaluate the forecasts, we set the end of the model fitting sample on March 31, 2020, and hence there are $N = 49$ forecasts to evaluate.

There are various models that can describe and predict S-shaped variables.[25] Model selection is not easy as these models are not nested.

For illustration, let us consider three models for S-shaped data. Denote the cumulative cases as y_t, for $t = 1, 2, 3, \ldots, T$, and denote m as the final cumulative number of cases, and $\alpha > 0$ and $\beta > 0$ as two unknown parameters.

The logistic curve is represented by

$$y_t = \frac{m}{1 + \exp\left(-\alpha\left(t - \beta\right)\right)}$$

The inflection point, or peak moment of new cases, is

$$y_t^i = \frac{1}{2}m$$

[25] Nigel Meade and Towhidul Islam (2006), Modeling and forecasting the diffusion of innovation – A 25 year review, *International Journal of Forecasting*, 22 (3), 529–545.

and it occurs at $t = \beta$. Adding an error term, the parameters (and associated standard errors) can be estimated using Nonlinear Least Squares (NLS).

A second function is the Gompertz curve represented by

$$y_t = m exp\big(-\alpha\big(\exp(-\beta t)\big)\big),$$

for which the inflection point

$$y_t^i = \frac{1}{e} m$$

occurs at

$$t = \frac{\ln \alpha}{\beta}$$

As the inflection point has a cumulative number of cases which is less than $\frac{1}{2} m$, the Gompertz curve is asymmetric. Again, NLS can be used to estimate the parameters.

The third and final function we consider here is the Bass (1969) growth curve,[26] which is represented by

$$y_t = m \frac{1 - \exp\big(-(\alpha + \beta)t\big)}{1 + \dfrac{\beta}{\alpha}\exp\big(-(\alpha + \beta)t\big)}$$

The inflection point occurs at

$$t = \frac{1}{\alpha + \beta} \ln \frac{\beta}{\alpha}$$

And the cumulative cases are then

$$y_t^i = m\left(\frac{1}{2} - \frac{\alpha}{2\beta}\right)$$

Again, this is an asymmetric curve as the latter expression is smaller than $\frac{1}{2} m$.

[26] Frank M. Bass (1969), A new product growth for model consumer durables, *Management Science*, 15 (5), 215–227.

We use each of these three models to recursively create one-step-ahead forecasts, and let us denote these as $y_{T+i|T+i-1}^{Logistic}$, as $y_{T+i|T+i-1}^{Gompertz}$ and as $y_{T+i|T+i-1}^{Bass}$, respectively. It might be useful to consider combined forecasts. A simple average forecast is

$$Average\ forecast = \frac{1}{3}\left(y_{T+i|T+i-1}^{Logistic} + y_{T+i|T+i-1}^{Gompertz} + y_{T+i|T+i-1}^{Bass}\right)$$

An alternative combination could consider the quality of the model in the "in-sample" period. One way to do so is to consider the in-sample posterior probabilities of each of the models given the data. When the prior probabilities of each of the models are equal, which seems reasonable here, it can be shown that the posterior probability (here for the Logistic curve for illustration) can be computed as:[27]

$$Prob(Logistic)$$

$$= \frac{\exp\left(-\frac{1}{2}BIC^{Logistic}\right)}{\exp\left(-\frac{1}{2}BIC^{Logistic}\right) + \exp\left(-\frac{1}{2}BIC^{Gompertz}\right) + \exp\left(-\frac{1}{2}BIC^{Bass}\right)}$$

where BIC is the Bayesian Information Criterion.[28] With the three posterior probabilities, the Bayesian average forecasts are

$$Bayesian\ average\ forecast = Prob(logistic)\,y_{T+i|T+i-1}^{Logistic}$$
$$+ Prob(Gompertz)\,y_{T+i|T+i-1}^{Gompertz} + Prob(Bass)\,y_{T+i|T+i-1}^{Bass}$$

As the forecasts are created recursively, one should also compute for each forecast the BIC again for the recursive samples. The Gompertz model seems to do best as we always want to minimize the BIC value. This model then also receives the largest weight in

[27] Adrian E. Raftery (1995), Bayesian model selection in social research, *Sociological Methodology*, 25, 111–163.

[28] Gideon Schwarz (1978), Estimating the dimension of a model, *Annals of Statistics*, 6 (2), 461–464. Further arguments why BIC can be useful are given on page 797 in Eric-Jan Wagenmakers (2007), A practical solution to the pervasive problems of p values, *Psychonomic Bulletin & Review*, 14 (5), 779–804.

Table 4.9 *Out-of-sample forecast performance of three nonlinear models and two combined forecasts*

Model	Forecast error		Absolute forecast error	
	Mean	Median	Mean	Median
Logistic	995	998	999	998
Gompertz	–170	–325	417	439
Bass	874	857	880	857
Average	567	485	580	485
Bayesian average	392	333	435	333

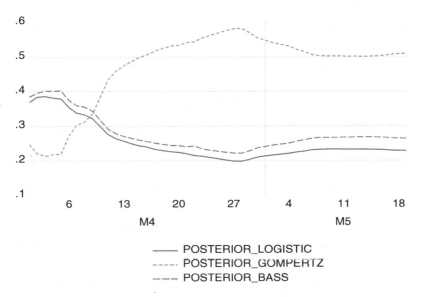

―― POSTERIOR_LOGISTIC
----- POSTERIOR_GOMPERTZ
――― POSTERIOR_BASS

FIGURE 4.9 Posterior probabilities (recursively computed) of each the three models.

the forecast combinations, see Figure 4.9. Table 4.9 reports the out-of-sample forecast accuracy of the three models separately, and of the two combined forecasts. Note that the Bayesian combination seems to do well with low forecast errors.

4.6 WHAT DID WE LEARN?

In this chapter we have argued and observed that we may want not to strive for one single model for inference and prediction. Trying to end up with a single model has all kinds of drawbacks. Various diagnostic tests and criteria are needed, and it is not certain which are the best tests and criteria. You may need to evaluate for unit roots, but relevant tests do not have much power. This lack of power can be misused in the sense that if you do not want the null hypothesis to be rejected, you simply resort to a test with low power.

It is thus better to maintain various models, at least models that stand various diagnostic tests, for inference and for forecasting, and to combine what can be learned from these models. Again, it is mandatory to report all model versions, and that you make explicit how you created the combinations.

4.7 FURTHER READING

In empirical finance, there is a wildly growing list of what are called market anomalies. "A market anomaly in a financial market is predictability that seems to be inconsistent with (typically risk-based) theories of asset prices."[29] Using various methods and techniques people seek to document these anomalies. One of them concerns calendar effects, such as the day-in-the-week effect or the month-in-the-year effect. In an illuminating study, Sullivan et al.[30] show that many of these calendar effects disappear when you correct for data mining effects.

So various of these reported anomalies do not truly exist.

---

[29] https://en.wikipedia.org/wiki/Market_anomaly.

[30] Ryan Sullivan, Allan Timmermann, and Halbert White (2001), Dangers of data mining: The case of calendar effects in stock returns, *Journal of Econometrics*, 105 (1), 249–286.

5   Estimation and Interpretation

In practice it may happen that a first-try econometric model is not appropriate because it violates one or more of the key assumptions that are needed to obtain valid results. There is a range of requirements for regression models, and violations of some of these requirements are more important than others. There should be no omitted but relevant variables, for example. In time series models, omitted relevant lags of the dependent variable will show up as autocorrelation in the residuals, and can lead to spurious results – as we will see in Chapter 7. On the other hand, approximate normality of the residuals is useful, but slight but symmetric nonnormality is not that harmful. Hence, again we should make choices for the use of diagnostics.

In case there is something wrong with the variables, such as measurement error or strong collinearity, we may better modify the estimation method or change the model. In the present chapter we deal with endogeneity, which can be caused, for example, by measurement error, and which implies that one or more regressors are correlated with the unknown error term. This is of course not immediately visible because the errors are not known beforehand and are estimated jointly with the unknown parameters. Endogeneity can thus happen when a regressor is measured with error, and, as we will see, when the data are aggregated at too low a frequency.

Another issue that affects estimation and interpretation occurs when variables are extremely correlated. This is called multicollinearity, and it is then difficult to disentangle (the statistical significance of) the separate effects. This certainly holds for levels and squares of the same variable, as we will see later.

All in all, it is thus important to apply diagnostic tests to a model to see if there are signs of misspecification and of issues with the variables. In Chapter 3 we discuss diagnostics for influential observations, and in this chapter, we mainly consider endogeneity and strong correlation.

The final part of this chapter deals with interpretation of model outcomes. One could be tempted to just report which parameters are significant, for example by presenting the p values. This is, however, not informative as to which variables contribute more than other variables to the final fit or forecast. Comparing p values or t test values related to the estimated parameters does not work, as these are correlated, which is because the variables are often correlated. At the end of this chapter, we propose a method that has become popular recently, particularly when models become large and complicated; it is based on so-called Shapley values.

5.1 MEASUREMENT ERRORS

We start our discussion on potential issues with regression model outcomes with a focus on measurement errors.[1] It seems that this issue is not often considered in practice, and this may be an underestimate of how important it can be. It is quite likely that not all variables we observe are free from measurement errors. Measurement errors in the dependent variable end up in the overall error term, but measurement errors in an explanatory variable have a different impact.

Consider a simple regression model for the variables y_i and x_i with $i = 1, \ldots, n$,

$$y_i = \alpha + \beta x_i^* + \varepsilon_i$$

where the true observations x_i^* are independent from ε_i but are measured with error, that is,

---

[1] A recent extensive and interesting account is given in Erik Meijer, Edward Oczkowski, and Tom Wansbeek (2021), How measurement error affects inference in linear regression, *Empirical Economics* 60 (1), 131–155.

$$x_i = x_i^* + v_i$$

Assume that the measurement error v_i with variance σ_v^2 is independent from x_i^* and from ε_i. Because we only have observed x_i, and not x_i^*, the regression model becomes

$$y_i = \alpha + \beta\left(x_i - v_i\right) + \varepsilon_i = \alpha + \beta x_i + \varepsilon_i - \beta v_i$$

The error term in this model with observed variables is $\varepsilon_i - \beta v_i$. In the latter regression model, we see that

$$Covariance\left(x_i, \varepsilon_i - \beta v_i\right) = Covariance\left(x_i^* + v_i, \varepsilon_i - \beta v_i\right) = -\beta\sigma_v^2$$

A key assumption for the OLS estimation method is thus violated as the error term is correlated with the regressor x_i. Indeed, we have the probability limit

$$plim\,\hat{\beta}_{OLS} = \frac{Covariance\left(x_i, y_i\right)}{Variance\left(x_i\right)} = \frac{\beta\sigma_{x^*}^2}{\sigma_{x^*}^2 + \sigma_v^2} \neq \beta$$

When the variance of the measurement error σ_v^2 gets large enough, the probability limit $plim\,\hat{\beta}_{OLS}$ converges to 0 and is always closer to 0 than β. A solution is now to resort to two-stage least squares (TSLS) with an instrumental variable, which we will illustrate for data on the Eurovision Song Contest in 2021.[2]

Before that, a brief refresher is perhaps relevant. TSLS (or Instrumental Variables estimation, IV) considers the regression model (in matrix notation):[3]

$$y = X\beta + \varepsilon$$

---

[2] https://en.wikipedia.org/wiki/Eurovision_Song_Contest_2021 says: "The Eurovision Song Contest 2021 was the 65th edition of the Eurovision Song Contest. It took place in Rotterdam, Netherlands, following the country's victory at the 2019 contest with the song "Arcade" by Duncan Laurence. The Netherlands was due to host the 2020 contest, before it was cancelled due to the COVID-19 pandemic. It was the fifth time that the Netherlands had hosted the contest, having previously done so in 1958, 1970, 1976 and 1980."

[3] The source is Christiaan Heij, Paul de Boer, Philip Hans Franses, Teun Kloek, and Herman van Dijk (2004), *Econometric Methods with Applications in Business and Economics*, Oxford: Oxford University Press, pages 379–383.

Suppose now that $E(X'\varepsilon) \neq 0$. Consider instrumental variables that are collected in Z. Regress X on Z, retrieve the fitted values $\hat{X}$ and next consider OLS for

$$y = \hat{X}\beta_{IV} + \omega$$

where ω is a new error term. Now, let us turn to the Eurovision Song Contest 2021, with the winner from Italy, Maneskin, with the song "Zitti e buoni." Some key statistics are in Table 5.1. The first column gives the ranks according to the sum of the scores of the professional jury and a public jury. The second column gives the moment of performance. Hence, a "1" means that this was the first song presented on television, while "26" is the final artist. The final two columns give the scores given by the jury and by the public, respectively.

The question we seek to answer is whether the professional jury and the public rate the contestants in a similar way. The scatter in Figure 5.1 concerning the last two columns in Table 5.1 seems to suggest a strong correlation, and this is indeed 0.618. We could perhaps expect that the regression line for the data in the scatter would have a slope equal to 1. This would match with a consensus of judgments.

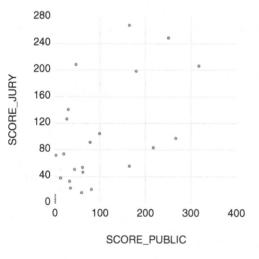

FIGURE 5.1 Scatter plot of score jury versus score public.
Source: Author's calculations

Table 5.1 *Some statistics of the Eurovision Song Contest, 2021*

Rank	Moment of performance	Score Jury	Score public
1	24	206	317
2	20	248	251
3	11	267	165
4	12	198	180
5	19	97	267
6	16	83	218
7	6	208	47
8	18	55	165
9	5	104	100
10	17	140	30
11	10	91	79
12	7	126	27
13	14	53	62
14	25	46	63
15	8	20	82
16	1	50	44
17	3	73	20
18	22	15	60
19	4	71	3
20	21	32	33
21	2	22	35
22	26	37	13
23	23	11	0
24	13	6	0
25	15	3	0
26	9	0	0

Source: Eurovision Song Contest – Wikipedia

When we apply OLS to the following model

$$Score\,jury_i = \alpha + \beta\,Score\,public_i + \varepsilon_i$$

the regression result (with standard errors in parentheses) is

$$a = 41.254(17.193)$$
$$b = 0.526(0.136)$$

The $R^2 = 0.382$. Looking at the estimate b, we see that the 95 percent confidence interval for β ranges from 0.254 to 0.798, and the value 1 is not included in that interval.

It could be that the public scores suffer from measurement error, which could be caused by so-called order effects. Such effects entail that the public remembers more from recent performances than from earlier ones, and hence may give higher scores to more recently performing artists.[4] Let us have a look at two auxiliary regressions (with standard errors in parentheses):

$$Score\ jury_i = \alpha + \beta\ Moment\ of\ performance_i + \varepsilon_i$$
$$a = 89.123(32.581)$$
$$b = -0.157(2.110)$$

and

$$Score\ public_i = \alpha + \beta\ Moment\ of\ performance_i + \varepsilon_i$$
$$a = 35.972(36.144)$$
$$b = 3.780(2.378)$$

We see that the moment of performance is not related to the score of the jury. However, the second regression result suggests that there is some positive effect of the moment of performance on the scores given by the public. Hence, the scores of the public have measurement errors.

We now need an instrument for the scores of the public. A reasonable instrument may now be the scores given by the bookmakers well in advance of the actual contest.[5] The winning probability (as a fraction of 100) and the rank (including semifinals before the contest, and therefore there are rank numbers such as 38) are presented in Table 5.2.

---

[4] Evgeny A. Antipov and Elena B. Pokryshevskaya (2017), Order effects in the results of song contests: Evidence from the Eurovision and the New Wave, *Judgment and Decision Making*, 12 (4), 415–419; Wändi Bruine de Bruin and Gideon Keren (2003), Order effects in sequentially judged options due to the direction of comparison, *Organizational Behavior and Human Decision Processes*, 92 (1), 91–101.

[5] Thanks to Christiaan Heij for alerting me to this possibility.

Table 5.2 *Scores by bookmakers, provided in advance of the contest*

Final rank	Winning probability	Rank (including earlier rounds)
1	10	4
2	17	1
3	13	3
4	8	6
5	2	9
6	2	11
7	16	2
8	2	8
9	2	14
10	2	12
11	9	5
12	1	19
13	0	22
14	2	10
15	0	25
16	3	7
17	1	17
18	1	15
19	1	20
20	1	21
21	0	38
22	2	13
23	0	30
24	0	37
25	0	27
26	0	23

Intuitively, as bookmaker scores precede the public votes, the variables in Table 5.2 should be exogenous. When we use the bookmakers' winning probabilities as an instrument for the regression

$$Score\ jury_i = \alpha + \beta\ Score\ public_i + \varepsilon_i$$

TSLS results in

$$a = -48.477(49.734)$$
$$b = 1.557(0.508)$$

and when we use the bookmakers' rank as an instrument, we get

$$a = -5.018(29.737)$$
$$b = 1.058(0.289)$$

We see that the 95 percent confidence intervals for β include the value of 1. And we also see confirmed that the measurement errors bias the OLS estimator for β towards zero. A test for the null hypothesis of exogeneity of the scores of the public yields for the two instruments in Table 5.2, 18.466 (p value 0.000) and 8.708 (p value 0.003), respectively.[6] Hence, indeed, it matters to take account of endogeneity of the regressor.[7]

In the example here, we could find a useful and relevant instrument. But often, good instruments are neither obvious nor easy to find. In other cases, one can choose between various instruments. It can also happen that the instruments themselves are observed with measurement error. When large rivers in the United States are used as an instrument for differences in competition across schools, then new and better coding of the rivers means that the instrument does not work anymore.[8] Generally, this is rather unfortunate.

Some people would claim that when instruments are needed, this is a sign of an improper research design,[9] and that one should

---

[6] For the test see Christiaan Heij, Paul de Boer, Philip Hans Franses, Teun Kloek, and Herman van Dijk (2004), *Econometric Methods with Applications in Business and Economics*, Oxford: Oxford University Press, pages 409–411.

[7] The so-called J test statistics that concern the null hypothesis that OLS and TSLS lead to the same results get a p value of 0.000 in both cases.

[8] Caroline M. Hoxby (2000), Does competition among public schools benefit students and taxpayers? *American Economic Review*, 90 (5), 1209–1238; Jesse Rothstein (2007), Does competition among public schools benefit students and taxpayers? Comment, *American Economic Review*, 97 (5), 2026–2037.

[9] Joshua D. Angrist and Jörn-Steffen Pischke (2009), *Mostly Harmless Econometrics*, Princeton: Princeton University Press; Joshua D. Angrist and Jörn-Steffen Pischke (2010), The credibility revolution in empirical economics: How better research design

better resort to other research designs involving, for example, randomized control trials,[10] or regression discontinuity designs.[11] Yet at the same time, it is not always easy to prevent endogeneity owing to measurement errors.

5.2 SIMULTANEITY OWING TO AGGREGATION

In many practical situations the proper aggregation level for analysis is unknown. Aggregation may lead to simultaneity, and this also leads to endogeneity. It can happen that the error term and a regressor are correlated because it is uncertain which of the variables should be on the left-hand side in a regression model and which on the right-hand side. This is called simultaneity, and it means that things may seem to happen at the same time, while they may not. Such simultaneity may be caused by temporal aggregation. It may then be better to consider higher frequency data, but these data may not be available. One may think that consumption (say of durable goods) may come after income when we observe the variables at, for example, a monthly level, but when the data are aggregated to yearly data, consumption and received income seem to happen at the same time.

To illustrate the consequences of aggregation with a simple case study, consider the median delays in departures versus median delays in arrivals at Amsterdam Schiphol airport for KLM flights, observed for January 1, 2016, 00.00 to January 31, 2016, 23.00. These 744 hourly observations are presented in a scatter plot in Figure 5.2. We put delays in departures on the vertical axis as it may seem plausible that when airplanes have arrived with a delay, one shall most likely depart with a delay.

The scatterplot in Figure 5.2 is not tremendously informative about potential relations between the two variables and leads and

is taking the con out of econometrics, *Journal of Economic Perspectives*, 24 (2), 3–30. See also Alberto Abadie and Matias D. Cattaneo (2018), Econometric methods for program evaluation, *Annual Review of Economics*, 10 (1), 465–503.

[10] https://en.wikipedia.org/wiki/Randomized_controlled_trial.

[11] https://dimewiki.worldbank.org/Regression_Discontinuity.

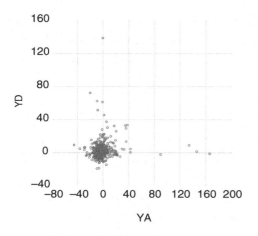

FIGURE 5.2 Median delays in departures (yd in minutes) versus median delays in arrivals (ya in minutes), hourly data.

lags cannot be observed. Hence, we try out the following regression model, where diagnostic tests suggest nonautocorrelated residuals, that is

$$Delays\ departures_t = \alpha + \beta_0 Delays\ arrivals_t + \beta_{1d} Delays\ departures_{t-1}$$
$$+ \beta_{2d} Delays\ departures_{t-2} + \beta_{1a} Delays\ arrivals_{t-1}$$
$$+ \beta_{2a} Delays\ arrivals_{t-2} + \varepsilon_t$$

OLS gives the following parameter estimates (with standard errors in parentheses)

$$a = 2.045(0.373)$$
$$b_0 = 0.036(0.025)$$
$$b_{1d} = 0.097(0.037)$$
$$b_{2d} = 0.083(0.038)$$
$$b_{1a} = 0.076(0.025)$$
$$b_{2a} = 0.030(0.025)$$

We see that the null hypothesis $\beta_0 = 0$ cannot be rejected. Backwards deleting insignificant terms results in

$$Delays\ departures_t = \alpha + \beta_{1d} Delays\ departures_{t-1}$$
$$+ \beta_{2d} Delays\ departures_{t-2}$$
$$+ \beta_{1a} Delays\ arrivals_{t-1} + \varepsilon_t$$

FIGURE 5.3 Median delays in departures (in minutes) versus median delays in arrivals (in minutes), daily data.

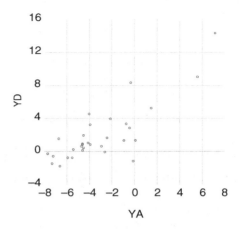

and OLS delivers

$$a = 1.788(0.349)$$
$$b_{1d} = 0.111(0.036)$$
$$b_{2d} = 0.097(0.037)$$
$$b_{1a} = 0.075(0.025)$$

Indeed, delays in departures seem not affected by delayed arrivals at the same time, at least when we consider these two variables at the hourly level.

Now suppose we aggregate the data to a daily level (by taking the averages of the hourly medians). The resultant thirty-one observations are presented in Figure 5.3.

This scatter plot shows that a linear link between the two variables seems visibly present. Indeed, when we consider a regression

$$Delays\ departures_t = \alpha + \beta_{0a} Delays\ arrivals_t + \varepsilon_t$$

OLS gives

$$a = 4.360(0.487)$$
$$b_{0a} = 0.798(0.106)$$

When we switch position of the two variables and consider

$$Delays\ arrivals_t = \alpha + \beta_{0d} Delays\ departures_t + \varepsilon_t$$

OLS delivers

$$a = -4.634(0.429)$$
$$b_{0d} = 0.827(0.110)$$

In both models no further lags are needed, according to diagnostic tests. It seems that the two types of delays happen "on the same day." This is of course caused by aggregation. It seems wise to replace OLS by TSLS and take, for example, *Delays departures*$_{t-1}$ and *Delays arrivals*$_{t-1}$ as instruments, although weather variables could also be considered. We then get for

$$Delays\ departures_t = \alpha + \beta_{0a} Delays\ arrivals_t + \varepsilon_t$$

the TSLS estimation results

$$a = 6.346(3.457)$$
$$b_{0a} = 1.496(1.182)$$

The validity of instruments is not rejected and the test for exogeneity of *Delays arrivals*$_t$ suggests some evidence of rejection of the null hypothesis.[12] In sum, temporal aggregation can make variables to be correlated at the same time, while they are not when we consider higher frequency observation of the variables.

5.3   MULTICOLLINEARITY

Another feature of an econometric model that, when ignored, can lead to misleading inference is multicollinearity. This involves a (very) strong correlation among the regressors, which makes it difficult to disentangle individual effects of the regressors.

To illustrate, let us create 100 observations with the following DGP, that is,

$$x_{1,i} \sim N(0,1)$$
$$x_{2,i} \sim N(0,1)$$

---

[12] The J test value is 0.649 (with a p value of 0.421), and the test for exogeneity of *Delays arrivals*$_t$ gives test value 0.823 (p value is 0.364).

$$v_i \sim N(0,1)$$
$$y_i = 10 + 2x_{1,i} + 2x_{2,i} + v_i$$

When we apply OLS to the regression

$$y_i = \alpha + \beta_1 x_{1,i} + \beta_2 x_{2,i} + \varepsilon_i$$

we get (at least for our simulation run using EViews)

$$a = 9.699 (0.115)$$
$$b_1 = 2.124 (0.113)$$
$$b_2 = 1.819 (0.110)$$

The parameters get estimated well because the standard errors (in parentheses) are small. If you want larger standard errors, then you can replace in the DGP v_i by $2v_i$ or more.

Before we continue with simulating more data, let us look at the concept called the Variance Inflation Factor (VIF). This is a statistic that can be computed for each regressor in a regression model. This VIF is a measure of the degree of multicollinearity. Consider the regression model

$$y_i = \mu + \beta_1 x_{1,i} + \dots + \beta_k x_{k,i} + \varepsilon_i$$

Now run $j = 1, \dots, k$ regressions like

$$x_{j,i} = \alpha + \gamma_1 x_{1,i} + \dots + \gamma_{j-1} x_{j-1,i} + \gamma_{j+1} x_{j+1,i} + \dots + \gamma_k x_{k,i} + \omega_i$$

and compute each time an R_j^2. The VIF factor for β_j is

$$VIF_j = \frac{1}{1 - R_j^2}$$

When the R_j^2 approaches 1, the VIF factor becomes large. Commonly, people set a VIF larger than 5 as a benchmark, which associates with an R_j^2 larger than 0.8. Note that to compute the VIF, one needs a regression model again. This suggests that looking at only pairwise correlations between variables is not useful, as there can be large correlations with multiple variables involved.

Let us see how this works by slightly changing the DGP in the simulation experiment; that is, we replace

$$x_{2,i} \sim N(0,1)$$

with

$$x_{2,i} = x_{1,i} + kw_i, \quad \text{with} \quad w_i \sim N(0,1)$$

The second variable is equal to the first with some measurement error. When we set $k = 0.5$, and run again the regression of y on a constant and x_1 and x_2, then the OLS (in our experiment) estimates become

$$a = 9.759(0.226)$$
$$b_1 = 1.900(0.581)$$
$$b_2 = 0.265(0.509)$$

Interestingly, the null hypothesis $\beta_2 = 0$ cannot be rejected. The uncentred (based on the raw and not demeaned data) VIF scores are 7.119 and 7.175, respectively. When we increase the degree of collinearity even further by setting $k = 0.1$, we get

$$a = 9.730(0.225)$$
$$b_1 = 0.036(2.603)$$
$$b_2 = 2.147(2.596)$$

While the $R^2 = 0.507$, we see that both the hypothesis $\beta_1 = 0$ and the hypothesis $\beta_2 = 0$ cannot be rejected. The associated VIF scores exceed 143, so these are telling numbers. In practice, it is thus wise to compute the VIF scores in regression models. At the same time, when the R^2 has a reasonably large value, while the parameters are all not significant, we have already a first sign of possible multicollinearity.

5.4 SOLUTIONS TO MULTICOLLINEARITY

What can we do about multicollinearity? If one variable measures about the same feature as one or more other variables, you can just as well delete this variable or take some average. Alternatively, you can resort to Ridge Regression,[13] which in matrix notation involves the estimator

$$b = (X'X + \lambda I_k)^{-1} X'y$$

with I_k is a $(k+1 \times k+1)$ identity matrix. The parameter $\lambda > 0$ shrinks parameters towards zero if they are less relevant.

Another alternative is to resort to Principal Components Analysis (PCA).[14] PCA seeks linear combinations of the regressors that maximize the variance of such combinations. These newly created variables can then be included in the so-called Principal Components Regression (PCR) replacing the original variables. It is often found that the first Principal Component comes close to an unweighted average of the relevant variables.

Specific versions of multicollinearity appear when we consider levels and squares of these levels in a regression model, often to describe nonlinear patterns. Think of correlating household holiday expenditure and age. When you are young you do not have much money and you cannot spend that much on holidays. With increasing age, and perhaps with increasing family size, you likely spend more. Later in life, when children do not join your trips anymore, you start to spend less. So, you may consider including Age_i and Age_i^2 in a regression model for such expenditures.

5.5 VARIABLES AND SQUARED VARIABLES

To see what happens if you include levels and squared levels in the same regression model, consider the following example. Look at the data in Figure 5.4, where we depict the levels of real GDP in Chile, where the data are indexed in 1950 equal to 100.

A possibly useful forecasting model for short-term forecasts could be

$$y_t = \alpha + \beta_1 t + \beta_2 t^2 + \rho y_{t-1} + \varepsilon_t$$

---

[13] https://en.wikipedia.org/wiki/Ridge_regression.
[14] https://en.wikipedia.org/wiki/Principal_component_analysis.

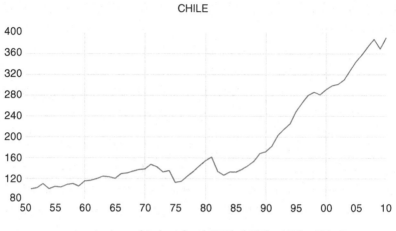

FIGURE 5.4   Annual index of real GDP of Chile, 1950 = 100.

where trend $t = 1, 2, 3, \ldots$. This is not to say that this would be the best possible model, but it could deliver accurate forecasts. Suppose one thus includes the quadratic trend (and not take logs) to capture the seemingly exponential pattern in the data. Applying OLS to this model results in

$$a = 20.033(9.634)$$
$$b_1 = -0.605(0.397)$$
$$b_2 = 0.022(0.001)$$
$$r = 0.862(0.062)$$

It is now good to know that the correlation between t and t^2 is close to 1. Hence, the apparent insignificance of β_1 may be attributable to this strong correlation. To avoid such multicollinearity,[15] one should better consider t and $\left(t - \bar{t}\right)^2$ as the correlation between t and $\left(t - \bar{t}\right)^2$ is 0. Note that $\left(t - \bar{t}\right)^2 = t^2 - 2\bar{t}t + \bar{t}^2$, and hence the parameter estimates for the intercept and the variable t will change when we consider

$$y_t = \alpha + \beta_1 t + \beta_2 \left(t - \bar{t}\right)^2 + \rho y_{t-1} + \varepsilon_t$$

---

[15] See also James Jaccard, Choi K. Wan, and Robert Turrisi (1990), The detection and interpretation of interaction effects between continuous variables in multiple regression, *Multivariate Behavioral Research*, 25 (4), 467–478.

Indeed, OLS gives

$$a = -1.338(2.764)$$
$$b_1 = 0.774(0.267)$$
$$b_2 = 0.022(0.001)$$
$$r = 0.862(0.062)$$

Note the switch of the sign of b_1 owing to $-2\beta_2 \bar{t}$ as additional coefficient value.

In all practical cases, one should be careful with quadratic regressions (with x_i is, for example, age) like

$$y_i = \alpha + \beta_1 x_i + \beta_2 x_i^2 + \varepsilon_i$$

and one should better use

$$y_i = \alpha + \beta_1 x_i + \beta_2 \left(x_i - \bar{x}\right)^2 + \varepsilon_i$$

Yet, at the same time, such a quadratic regression does enforce a strong (partial) symmetric parabolic effect of a variable. In some cases, it may perhaps be recommended to use two interrupted regression lines,[16] like

$$y_i = \alpha + \beta_1 x_i I\left(x_i < \tau\right) + \beta_2 x_i I\left(x_i \geq \tau\right) + \varepsilon_i$$

5.6 UNANTICIPATED SIGNS

It is sometimes thought that multicollinearity can lead to unanticipated signs of the estimated parameters. And as such, bearing in mind what we discuss in Chapter 2, that such multicollinearity may lead to harking, and hence lowering the quality of the knowledge base. But it is easy to show that estimated parameters do *not* get an unanticipated sign owing to collinearity across included variables in reasonably large samples.[17]

---

[16] Uri Simonsohn (2018), Two lines: A valid alternative to the invalid testing of U-shaped relationships with quadratic regressions, *Advances in Methods and Practices in Psychological Science*, 1 (4), 538–555.

[17] Based on Philip Hans Franses and Christiaan Heij (2003), Estimated parameters do not get an unanticipated sign due to collinearity across included variables, *Canadian Journal of Marketing Research*, 21 (1), 79–81.

Consider, for example,

$$y_i = \beta_1 x_{1,i} + \beta_2 x_{2,i} + \varepsilon_i$$

Assume $\varepsilon_i \sim N(0,1)$ and that it is uncorrelated with $x_{1,i}$ and $x_{2,i}$, and assume that

$$\begin{pmatrix} x_{1,i} \\ x_{2,i} \end{pmatrix} \sim N\left(\begin{pmatrix} 0 \\ 0 \end{pmatrix}, \begin{pmatrix} 1 & \rho \\ \rho & 1 \end{pmatrix} \right)$$

The collinearity appears in the t statistics. For the first variable, the t statistic is

$$t_1 \approx b_1 \sqrt{n} \sqrt{1 - \rho^2}$$

With large enough n, even for ρ close to 1, the sign does not change, and the estimated parameter can be significant, but it can also be insignificant, as we saw earlier.

However, problems potentially appear when the DGP is

$$y_i = \beta_1 x_{1,i} + \beta_2 x_{2,i} + \varepsilon_i$$

but one considers

$$y_i = \gamma x_{1,i} + \omega_i$$

which means that a variable $x_{2,i}$ is omitted. In that case, OLS for γ concerns (for these similarly scaled variables)

$$\gamma \approx \beta_1 + \beta_2 \rho$$

And it is here where it can happen that γ gets estimated with a different sign than β_1. In sum, "wrong signs" can appear when there are omitted variables that are more important than the included variables.

5.7 DIAGNOSTIC TESTS

There are many diagnostic tests for various features of regression models, and such tests also exist for all kinds of other econometric models, such as the logit and probit models for binary variables, multinomial models, and ordered regression models; there are many more.

These diagnostic tests challenge the underlying assumptions needed for proper statistical inference. In time series models, tests for residual autocorrelation are very important. When there is such ignored autocorrelation, then the forecasts from time series models can be improved as not all information is incorporated. Tests for structural breaks, can be relevant, as can tests for the constancy of parameters and for constant variance of the error terms. One may want to check for normality, although it is perhaps more useful to straightaway consider the potential presence of influential observations.

There are various studies that use simulation experiments to see if tests have the proper type 1 error and a low type 2 error, and hence a large power. Tests for unit roots are notorious for having low power, and there it seems that perhaps models with and without unit roots should be entertained, as for the airline data in Chapter 4, for example when looking at out-of-sample forecasts.[18]

On the other hand, running too many tests can also be problematic as there might always be some aspect of a model that does not fully comply with all assumptions.[19] There are various assumptions for OLS to work for models such as

$$y_i = \beta_1 x_{1,i} + \beta_2 x_{2,i} + \varepsilon_i$$

And there are various diagnostic tests for each of these assumptions.[20]

5.8 PROPER SCIENTIFIC CONDUCT

In sum, it is relevant to check the main assumptions of an econometric model.

---

[18] In any case, an interesting quote is "A test that is never used has zero power" in Michael McAleer (1994), Sherlock Holmes and the search for truth: A diagnostic tale, *Journal of Economic Surveys*, 8 (4) 317–370, at page 334. Michael McAleer passed away on 8 July 2021. For a long time, he was affiliated with the Econometric Institute in Rotterdam.

[19] See, for example, Edward E. Leamer (1988), Things that bother me, *Economic Record*, 64 (4), 331–335, at page 332; and Peter C. B. Phillips (1988), Reflections on econometric methodology, *Economic Record*, 64 (4), 344–359, at page 349.

[20] See Christiaan Heij, Paul de Boer, Philip Hans Franses, Teun Kloek, and Herman van Dijk (2004), *Econometric Methods with Applications in Business and Economics*, Oxford: Oxford University Press, chapter 5.

Variables for which "a wrong sign" of the parameter is obtained should not be excluded from the analysis, and should also not be thought of as being caused by multicollinearity. In fact, when a "wrong sign" occurs, one should look for any initially omitted variables. This holds also in the case of endogeneity and omitted equations. Indeed, it is perhaps then better to include too many than too few variables. A recent tendency in macroeconomic forecasting, for example while forecasting inflation, is to include hundreds of potential regressors and let the data tell which variables to keep in a final forecasting model. On the downside, this can lead to data mining.

We also learnt that one should be careful with quadratic regressions, and the interpretation of parameters. A modified version of a quadratic regression, where care is taken of the average of the regressor to be squared, seems more appropriate for interpretation as collinearity decreases.

5.9 INTERPRETATION

We conclude this chapter with a few words about the interpretation of estimated regression models. Rarely, we just present the parameter estimates and their associated standard errors and leave it up to the advisee to draw suitable inference. In fact, we need to provide an interpretation of the presented numbers. This is not that straightforward owing to the ceteris paribus conditions, and perhaps a useful tool concerns the Shapley values, which are presented and illustrated in Section 5.10.

Before doing so, it is good to be reminded that statistical significance does not necessarily mean practical relevance. Consider the following case study.[21] Since 1901, a record has been kept of the day in the year on which the first lapwing egg was found in the Netherlands. In 1901 it was day 84 and in 2020 it was day 62. It

---

[21] Exercise 7.1 from Philip Hans Franses (2021), *Quantitative Insights for Lawyers*, The Hague: Eleven.

has been believed that in recent times these eggs seem to be discovered earlier in the year, which could perhaps be a sign of global warming.

To examine a potential downward tendency, one can consider the following regression model, here applied to the data from 1901 to 2010, that is,

$$Number\ of\ days_t = \alpha + \beta\,Trend_t + \varepsilon_t$$

where $Trend_1 = 1$ for 1901, $Trend_2 = 2$ for 1902, and so on. Application of OLS gives

$$a = 81.553(1.061)$$
$$b = -0.081(0.017)$$

The hypothesis $\beta = 0$ is clearly rejected.

But now look at the multi-step-ahead forecasts for 2011 to 2020. It so turns out that all these forecasts are equal to 72. Hence, even though the downward trend is statistically significant, it does not seem to matter much for forecasting ten years ahead.

5.10 SHAPLEY VALUES

A promising tool to assign interpretation to regression results relies on so-called Shapley values.[22] These can be used to indicate how important variables are in their contribution to the R^2. Comparing t values is cumbersome as these are related through the correlation among the included variables.

Start with a regression with only two variables, such as

$$y_i = \alpha + \beta_1 x_{1,i} + \beta_2 x_{2,i} + \varepsilon_i$$

---

[22] https://en.wikipedia.org/wiki/Lloyd_Shapley; https://en.wikipedia.org/wiki/Shapley_value; Lloyd Shapley (1953), A value for n-person games, In H. W. Kuhn and A. W. Tucker (eds.), *Contributions to the Theory of Games* volume II, Princeton: Princeton University Press, 307–317; Lloyd Shapley and Martin Shubik (1954), A method for evaluating the distribution of power in a committee system, *American Political Science Review* 48 (3), 787–792; Xingwei Hu (2020), A theory of dichotomous valuation with applications to variable selection, *Econometric Reviews*, 39 (10), 1075–1099.

and use OLS to estimate the parameters. The fit of this model is measured by R_{12}^2, where the subscript "12" means the inclusion of the two predictors. When the model would include only x_1, we have R_1^2, and when it includes only x_2, we have R_2^2.

The contribution of x_1 to the overall fit, taking on board the correlation between x_1 and x_2, is now defined as

$$\frac{1}{2}R_1^2 + \frac{1}{2}\left(R_{12}^2 - R_2^2\right)$$

and the associated Shapley value is

$$S_1 = \frac{\dfrac{1}{2}R_1^2 + \dfrac{1}{2}\left(R_{12}^2 - R_2^2\right)}{R_{12}^2}$$

For x_2 we have

$$S_2 = \frac{\dfrac{1}{2}R_2^2 + \dfrac{1}{2}\left(R_{12}^2 - R_1^2\right)}{R_{12}^2}$$

Clearly, $S_1 + S_2 = 1$.[23]

To illustrate with an example,[24] consider a regression of the natural logarithm of citations (to reduce the variance) to articles in a top journal called *Marketing Science* (in case citations are nonzero) on a constant, the number of pages of an article, the number of references in the papers, and the number of revisions. One may now wonder which factors lead to more citations. More precisely, one may

---

[23] Expressions for K variables can be found in Frederic Chantreuil and Alain Trannoy (2011), Inequality decomposition values, *Annals of Economics and Statistics*, 101/102 (January/June), 13–36. Alternative computational approaches are presented in Stan Lipovetsky and Michael Conklin (2001), Analysis of regression in game theory approach, *Applied Stochastic Models in Business and Industry*, 17 (4), 319–330; Anthony F. Shorrocks (2013), Decomposition procedures for distributional analysis: A unified framework based on the Shapley value, *Journal of Economic Inequality*, 11 (1), 99–126; and Kjersti Aas, Martin Jullum, and Anders Løland (2021), Explaining individual prediction when features are dependent: More accurate approximations to Shapley values, *Artificial Intelligence*, 298, 103502.

[24] This example is taken from Philip Hans Franses (2018), *Enjoyable Econometrics*, Cambridge: Cambridge University Press.

wonder whether perhaps more revisions before publication lead to more citations. The regression model is

$$\log Citations_i = \alpha + \beta_1 Pages_i + \beta_2 References_i$$
$$+ \beta_3 Revisions_i + \varepsilon_i$$

For 208 observations, OLS gives

$$a = -1.358(0.284)$$
$$b_1 = 0.048(0.013)$$
$$b_2 = 0.009(0.004)$$
$$b_3 = 0.199(0.073)$$

The influence statistics in Figure 5.5 suggest that this model does not suffer from influential observations, so we can move on.

We see that all parameters seem statistically significant (at the 5 percent level), but the coefficients vary in size and so do the t values. So, how relevant is $Revisions_i$?

To compute the Shapley values for each of the regressors, we do the following. We start with computing regressions using all combinations of the predictors, that is,

Predictors	R^2
No predictors	0
Pages	0.103
References	0.056
Revisions	0.029
Pages and References	0.120
References and Revisions	0.091
Pages and Revisions	0.130
Pages, References and Revisions	0.151

To see what each predictor adds, we compare the R^2 values. On its own, the variable Pages gives an R^2 of 0.103. When Pages is added to References, the R^2 increases from 0.056 to 0.120. When Pages is added to Revisions, the R^2 increases from 0.029 to 0.130. And when

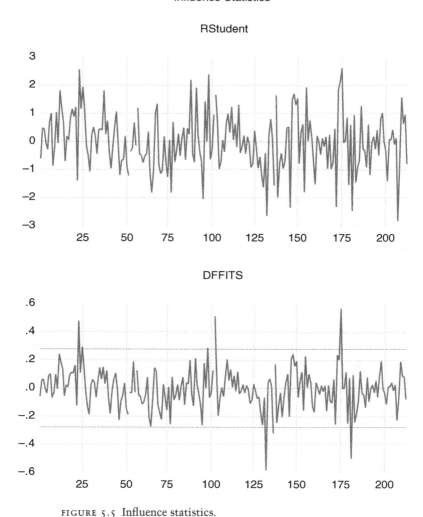

FIGURE 5.5 Influence statistics.

Pages is added to References and Revisions, the R^2 increases from 0.091 to 0.151. As there are two models at the end of the spectrum (only Pages or one of the other variables versus all variables), these models get a weight of $\frac{1}{3}$, while the middle two options each get a weight of $\frac{1}{6}$. In sum, the total contribution of Pages is

$$\frac{1}{3}(0.103) + \frac{1}{6}(0.120 - 0.056) + \frac{1}{6}(0.130 - 0.029)$$
$$+ \frac{1}{3}(0.151 - 0.091) = 0.0818$$

Similarly, the contribution of References is

$$\frac{1}{3}(0.056) + \frac{1}{6}(0.120 - 0.103) + \frac{1}{6}(0.091 - 0.029)$$
$$+ \frac{1}{3}(0.151 - 0.130) = 0.0388$$

And the contribution of Revisions is

$$\frac{1}{3}(0.029) + \frac{1}{6}(0.130 - 0.103) + \frac{1}{6}(0.091 - 0.029)$$
$$+ \frac{1}{3}(0.151 - 0.120) = 0.0297$$

Scaling up to a total 100% gives

Pages	0.0818	54.4%
References	0.0388	25.8%
Revisions	0.0297	19.8%

In other words, Pages contributes to more than "half of the fit," according to this method, while the contribution of Revisions is just about 20 percent. Note that this could not have been seen from the parameter estimates or the t test values.

5.11 WHAT DID WE LEARN?

In this chapter we have addressed a few issues concerning estimation and interpretation. Measurement errors are often around, but perhaps too often not taken care of. We have seen that inference can change dramatically. Key is to have the proper instruments. When collecting data, one should strive to better measure the data, although this may not always easy. Some would say that it all begins with better research designs, and perhaps this is indeed the way to go in some areas.

Interpretation of model outcomes is not straightforward owing to correlation between regressors. Shapley values can help. And if the correlation is too strong, when there is multicollinearity, there are various ways to improve the model. Definitively, though, apparent wrong signs of estimated parameters should not be interpreted as caused by strong correlation. In that case one may have misspecified the model, thereby excluding relevant variables. Harking is then not the way to go; looking for more relevant variables is.

FURTHER READING

One of the features of econometric analysis that might be associated with the holy grail concerns how to cope with endogeneity. IV estimation is the standard practice, as is also done in this chapter, but finding proper instruments is not often successful. One often ends up with weak instruments, and see what happens then in:

John Bound, David A. Jaeger, and Regina M. Baker (1995), Problems with instrumental variables estimation when the correlation between the instruments and the endogenous explanatory variable is weak, *Journal of the American Statistical Association*, 90 (June), 443–450.

A recent potentially successful approach is advocated in

Sungho Park and Sachin Gupta (2012), Handling endogenous regressors by joint estimation using copulas, *Marketing Science*, 31 (4), 567–586.

Simulations experiments give hopeful results, but in:

Fredrik Falkenström, Sungho Park, and Cameron N. McIntosh (2021), Using copulas to enable causal inference from non-experimental data: Tutorial and simulation results, *Psychological Methods*, in print.

and

Christine Eckert and Jan Hohberger (2022), Addressing endogeneity without instrumental variables: An evaluation of Gaussian copula approach for management research, *Journal of Management*, https://doi.org/10.1177/01492063221085913.

it is shown using other simulation experiments that the assumptions for this method are not always met in practice. This shows how econometrics as an academic discipline proceeds. New methods are proposed. These are tested and applied, and after a while it is established if such a new method will stay in the toolkit.

6   Missing Data

This chapter deals with missing data and a few approaches to managing it. There are several reasons why data can be missing. An example is that people can have thrown away older data, which can be a sensible thing to do in some cases. It can also occur that you want to analyze a phenomenon that occurs at an hourly level while you have data only at the daily level; the hourly data are missing. It can also be that a survey is simply too long: If people get tired they may not answer all the questions.[1]

In this chapter we will review various situations where data are missing and how we can recognize such situations. Sometimes we know how to manage missing data. Often there is no need to panic and modifications of models and/or estimation methods can be used. We will even encounter a case where data can be made to be missing on purpose, by selective sampling, to facilitate empirical analysis. If subsequent analysis explicitly takes account of the missingness, the impact of missing data can become minor, as we will see.

It is not the purpose of this chapter to educate on all strategies that follow. That would simply be too much. There will be some references to articles that you may wish to consult. The main intention is to create awareness that missing data can happen and which potential actions can be taken next. When you pursue your own empirical analysis, it is important that you clearly indicate how you dealt with the missing data.

---

[1] For a recent account on living standards measurement surveys, see Dahyeon Jeong, Shilpa Aggarwal, Jonathan Robinson, Naresh Kumar, Alan Spearot, and David Sungho Park (2022), Exhaustive or exhausting? Evidence and respondent fatigue in long surveys, NBER Working paper No. 30439.

This chapter gives a succinct overview of what can happen and what in some cases you can do. There are several reasons why data can be missing, and it is good to be aware of those reasons. A next step concerns what one can do when data are missing. One may wish to interpolate the missing data from the available data, over time or within cross sections, but we will see that interpolation has nonnegligible consequences, and understanding these consequences is one of the key themes of this book. For example, for time series data we will see that the autocorrelations are enlarged values. On the other hand, missing data can also be convenient when surveys are costly or when there is a risk of attrition (people leaving the surveys). The creation of a database with missing data on purpose can therefore be useful, at least if the subsequent model and estimation method is changed. Finally, we will see that data can become missing owing to temporal aggregation. However, when the relevant model for the aggregated data is adapted, one can still learn about the parameters in a more realistic model for the less aggregated data.

6.1   DOES IT MATTER?

To show that dealing with missing data can matter, and to illustrate what can go wrong if such consequences are ignored, let us look at the following case.[2]

Clark and colleagues requested that their article be retracted out of concern that some of the measures used in the research were invalid. Specifically, they noted that

> the National IQ data used in their analyses, based on Lynn
> and Vanhanen's (2012) compilation,[3] are plagued by lack of

---

[2] C. J. Clark, B. M. Winegard, J. Beardslee, R. F. Baumeister, and A. F. Shariff, (2020), Declines in religiosity predict increases in violent crime – But not among countries with relatively high average IQ. *Psychological Science*, 31, 170–183, https://journals .sagepub.com/doi/full/10.1177/0956797619897915.

[3] Richard Lynn and Tatu Vanhanen (2012), *Intelligence: A Unifying Construct for the Social Sciences*, London: Ulster Institute for Social Research; Richard Lynn and Tatu Vanhanen (2002), *IQ and the Wealth of Nations*, Westport, CT: Praeger/Greenwood Publishers, https://en.wikipedia.org/wiki/IQ_and_the_Wealth_of_Nations.

representativeness of the samples, questionable support for some of the measures, an excess of researcher degrees of freedom, and concern about the vulnerability of the data to bias. They also noted that the cross-national homicide data used in the research are unreliable, given that many countries included in the data set provided no actual data on homicides that had occurred. Instead, in these countries, homicide rates were estimated on the basis of other variables that may or may not be closely related to homicide rates. Importantly, some of the variables used to create the estimates were confounded with variables of interest in the research. When the authors reanalyzed the data *without the imputed values* [emphasis added], the reported effects *were no longer apparent* [emphasis added].

The editor-in-chief Patricia J. Bauer continues:

In the conclusion of their request for retraction, the authors reflected that although articles with certain types of errors may still be helpful to have in the literature, they do not believe theirs falls into that category. They explicitly expressed concern that leaving the article in the literature could prolong the use of Lynn & Vanhanen's cross-national IQ measures. As Editor of *Psychological Science*, I have decided to honor the authors' request and retract this article. I hope that this action on the part of the authors and the journal will encourage all researchers to exercise extreme care in selection and use of the data sets on which they base their analyses, conclusions, and interpretations. Critiques of Lynn and Vanhanen's (2012) National IQ data were available in the literature prior to the publication of Clark et al. (2020). It is unfortunate that these critiques were not consulted, thereby potentially avoiding publication and the necessity for retraction.

Here we see a retraction of a paper from a top journal. This is too bad, but this case study illustrates how important it is to check the data, in various dimensions, before you perform your analysis. In this case, replacing the missing data with new imputed data is the culprit.

6.2 WHY ARE DATA MISSING IF THEY ARE?

There are several reasons why data can be missing.

People can make mistakes while recording data. Typographical errors can be made, and other users of the dataset may delete these upon screening.

It may be that older data have been deleted because people thought they would not be relevant for further analysis. Note that this could be a sound strategy in some cases, for example where products in supermarkets simply do not exist after a few years have passed. Moreover, individual preferences ten years ago, for example concerning internet offers for travels, may have changed so much for individuals over time that including such information in present-day models may be confusing instead of informative.

It may be believed that it is too expensive to measure and store high frequency data or highly detailed data. In principle, using loyalty cards from retailers, one could keep track of all purchases ever made by an individual, and everything that person did not purchase. Storing all these data can be expensive and difficult to maintain, and hence one may move to keeping store-level data instead of individual consumer data. When there are too many stores, one could decide to collect data at county level instead of store level.

Survey participants may decide not to answer all questions, for example when questions deal with sensitive issues. Not everyone is keen on answering questions such as "Do you use drugs?" or "Do you drink more than six glasses alcohol per day?" Questions on income and gender can also be ignored on purpose.

When people are included in a household panel, where the purpose is to learn what individual households purchase when and where, attrition may happen. Attrition implies that people leave the panel because of boredom or because of an unpleasant feeling of "being watched." Additionally, reporting every day what you buy may also lead to a feeling that you should change your eating or drinking habits. If that happens, your behavior changes just because you are a member of a household panel.

As a macroeconomic example, consider national accounts. It took quite a while into the 1990s for national statistical agencies to recognize that computers were contributing to Gross National Product (GNP). With hindsight, the national accounts were modified for those years. This is an example of missing information in the earlier data on GNP. It may have taken a while for people to recognize that it might have been important to collect some data earlier.

6.3   HOW CAN DATA BE MISSING?

Data can be missing completely at random.[4] This is defined as the "Missing mechanism is independent from the observable variables and the parameters to be estimated." Data can be missing at random, which is defined as the "Missing mechanism is dependent on one or more of the observable variables." For example, younger people may be less likely to fill in some survey questions than older people, or the other way around. The third situation is that the data are missing not at random. An example is that smokers may not fill in surveys on the health aspects of smoking.

6.4   HOW TO DEAL WITH (OR PREVENT) MISSING DATA

Before we zoom in on some specific case studies, here are a few general approaches that we can follow when data is missing. A first is to redesign surveys by asking better questions. You can also use randomized surveys in the case of sensitive questions that people can be reluctant to answer. For example, you can make the participant toss a coin (without you seeing it), and agree that when it is "heads" the answer will be an honest one.

It may also be possible to adapt the estimation procedure,[5] or to change the model. A two-step model, such as the so-called Tobit

---

[4] Roderick J. A. Little (1992), Regression with missing X's: A review, *Journal of the American Statistical Association*, 87 (420), 1227–1237.

[5] Theo Nijman and Marno Verbeek (1992), Nonresponse in panel data – The impact on estimates of a life-cycle consumption function, *Journal of Applied Econometrics*, 7 (3), 243–257; James H. Albert and Siddhartha Chib (1993), Bayes inference via Gibbs sampling of autoregressive time series subject to Markovian mean and variance shifts, *Journal of Business & Economic Statistics*, 11 (1), 1–15.

model,[6] can also be considered, in which the model contains a part that deals with the probability of being observed and where a second part is a regression model for factual observation.

One may also decide to interpolate the missing data. In a cross section, one can replace missing data on a certain variable by the average of that variable for all nonmissing data. Note that this effectively means a reduction of the variance of these observations. For time series, one can choose to "connect the points" by replacing the missing observations by those that are on a (straight or curved) line between the earlier and later observed data points. This does have consequences though, as we will see.

It is important to be aware that aggregation of data can imply changes to a model. The well-known example, again to be discussed later in this chapter, is that temporally aggregating a random walk process leads to a random walk with an additional moving average term. In practice this may suggest predictability, but it only means that the data are aggregated to a too low frequency.

6.5 INTERPOLATION AND AUTOCORRELATION

To understand what interpolation does to the time series properties of variables,[7] consider the following four observations

$$\varepsilon_1, \varepsilon_2, \varepsilon_3, \varepsilon_4$$

and assume that each observation is a draw from a zero-mean uncorrelated process with variance σ^2, that is, the correlation between any ε_i and ε_j for $i \neq j$ is zero. It follows that the empirical first-order autocorrelation for this short series of observations can be calculated as

$$r_1 = \frac{\frac{1}{3}\sum_{t=2}^{t=4} E(\varepsilon_t \varepsilon_{t-1})}{\frac{1}{3}\sum_{t=2}^{t=4} E(\varepsilon_t)^2} = \frac{0}{\sigma^2} = 0$$

---

[6] https://en.wikipedia.org/wiki/Tobit_model.

[7] Based on Philip Hans Franses (2021), Interpolation and correlation, *Applied Economics*, 54 (14), 1562–1567.

Suppose now that ε_2 is (made) missing and is interpolated using ε_1 and ε_3. In this case, the new data series becomes

$$\varepsilon_1, \frac{1}{2}\varepsilon_1 + \frac{1}{2}\varepsilon_3, \varepsilon_3, \varepsilon_4$$

We call these observations ε_t^*. For this new data series, it holds that

$$\frac{1}{3}\sum_{t=2}^{t=4} E(\varepsilon_t^* \varepsilon_{t-1}^*) = \frac{1}{3}\left(\frac{1}{2}\sigma^2 + \frac{1}{2}\sigma^2 + 0\right) = \frac{1}{3}\sigma^2$$

and that

$$\frac{1}{3}\sum_{t=2}^{t=4} E(\varepsilon_t^*)^2 = \frac{1}{3}\left(\frac{1}{4}\sigma^2 + \frac{1}{4}\sigma^2 + \sigma^2 + \sigma^2\right) = \frac{5}{6}\sigma^2$$

Hence, the first order autocorrelation becomes

$$r_1 = \frac{\frac{1}{3}\sum_{t=2}^{t=4} E(\varepsilon_t^* \varepsilon_{t-1}^*)}{\frac{1}{3}\sum_{t=2}^{t=4} E(\varepsilon_t^*)^2} = \frac{\frac{1}{3}}{\frac{5}{6}} = \frac{2}{5} = 0.4$$

In a second case, suppose ε_2 and ε_3 are missing and are interpolated using ε_1 and ε_4. When there are two observations missing, a linear interpolation method results in the new observations

$$\varepsilon_1, \frac{2}{3}\varepsilon_1 + \frac{1}{3}\varepsilon_4, \frac{1}{3}\varepsilon_1 + \frac{2}{3}\varepsilon_4, \varepsilon_4$$

We now have that

$$\frac{1}{3}\sum_{t=2}^{t=4} E(\varepsilon_t^* \varepsilon_{t-1}^*) = \frac{1}{3}\left(\frac{2}{3}\sigma^2 + \frac{2}{9}\sigma^2 + \frac{2}{9}\sigma^2 + \frac{2}{3}\sigma^2\right) = \frac{16}{27}\sigma^2$$

and that

$$\frac{1}{3}\sum_{t=2}^{t=4} E(\varepsilon_t^*)^2 = \frac{1}{3}\left(\frac{5}{9}\sigma^2 + \frac{5}{9}\sigma^2 + \sigma^2\right) = \frac{19}{27}\sigma^2$$

The first-order autocorrelation of the new interpolated series becomes

$$r_1 = \frac{\frac{1}{3}\sum_{t=2}^{t=4} E(\varepsilon_t^* \varepsilon_{t-1}^*)}{\frac{1}{3}\sum_{t=2}^{t=4} E(\varepsilon_t^*)^2} = \frac{16}{19} = 0.84$$

Finally, suppose ε_2 is missing and is interpolated using ε_1 and ε_3, while there are now five instead of four observations, that is,

$$\varepsilon_1, \frac{1}{2}\varepsilon_1 + \frac{1}{2}\varepsilon_3, \varepsilon_3, \varepsilon_4, \varepsilon_5$$

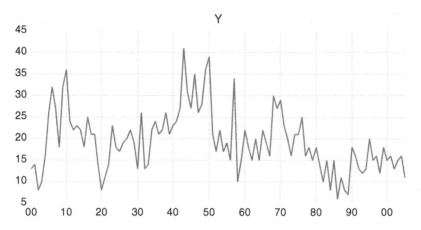

FIGURE 6.1 The number of earthquakes on earth with magnitude (≥7) per year, 1900–2005.
Source: https://en.wikipedia.org/wiki/Lists_of_earthquakes

For this series, we have

$$\frac{1}{4}\sum_{t=2}^{t=5} E(\varepsilon_t^{\bullet}\varepsilon_{t-1}^{\bullet}) = \frac{1}{4}\left(\frac{1}{2}\sigma^2 + \frac{1}{2}\sigma^2 + 0 + 0\right) = \frac{1}{4}\sigma^2$$

and

$$\frac{1}{4}\sum_{t=2}^{t=5} E(\varepsilon_t^{\bullet})^2 = \frac{1}{4}\left(\frac{1}{4}\sigma^2 + \frac{1}{4}\sigma^2 + \sigma^2 + \sigma^2 + \sigma^2\right) = \frac{7}{8}\sigma^2$$

resulting in

$$r_1 = \frac{\frac{1}{4}\sum_{t=2}^{t=5} E(\varepsilon_t^{\bullet}\varepsilon_{t-1}^{\bullet})}{\frac{1}{4}\sum_{t=2}^{t=5} E(\varepsilon_t^{\bullet})^2} = \frac{2}{7} \cong 0.29$$

Hence, when the number of noninterpolated data increases, the first-order autocorrelation in the case of one interpolated observation decreases.

In sum, we see that interpolation introduces autocorrelation among otherwise uncorrelated observations. When the data to be interpolated already have some autocorrelation, one may expect that autocorrelations further increase. To see whether this is the case, consider the annual time series in Figure 6.1, which depicts the number of major

Table 6.1 *Estimated autocorrelations*

Lag	All data	Case 1	Case 2
1	0.564	0.569	0.548
2	0.444	0.464	0.476
3	0.424	0.456	0.415
4	0.373	0.404	0.401
5	0.295	0.317	0.353
6	0.247	0.268	0.252
7	0.251	0.272	0.181
8	0.139	0.170	0.201
9	0.035	0.091	0.168
10	−0.015	0.052	0.125

Source: Author's calculations

earthquakes worldwide for 1900 to and including 2005. The first ten autocorrelations of this series are given in the first column of Table 6.1.

Next, if we look at the data, we see that the observation in 1912 is 22 and in 1928 it is also 22. Let us now proceed as if the data are missing and set all observations in between these two years at 22. The autocorrelations of this partly interpolated series are in the second column of Table 6.1 (Case 1). We see that these are all larger than in the first column. We can now extend the interpolated period to 1953, where the observation is also 22, and the autocorrelations of this interpolated series are to be found in the final column (Case 2). Most of these autocorrelations are also larger than those in the first column. Indeed, interpolation may make the auto-correlation increase and hence increase the persistence of shocks.

An alternative to interpolating the data can be to modify the model and the estimation method. This is what we will do in the next illustration.

6.6 ESTIMATING PERSISTENCE (IN CASE DATA ARE MISSING)

Suppose a first order autoregression is observed at times t_i where $i = 1, 2, 3, \ldots, N$. A general expression for a first order autoregression with arbitrary time intervals is

$$y_{t_i} = \alpha_i y_{t_{i-1}} + \varepsilon_{t_i}$$

with

$$\alpha_i = \exp\left(-\frac{t_i - t_{i-1}}{\tau}\right)$$

with $\tau > 0$.[8] For ease of analysis, it is assumed here that ε_{t_i} is a white noise process with mean zero and common variance σ^2. The τ is as a measure of memory. When we define

$$\alpha = \exp\left(-\frac{1}{\tau}\right)$$

the general first order autoregression can be written as

$$y_{t_i} = \alpha^{t_i - t_{i-1}} y_{t_{i-1}} + \varepsilon_{t_i}$$

When the data would be regularly spaced with interval one, then $t_i - t_{i-1} = 1$. The model then becomes

$$y_t = \alpha y_{t-1} + \varepsilon_t$$

Suppose the data is unequally spaced because of selectively sampling each second observation, and that all the in-between observations are assumed as missing, then $t_i - t_{i-1} = 2$, and the model reads as

$$y_t = \alpha^2 y_{t-2} + \varepsilon_t^*$$

Note that the error term ε_t^* is now heteroskedastic as the variance alternates between σ^2 and $\left(1 + \alpha^2\right)\sigma^2$, and hence we need to rely on the Newey-West heteroskedasticity and autocorrelation consistent (HAC) estimator for standard errors.[9] This is the case when the models alternate over time. When the models are kept constant, there is no heteroskedasticity.

---

[8] Peter M. Robinson (1977), Estimation of a time series model from unequally spaced data, *Stochastic Processes and their Applications*, 6 (1), 9–24; Michael Schulz and Manfred Mudelsee (2002), REDFIT: Estimating red-noise spectra directly from unevenly spaced paleoclimatic time series, *Computers & Geosciences*, 28 (3), 421–426. See also Philip Hans Franses (2021), Estimating persistence for irregularly spaced historical data, *Quality and Quantity*, 55 (6), 2177–2187.

[9] Whitney K. Newey and Kenneth D. West (1987), A simple, positive semi-definite, heteroskedasticity and autocorrelation consistent covariance matrix, *Econometrica*, 55 (3), 703–708.

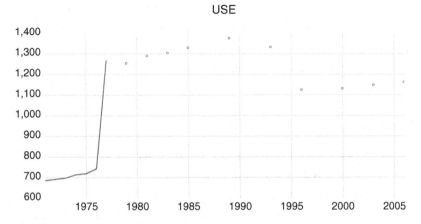

FIGURE 6.2 Land used for transport in the Netherlands, 1970–2006.
Source: Statistics Netherlands

As an illustration, consider the data in Figure 6.2, which concerns the land used for transport in the Netherlands, 1970–2006, where the data source is the Statistics Netherlands (CBS). These measurements were done annually for 1970–1977, and after that only irregularly.

For 1972 to 1977, we consider the model

$$Use_t = \alpha + \beta Use_{t-1} + \varepsilon_t$$

OLS gives

$$a = -5673(2151)$$
$$b = 9.144(3.035)$$

This b is exceptionally large, owing to an explosion in infrastructure works in that period. When we incorporate the more recent years in the following model for all observations

$$Use_{t_i} - \alpha = \beta^{t_i - t_{i-1}} \left(Use_{t_{i-1}} - \alpha \right) + \varepsilon_{t_i}$$

we get

$$a = 1230.6(65.62)$$
$$b = 0.841(0.122)$$

where the numbers in parentheses are the HAC standard errors. Now the value of b seems more appropriate. This illustration shows that one not always has to interpolate the missing data; one can also change the model and the estimation methods.[10]

6.7 CHANGE DATA COLLECTION AND ADJUST MODEL AND ESTIMATION METHOD

In some cases, it can be beneficial to create periods of missing data, for example to reduce attrition. If people get requests to participate in surveys very frequently, then attrition is likely. If you ask people to join consumer confidence surveys each month, it is likely that at some point they will not wish to participate anymore.

One way to avoid this is to ask a different group of individuals each period, as in Figure 6.3.

These data are in fact repeated cross sections. A problem with this approach is that you cannot observe individuals' switching behavior, for example when they switch their votes for political parties, or switch to other brands, or change their opinions.

To observe switching behavior, for example concerning consumer confidence, one may consider the data collection illustrated in Figure 6.4.

It may be that there are extended periods of time in between surveying the same individuals. An alternative method would be to

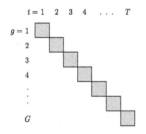

FIGURE 6.3 Repeated cross sections.
Source: Author's drawing

---

[10] A related issue concerns the situation when the dependent variable can sometimes take a value 0, while the model requires a natural log transformation: see Christophe Bellégo, David Benaita, and Louis-Daniel Pape (2022), Dealing with logs and zeros in regression models, arXiv:2203.11820.

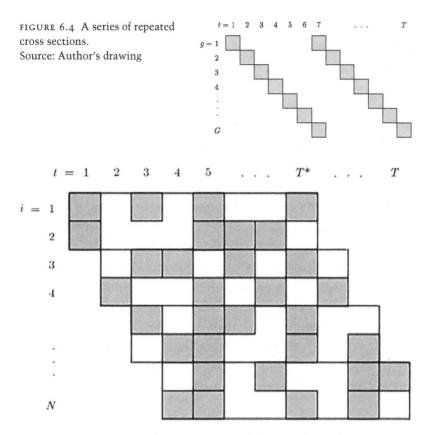

FIGURE 6.4 A series of repeated cross sections.
Source: Author's drawing

FIGURE 6.5 A randomized rotating panel.
Source: Author's drawings

collect, for example, consumer confidence data at individual level using a randomized rotating panel.[11] An illustrative design appears in Figure 6.5.

To statistically analyze the dynamic correlation of a new consumer confidence index and to draw inferences about transition rates, a Markov transition model can be developed. This enables the computation of a weekly consumer confidence indicator as if the entire panel were surveyed every week.

[11] Bert de Bruijn, René Segers, and Philip Hans Franses (2017), A novel approach to measuring consumer confidence, *Econometrics and Statistics*, 4 (October), 121–129.

This is an example where missing values are effectively created to avoid annoying survey respondents. By proposing a suitable model and associated estimation method, one can still retrieve switching behavior.

6.8   TOO FEW ONES AND TOO MANY ZEROES: WHAT TO DO?

Another situation where one may want to select data, here by selective sampling, is a situation in which there is a small set of observations of relevance and many more that are not directly of interest. Think of analyzing why certain companies go bankrupt. Usually this is a small number of companies within a certain sample frame, because most companies do not go bankrupt. If you need to collect data on these companies, you may want to reduce efforts in data collection in advance. More precisely, if bankrupt companies are labeled as 1 and all other non-bankrupt companies as 0, then there are just a few observations $y_i = 1$ while there are many observations $y_i = 0$.

To describe such data, and correlate "yes" or "no" bankruptcy with k explanatory variables (including an intercept) collected in X, then one might consider the logit model as a DGP, which reads as

$$Prob(y_i = 1) = \frac{\exp(X_i\beta)}{1 + \exp(X_i\beta)}$$

Suppose now that you ignore a fraction $1 - \delta$ of the $y_i = 0$ observations by random sample selection. Then it can be shown that the logit model as a DGP for the new reduced sample reads:[12]

$$Prob(y_i = 1) = \frac{\exp(-\ln\delta + X_i\beta)}{1 + \exp(-\ln\delta + X_i\beta)}$$

This means that in both cases the parameter estimators for β, except for the constant, do not change and measure the same parameter, and that the only thing that changes is the intercept, with $-\ln\delta$. Of course, with a decrease in the effective sample size, standard errors get affected upwards.

---

[12] Charles Manski and Steven R. Lerman (1977), The estimation of choice probabilities from choice-based samples, *Econometrica*, 45 (8), 1977–1988.

Table 6.2 *Parameter estimates and standard errors (in parentheses) in three logit models for different sample sizes*

	Number of observations		
Variable	2976	16368	293880
Constant	−4.848 (0.120)	−4.810 (0.083)	−4.874 (0.080)
Loyalty	−0.287 (0.100)	−0.295 (0.073)	−0.264 (0.067)
Log savings	0.470 (0.035)	0.476 (0.025)	0.460 (0.022)
Share index	1.388 (0.528)	1.411 (0.378)	1.514 (0.353)
Interest	−1.198 (0.156)	−1.087 (0.118)	−1.208 (0.116)
New product	0.846 (0.084)	0.815 (0.057)	0.755 (0.053)

Source: Cramer, Franses and Slagter (1999)

With less observations to estimate the parameters, there may be a loss of efficiency. To see that this loss does not have to be large, consider the following case study.[13] Consider a logit model where the variable of interest is whether a customer of a large Rotterdam-based investment firm makes a switch from savings to investment ($y_i = 1$) or not ($y_i = 0$). The full sample concerns 293,880 individuals, out of whom only 1,488 make that switch. Table 6.2 reports on the estimation results for a logit model when those 1,488 individuals are matched randomly with 1,488 individuals who did not switch (second column), are matched with ten times 1,488 individuals who did not switch (third column), and all individuals (final column). The estimates for the intercept have been adjusted by adding as δ is known.

When we look at the standard errors, we see that the full data set gives the smallest standard errors and that the smallest dataset is associated with larger standard errors, although the differences are not exceptionally large. Hence, loss of efficiency can be small. We also see from Table 6.2 that the estimated β parameters do not vary much across the samples, which is what we expected. The ethics here come in by saying from the onset that you chose for a certain value of δ.

---

[13] Cramer Mars (J.S.), Philip Hans Franses, and Erica Slagter (1999), Censored regression analysis in large samples with many zero observations, Econometric Institute Report 9939/A, Erasmus University Rotterdam.

6.9   CONSEQUENCES OF AGGREGATION

The aggregation of data can have various consequences. For example, suppose that you wish to examine if price changes or promotions improve the market share M_t of a product. Suppose further that there are three brands and that the number of people who buy these brands is the same over time. In Figure 6.6 we display two sequential market shares in week 1 and week 2. From week 1 to week 2 we indicate which type of switching behavior could be associated with the two sets of market shares. These switches are quite different, but they do lead to the same market shares in week 2. When you wish to examine the effect of changing prices, you need the transition process as well. Unfortunately, this transition process is not observed when you only have market shares (and no individual purchase data), and the model must then somehow include such a latent transition process.

For the data in Figure 6.6, we thus have

$$M_{t-1} = \begin{pmatrix} 0.30 \\ 0.50 \\ 0.20 \end{pmatrix}$$

$$M_t = \begin{pmatrix} 0.36 \\ 0.38 \\ 0.26 \end{pmatrix}$$

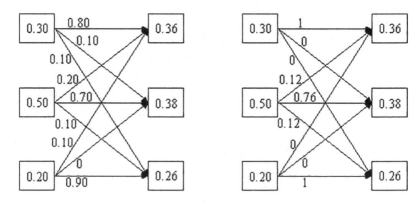

FIGURE 6.6 Two ways in which market shares can become different. Source: Author's calculations

and switching matrix in Figure 6.6 on the left-hand side is

$$S_t = \begin{pmatrix} 0.80 & 0.10 & 0.10 \\ 0.20 & 0.70 & 0.10 \\ 0.10 & 0.00 & 0.90 \end{pmatrix}$$

such that $M_t = S'_t M_{t-1}$.

A model to study the impact of marketing efforts on market shares must then become something like

$$\sum_{k=1}^{3} s_{l,k,t} = 1 \text{ for } l = 1,\ldots,3$$

$$M_{k,t} = \sum_{l=1}^{3} s_{l,k,t} M_{l,t-1} \text{ for } k = 1,\ldots,3$$

The latter equation reads in matrix notation

$$M_t = S'_t M_{t-1}$$

A next step is then to propose a model description for the switching matrix.[14] Details on this are not relevant here, but what is important is to recognize that when you want to see the effect of prices and promotions on changes in market shares, you need to define an unobserved switching process, as this process is missing.

6.10   FURTHER CONSEQUENCES OF TEMPORAL AGGREGATION

To stick to cases in marketing, consider the situation where you want to study the impact of advertising on sales. A useful model for measuring current and carry-over effects is the geometric lag model (sometimes called the Koyck model).[15] Consider sales S_t and

[14] Examples of such models are presented in Peter S. H. Leeflang (1974), *Mathematical Models in Marketing*, Leiden: Stenfert Kroese; and Peter S. H. Leeflang, Dick R. Wittink, Michel Wedel, and Philippe A. Naert (2000), *Building Models for Marketing Decisions*, Dordrecht: Kluwer Academic Publishers.

[15] Leendert M. Koyck (1954), *Distributed Lags and Investment Analysis*, Amsterdam: North Holland; Philip Hans Franses and Rutger van Oest (2007), On the econometrics of the geometric lag model, *Economics Letters*, 95 (2), 291–296.

advertising A_t. The Koyck model assumes that the link between the two variables is

$$S_t = \mu^* + \beta\left(A_t + \lambda A_{t-1} + \lambda^2 A_{t-2} + ...\right) + \varepsilon_t$$

with $0 < \lambda < 1$ and ε_t a white noise error term, which means that it has mean zero, common variance σ_ε^2, and zero autocorrelations. The so-called Koyck transformation, that is, subtracting λS_{t-1} from both sides, gives

$$S_t = \mu + \beta A_t + \lambda S_{t-1} + \varepsilon_t - \lambda \varepsilon_{t-1}$$

with $\mu = (1-\lambda)\mu^*$. The current effect of advertising is β, and the carry-over (or long-run) effect is $\dfrac{\beta}{1-\lambda}$, and the $(100\alpha)\%$ duration interval is defined as the period τ_α during which $(100\alpha)\%$ of the cumulative effect has taken place. For the Koyck model this τ_α is

$$\tau_\alpha = \frac{\ln(1-\alpha)}{\ln\lambda} - 1$$

Before we continue with temporal aggregation, it is interesting to note that there is something special about the Koyck model. Look again at

$$S_t = \mu^* + \beta\left(A_t + \lambda A_{t-1} + \lambda^2 A_{t-2} + ...\right) + \varepsilon_t$$

Suppose one wants to test for the significance of the advertising effects, that is, to test the null hypothesis $\beta = 0$. Under this null hypothesis of interest, that is, $\beta = 0$, the model becomes

$$S_t = \mu^* + \varepsilon_t$$

This shows that the parameter λ cannot be identified under the null hypothesis. This is what is known as the Davies problem,[16] and it seriously complicates statistical analysis. The issue is that the usually considered t test depends on the true λ but it is not known which value it takes.

Now let us go back to temporal aggregation. If it is assumed that there is a relation between sales and advertising at frequency t (e.g., days), but that one does not observe daily frequency data, but one observes data at a lower frequency T (e.g., weeks), and suppose one considers the same model specification for the lower frequency data, that is,

$$S_T = \mu^{**} + \beta^* A_T + \lambda^* S_{T-1} + \varepsilon_T - \lambda^* \varepsilon_{T-1}$$

It then occurs that the carry-over effect will be grossly overestimated.[17] This is because temporal aggregation (from days to weeks) makes the model specification change, as we will see.

Before we turn to that, let us have a look at the classic study on a random walk that can be used to illustrate the change of model after aggregation.[18] Suppose that there is a variable y_τ where τ is of a higher frequency than t. Suppose further that the variable at the higher frequency τ obeys a random walk model

$$y_\tau = y_{\tau-1} + \varepsilon_\tau$$

with ε_τ is a zero-mean white noise process. Suppose that this high frequency random walk is temporally aggregated to a variable with frequency t and suppose that this aggregation involves m steps. For example, aggregation from months to years would imply that $m = 12$. It can be shown that such temporal aggregation results in the following model

$$y_t = y_{t-1} + u_t$$

where the first order autocorrelation of u_t, say, ρ_1^u is the only non-zero valued autocorrelation, and this autocorrelation can be shown to equal

$$\rho_1^u = \frac{m^2 - 1}{2(2m^2 + 1)}$$

When $m \to \infty$, $\rho_1^u \to \frac{1}{4}$. When $m = 2$, $\rho_1^u = \frac{1}{6}$. Hence, aggregation of a high frequency random walk leads to a so-called Integrated Moving Average [IMA (1,1)] model.

---

[17] Darral G. Clarke (1976), Econometric measurement of the duration of advertising effect on sales, *Journal of Marketing Research*, 8 (November), 345–357.

[18] Holbrook Working (1960), Note on the correlation of first differences of averages in a random chain, *Econometrica*, 28 (4), 916–918.

Back to the Koyck model, what can we do in case of temporal aggregation?[19] Suppose again that $S_t = \beta A_t + \lambda S_{t-1} + \varepsilon_t - \lambda \varepsilon_{t-1}$ is valid for the true frequency t, and assume that an advertising impulse occurs only once in each K-th period, and at the same moment within that K-th period. It can then be shown that temporal aggregation to frequency T leads to a change in the Koyck model as it becomes

$$S_T = \lambda^K S_{T-1} + \beta_1 A_T + \beta_2 A_{T-1} + \varepsilon_T - \lambda^K \varepsilon_{T-1}$$

with an additional term $\beta_2 A_{T-1}$. With this model, it can be shown that

$$\frac{\beta_1 + \beta_2}{1 - \lambda^K}$$

Hence, in case aggregation is necessary, one should collect data such that the key assumptions on the advertising process holds, and then one can retrieve the original β and λ in the model for the high frequency data, and hence compute the correct carry-over effects.

6.11 MIDAS (MIXED DATA SAMPLING)

A final word on temporal aggregation is that there is no need to aggregate alle variables to a certain aggregation level if one or a few of the variables can only be observed after aggregation. In fact, recently, a class of models has become quite popular as this explicitly involves linking variables with different sampling frequencies, called MIDAS.[20] As these models can involve many parameters, one needs to make choices.

For example, think of T as week and j as an hour within a week, so, $j = 1, 2, 3, \ldots, 168$, then one can have for example

$$y_T = \alpha + \sum_{j=1}^{p} \beta_j x_{T,j} + \varepsilon_T$$

[19] Gerard J. Tellis and Philip Hans Franses (2006), Optimal data interval for estimating advertising response, *Marketing Science*, 25 (3), 217–229.

[20] Jörg Breitung and Christoph Roling (2015), Forecasting inflation rates using daily data: A Nonparametric MIDAS approach, *Journal of Forecasting*, 34 (7), 588–603; Eric Ghysels, Pedro Santa-Clara, and Rossen Valkanov (2002), The MIDAS touch: Mixed data sampling regression models, Working paper, UNC, and UCLA; Eric Ghysels, Arthur Sinko, and Rossen Valkanov (2007), MIDAS regressions: Further results and new directions, *Econometric Reviews*, 26 (1), 53–90.

with $p \le 168$. As there are many parameters to estimate, the literature presents various restrictions on β_j. The choice for these restrictions has consequences and implications for interpretation. MIDAS models are often considered in case the dependent variable is not often observed, such as real GDP growth (per quarter), while the explanatory variable is observed with a much higher frequency, such as weekly money supply by a central bank. MIDAS models are useful for so-called nowcasting as we can try to estimate real GDP figures based on incoming weekly money supply figures.

6.12 WHAT DID WE LEARN? HOW SHOULD WE CONDUCT OURSELVES?

In this chapter we have considered various cases of how to deal with missing values. Missing values can occur frequently, and we have also seen that we can create missing values, or better select data, by selective sampling to reduce subsequent data collection and modeling efforts.

We have seen that interpolation has consequences for autocorrelations, and hence that it is important to be informative on how interpolation took place.

In various cases, we have seen that missing data, through aggregation or data collection methods, require that the model must be modified and the parameter estimation method be adapted. In practice, this must be done on a case-by-case basis, as there are no general guidelines about how to proceed. It is good, though, to know that aggregation can have dire consequences.

Finally, data can be selectively sampled, to facilitate analysis. And there again, models and estimation methods can (and must) be adapted.

We see that there is a range of settings concerning missing or selected data. Each requires follow-up actions, and these are data-dependent and model-dependent. Again, the choices made should be reported.

FURTHER READING

Some interesting studies on the impact of various imputation methods, which are methods that replace missing data by newly created data, in a variety of disciplines are the following:

Marianne Riksheim Stavseth, Thomas Clausen, and Jo Røislien (2019), How handling missing data may impact conclusions: A comparison of six different imputation methods for categorical questionnaire data, *Sage Open Medicine*, 7, 1–12.

Alireza Farhangfar, Lukasz Kurgan, and Jennifer Dy (2008), Impact of imputation of missing values on classification error for discrete data, *Pattern Recognition*, 41 (12), 3692–3705.

Ranjit Lall (2016), How multiple imputation makes a difference, *Political Analysis*, 24, 414–433.

A study on how data are (selectively) collected by behavioral scientists is

Joseph Henrich, Steven J. Heine, and Ara Norenzayan (2010), The weirdest people in the world? *Behavioral and Brain Sciences*, 33 (2–3), 61–135.

In their article, the authors address the following:

> Behavioral scientists routinely publish broad claims about human psychology and behavior in THE world's top journals based on samples drawn entirely from Western, Educated, Industrialized, Rich, and Democratic (WEIRD) societies. Researchers often implicitly assume that either there is little variation across human populations, or that these "standard subjects" are as representative of the species as any other population. Are these assumptions justified?

7   Spurious Relations

In practice we do not always have a clear guidance from economic theory about the econometric model to specify. At the extreme, it may occur that we "let the data speak." It is then good to know when "they speak" that what the data say makes sense. We must be aware of a particularly important phenomenon in empirical econometrics, and this concerns a spurious relationship.

Wikipedia says:

> In statistics, a spurious relationship. or spurious correlation is a mathematical relationship in which two or more events or variables are associated but *not* causally related, due to either coincidence or the presence of a certain third, unseen factor (referred to as a "common response variable," "confounding factor," or "lurking variable").[1]

If you encounter a spurious relationship. but do not recognize it as such, you may inadequately consider such a relationship for hypothesis testing or for the creation of forecasts. A spurious relationship appears when the model is not well specified. In this chapter, we will see from a case study that people can draw strong but inappropriate conclusions if the econometric model is not well specified. More precisely, we will see that if you a priori hypothesize a structural break at a particular moment in time, and based on that very assumption analyze the data, then it is easy to draw inaccurate conclusions. As with influential observations, the lesson here is that one should first create an econometric model, and given that model, investigate whether there could have been a structural break. For

[1] https://en.wikipedia.org/wiki/Spurious_relationship.

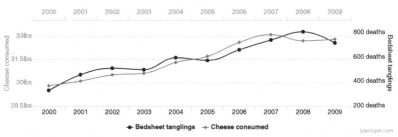

FIGURE 7.1 An amusing spurious correlation for annual data.
Source: www.tylervigen.com/spurious-correlations

the case study, we will see that the initially hypothesized structural break does not exist.

Spurious relations can happen when we ignore relevant variables. As an example, such a relevant variable can create a trend in the data. When two variables have such trends, one may think these variables are somehow associated. This can lead to amusing correlations as in Figure 7.1. Obviously, there is no true nonzero correlation between the two variables in the graph. In fact, this could become visible when we correct for the underlying trends in the data.

In a classic study,[2] the author David Hendry presents evidence of a mysterious factor partly driving inflation. The article starts with a serious tone:

> A second example will clarify this issue. Hendry's theory of inflation is that a certain variable (of great interest in this country) is the "real cause" of rising prices. I am "certain" that the variable (denoted C) is exogenous, that causality is from C to P only and (as far as I am aware) that C is outside government control although data are readily available in government publications.

[2] David F. Hendry (1980), Econometrics: Alchemy or science? *Economica*, 47 (188), 387–406. Theoretical underpinnings of the empirical results in this study are provided in Peter C. B. Phillips (2003), Laws and limits of econometrics, *The Economic Journal*, 113 (March), C26–C52.

But towards the end of the article the author reveals the true nature of that factor:

> My theory performs decidedly better than the naive version of the monetary one, but, alas, the whole exercise is futile as well as deceitful since C is simply *cumulative rainfall* [emphasis added] in the UK. It is meaningless to talk about "confirming" theories when spurious results are so easily obtained.

How we can detect spurious relations and how we can sometimes prevent them from happening is the key topic of this chapter.

7.1 OUTLINE

We begin with a demonstration that spurious relations can occur owing to model misspecification, here because of omitted variables. A particular example of such a variable concerns the first lag of the dependent variable. We will see that ignoring autocorrelation can have dire consequences. A classic case is the regression of two random walks on one another, resulting in large R^2 values, large and significant t values, and exceptionally low Durbin Watson values, which means large autocorrelation in the residuals.[3] We will learn that an important initial diagnostic for a regression model with time series variables is this Durbin Watson value.[4] Values close to zero indicate strong auto-correlation in the residuals and ignoring such autocorrelation results in spurious relations. This not only holds for random walks, but also even for moderately sized autocorrelation. And when we look at so-called cohort analysis, this can lead to excessive amounts of "significant" findings, as we will see.

---

[3] Clive W. J. Granger and Paul Newbold (1974), Spurious regression in economics, *Journal of Econometrics*, 2 (2), 111–120.

[4] A recent alternative methodology to detect spurious correlations is presented in Paravastu Swamy, Peter von zur Muehlen, Jantider Singh Mehta, and I-Lok Chang (2022), The state of econometrics after John W. Pratt, Robert Schlaifer, Brian Skyrms, and Robert L. Basmann, *Sankhya B: The Indian Journal of Statistics*, 84 (2), 627–654.

7.2   MODEL MISSPECIFICATION

Let us begin with a simple bivariate case, and if you wish you can call y_t sales and x_t advertising. Consider the DGP

$$y_t = \rho y_{t-1} + \varepsilon_t \text{ with } |\rho| < 1$$
$$x_t = \delta y_{t-1} + \omega_t$$

with ε_t and ω_t mutually independent white noise series. In other words, sales depend on past sales, and more past sales lead to more advertising (owing to more budget). Note, however, that sales are not driven by advertising, as it is in fact the other way around. Now suppose you consider the following regression model (to see if sales and advertising are correlated), that is,

$$y_t = \beta x_t + u_t$$

and you use OLS to estimate β. Given knowledge of the DGP, we can derive the expected values (E)

$$var(x_t) = E\left[(\delta y_{t-1} + \omega_t)(\delta y_{t-1} + \omega_t)\right] = \frac{\delta^2 \sigma_\varepsilon^2}{1 - \rho^2} + \sigma_\omega^2$$

$$cov(y_t x_t) = E\left[(\rho y_{t-1} + \varepsilon_t)(\delta y_{t-1} + \omega_t)\right] = \frac{\rho \delta \sigma_\varepsilon^2}{1 - \rho^2}$$

and hence that

$$plim(b) = \frac{cov(y_t x_t)}{var(x_t)} = \frac{\rho \delta}{\delta^2 + (1 - \rho^2)\frac{\sigma_\omega^2}{\sigma_\varepsilon^2}}$$

When it holds that $\rho \neq 0$ and $\delta \neq 0$, then $plim(b) \neq 0$. Hence, you will find a correlation between, say, sales and advertising.

7.3   EXERCISE

As an exercise, you can create your own artificial data (e.g., for $n = 100$) from

$$y_t = \rho y_{t-1} + \varepsilon_t \text{ with } |\rho| < 1$$
$$x_t = \delta y_{t-1} + \omega_t$$

with ε_t and ω_t draws from a $N(0,1)$ distribution, where you set $y_0 = 0$, for $\rho = 0.5, 0.8, 0.95$ and $\delta = 1, 5, 10$. What do you see if you apply OLS to

$$y_t = \beta x_t + u_t$$

across the various configurations?

The simple solution to prevent spurious correlations from happening in this case is not to look at the regression model $y_t = \beta x_t + u_t$, but to look at a so-called vector autoregression of order 1 (VAR (1)), that is here,

$$y_t = \alpha_{11} y_{t-1} + \alpha_{12} x_{t-1} + \varepsilon_{1,t}$$
$$x_t = \alpha_{21} y_{t-1} + \alpha_{22} x_{t-1} + \varepsilon_{2,t}$$

and to apply OLS to each equation. Then you will see in most cases that the hypothesis $\alpha_{12} = 0$ cannot be rejected, nor can the hypothesis $\alpha_{22} = 0$ be rejected in most cases.

Create again artificial data ($n = 100$) from

$$y_t = \rho y_{t-1} + \varepsilon_t \text{ with } |\rho| < 1$$
$$x_t = \delta y_{t-1} + \omega_t$$

with ε_t and ω_t draws from a standard normal distribution, with $y_0 = 0$, for $\rho = 0.5, 0.8, 0.95$ and $\delta = 1, 5, 10$. Now, what do you see if you estimate the parameters in a VAR(1) model as previously for y_t and x_t?

7.4 AUTOCORRELATION, UNIT ROOTS

Autocorrelation concerns an interesting case.[5] A classic study considers the following situation.[6] Consider the simple regression model

$$y_t = \alpha + \beta x_t + \varepsilon_t$$

while the DGP consists of

$$y_t = y_{t-1} + u_t$$
$$x_t = x_{t-1} + w_t$$

---

[5] An early study is Udny G. Yule (1926), Why do we sometimes get nonsense correlations between time series? A study in sampling and the nature of time series, *Journal of the Royal Statistical Society*, 89 (1), 1–64. See also David G. Champernowne (1960), An experimental investigation of the robustness of certain procedures for estimating means and regression coefficients, *Journal of the Royal Statistical Society. Series A (general)*, 123 (4), 398–412.

[6] Clive W.J. Granger and Paul Newbold (1974), Spurious regression in economics, *Journal of Econometrics*, 2 (2), 111–120.

where u_t and w_t are mutually independent white noise variables, that is, the DGP constitutes of two independent random walks. With simulation experiments it is shown that,[7] for the simple regression model, you find "significant" estimates of β, large t values, high R^2 values (even close to 1), and, this is important, also low values for the Durbin Watson test statistics. As we have seen in an earlier chapter, when t values get exceptionally large in moderately large samples, there is something to look at more closely. And indeed, years later, the asymptotic theory for the regression model for that DGP was developed,[8] and it was found that this theory is far from standard asymptotic theory. In fact, the t test statistic does not follow a t distribution at all anymore.

7.5 AUTOCORRELATION, $0 < \rho < 1$

Years later, the asymptotic distribution of the t test was derived for the parameter β,[9] in the simple regression

$$y_t = \alpha + \beta x_t + \varepsilon_t$$

where the DGP is

$$y_t = \rho y_{t-1} + u_t$$
$$x_t = \rho x_{t-1} + w_t$$

with $|\rho| < 1$, that is, the two variables are independent first order autoregressive time series with the same parameter ρ. This asymptotic distribution for b under the null hypothesis that $\beta = 0$ is a normal distribution, but not a standard normal distribution. In fact, it is

$$t_b \sim N\left(0, \frac{1 + \rho^2}{1 - \rho^2}\right)$$

Only when $\rho = 0$, does one get the commonly considered $N(0,1)$ distribution. Clearly,

---

[7] Granger and Newbold, Spurious regression in economics.

[8] Peter C. B. Phillips (1986), Understanding spurious regressions in econometrics, *Journal of Econometrics*, 33 (3), 311–340.

[9] Clive W.J. Granger, Namwon Hyung, and Yongil Jeon (2001), Spurious regressions with stationary series, *Applied Economics*, 33 (7), 899–904.

$$\frac{1+\rho^2}{1-\rho^2} > 1$$

and hence a substantial amount of t values will be larger than 2 or more negative than –2, more than the 5 percent when you test the null hypothesis at the 95 percent level. Hence, significant test values will often be found. When, for example,[10] $\rho = 0.7$, one will obtain around 23 percent significant t test values (at the nominal 5 percent significance level). Note that of course the proper empirical strategy would have been not to consider $y_t = \alpha + \beta x_t + \varepsilon_t$ but again a VAR model as above.

7.6 INTERPOLATION (AND SPURIOUS RELATIONS)

In Section 6.5 we showed that interpolation of time series variables influences the autocorrelations. That is, they become larger. So, one may understand that ignoring autocorrelations for interpolated series may also have a substantial effect.

To demonstrate this effect, consider for example the data on GDP in Holland and the Dutch Republic for the sample 1738–1779.[11] The two variables in Figure 7.2 measure the contribution to GDP in Holland (in thousands of guilders) for domestic production, trade, and shipping (DPTS) and Army and Navy (AN). It often occurs in historical data that data are missing owing to the absence of archives, either through accidental or deliberate destruction or because documents were not well kept, and then one may wish to look at interpolated data.

Let us look at the two variables in Figure 7.2, and suppose we are interested in their potential relationship. Note that this is not the purpose of the original article, so we use it here for illustrative purposes. The sample correlation between these two variables as they

---

[10] Philip Hans Franses (2018), *Enjoyable Econometrics*, Cambridge: Cambridge University Press, Table 5A1, page 146.

[11] Pepijn Brandon and Ulbe Bosma (2019), Calculating the weight of slave-based activities in the GDP of Holland and the Dutch Republic – Underlying methods, data, and assumptions, *The Low Countries Journal of Social and Economic History*, 16 (2), 5–45.

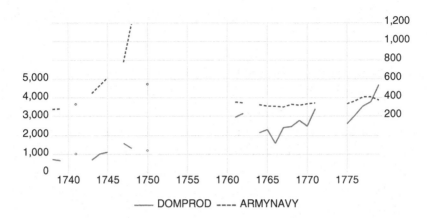

FIGURE 7.2 Domestic production, trade, and shipping (DOMPROD)
(left-hand axis) and Army and Navy (ARMYNAVY) (right-hand axis),
1738–1779.
Source: Brandon and Bosma (2019)

are presented in Figure 7.2 is –0.269. When we consider a simple
regression model (for the available and not interpolated data), and we
apply OLS to

$$DPTS_t = \alpha + \beta\, AN_t + \varepsilon_t$$

we obtain the estimation results

$$a = 2834(531.9)$$
$$b = -1.494(0.713)$$

where the numbers in parentheses are the HAC standard errors. The
estimated t statistic for the hypothesis that $\beta = 0$ is –2.097, with a p
value 0.048. The Durbin Watson test statistic has a value of 0.216,
which is close to zero.

Now, let us create the interpolated series by taking linear
trends in between the available points. The contribution to GDP in
Holland (in 1,000 guilders) for the Army and Navy, after interpolation (linearly between available points) are presented in Figure 7.3.

The correlation between these two interpolated series is –0.333,
a slight decrease relative to the –0.269 before. When we consider a
simple regression model and apply OLS to

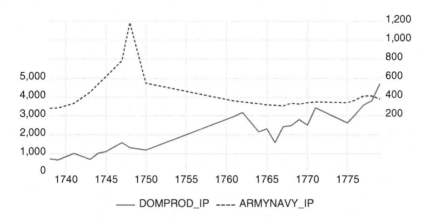

FIGURE 7.3 The contribution to GDP in Holland (in one thousand guilders) for the Army and Navy, after interpolation (linearly between available points).

$$DPTS\_interpolated_t = \alpha + \beta \ AN\_interpolated_t + \varepsilon_t$$

we obtain the estimation results

$$a = 2924(534.0)$$
$$b = -1.817(0.773)$$

with again the HAC standard errors. The t statistic on $\beta = 0$ is -2.351, and hence there seems to be a significant relationship, with a p value of 0.024. The Durbin Watson test statistic value for the forty-two residuals is 0.186, which is now even closer to zero.

As indicated before, a simple remedy to prevent spurious results is to explicitly incorporate the lags of the variables. In this illustrative example, this means that we move from

$$DPTS\_interpolated_t = \alpha + \beta \ AN\_interpolated_t + \varepsilon_t$$

to

$$DPTS\_interpolated_t = \alpha + \beta \ AN\_interpolated_t$$
$$+ \gamma DPTS\_interpolated_{t-1} + \varepsilon_t$$

The OLS estimation results for this extended model are

$$a = 179.3(206.8)$$
$$b = -0.141(0.229)$$
$$c = 0.990(0.085)$$

The parameter β for Army Navy is now insignificant. Given the close-to -1 estimate of 0.990 for γ, one can also correlate the differences of the two variables. Then the regression for the differences looks like

$$DPTS\_interpolated_t - DPTS\_interpolated_{t-1} =$$
$$\alpha + \beta \left(AN\_interpolated_t - AN\_interpolated_{t-1} \right) + \varepsilon_t$$

and the OLS estimation results (with HAC standard errors) are

$$a = 97.76(53.28)$$
$$b = -0.082(0.247)$$

There is no significant link between the two differenced variables. Note that investigating levels and differences at the same time can also be informative. Evidence for relationships between variables becomes stronger if they are present for the levels and for the differences, at the same time. We saw such evidence in Chapter 3 for the error correction model for Madagascar consumption and income, where the growth rates and the levels were jointly included in a model.

7.7   CASE STUDY: "WHEN DID GLOBALIZATION BEGIN?"

Let us turn to a case study.[12] The next analysis is not about wrong or right, but it is about how difficult empirical work can be, and how much there is to be known by an econometrician in order to conduct proper econometric analysis. It also highlights how many choices can and must be made. A key issue in this case study is the a priori decision on a break date. We will see that this decision should have better been taken after constructing an econometric model.

---

[12] Kevin H. O'Rourke and Jeffrey G. Williamson (2002), When did globalization begin? *European Review of Economic History*, 6 (1), 23–50.

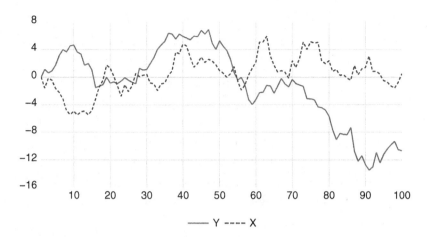

FIGURE 7.4 Two independent random walks.

But before we turn to the case study in more detail, consider the two (newly created) independent random walks in Figure 7.4. Suppose that we again consider the regression model

$$y_t = \alpha + \beta x_t + \varepsilon_t$$

For the full sample with all 100 observations, OLS gives

$$a = -5.493(0.389)$$
$$b = 0.201(0.050)$$

The Durbin Watson test value has a low value, as expected, and here it is 0.160, and the $R^2 = 0.160$. Suppose further that we a priori believe that there was a structural break at $t = 50$. When we consider the first fifty observations, OLS gives

$$a = -3.056(0.653)$$
$$b = -0.577(0.139)$$

with a Durbin Watson test value of 0.200, and the $R^2 = 0.265$. For the second fifty observations OLS gives

$$a = -5.005(0.377)$$
$$b = 0.234(0.038)$$

with a Durbin Watson test value of 0.376 and the $R^2 = 0.447$. Comparing the two subsample regressions, we see that in both cases the hypothesis $\beta = 0$ is firmly rejected (incorrectly, as we know the DGP), and notably that the sign of the estimate for β has switched.

Back to the case study. Let us have a look at the following estimation results,[13] here with t statistics in parentheses. A definition of the variables follows soon, but let us focus first on the two subsamples, the different parameter estimates across the two samples, and most importantly, let us look at the Durbin Watson values.

Time period	1565–1828	1828–1936
C	0.053 (0.047)	-4.500 (-1.691)
LANDLAB	0.666 (5.481)	1.013 (3.706)
PAPM	0.158 (1.560)	-0.770 (-5.496)
TREND	-0.002 (-6.092)	0.024 (7.268)
Durbin Watson	0.134	0.321

There are differences across the two samples' estimates, but the low Durbin Watson values give a warning signal. Yet these results could be viewed as evidence that around 1828 globalization began, as there seems to be a break in the results.

It is now interesting to see if we can create a suitable econometric model for the data, and after estimating the parameters see if the 1828 break date still stands. Figure 7.5 presents the relevant variables for the first subsample.

Figure 7.6 presents the data for the second subsample.

Figure 7.7 presents the data for the full sample. We see signs of trends, even of quadratic trends, signs of interpolation, and in fact

---

[13] Kevin H. O'Rourke and Jeffrey G. Williamson (2002), When did globalization begin? *European Review of Economic History*, 6 (1), 23–50, Table 3, page 45.

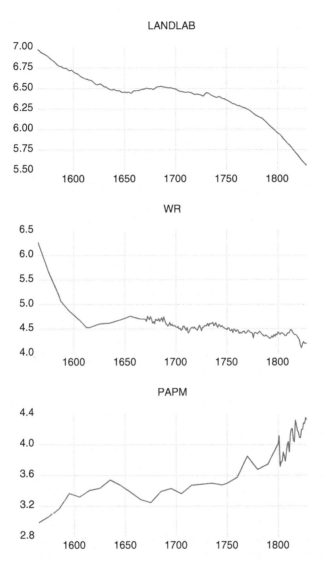

FIGURE 7.5 Trends in land-labor ratios (LANDLAB), wage-rental ratios (WR), and relative prices of agricultural goods (PAPM): England, 1565–1828.
Source: O'Rourke and Williamson (2002)

erratic patterns over time. At first sight, 1828 does not seem to be the immediate choice for a break date. When we run various simple regressions, we get the results in Table 7.1.

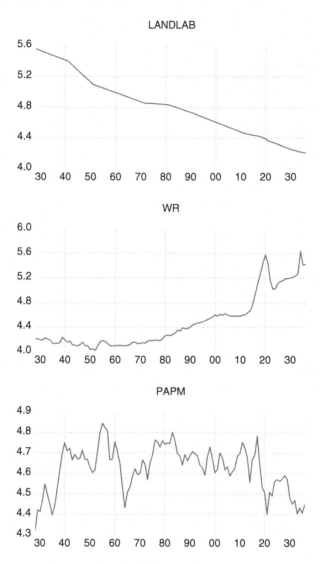

FIGURE 7.6 Trends in land-labor ratios (LANDLAB), wage-rental ratios (WR), and relative prices of agricultural goods (PAPM): England, 1828–1936.

The table shows sign switches, but most notably we see that there are extremely small Durbin Watson values.

Let us now try to create an econometric model. When we consider the Johansen cointegration tests (trace and eigenvalue) for the

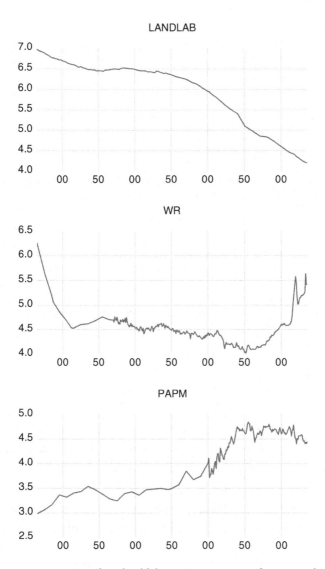

FIGURE 7.7 Trends in land-labor ratios, wage-rental ratios, and relative prices of agricultural goods: England, 1565–1936 full sample.

full sample (first lagged growth rates included), that is for the years 1565 to 1936, which amounts to 372 observations, we see that there can be one or two cointegrating relations across the variables WR, LAND, and PAPM, as reported in Table 7.2.

Table 7.1 *Regression results*

	PAPM (1565–1828)	PAPM (1565–1800)	WR (1565–1828)	WR (1828–1936)	PAPM (1828–1936)
LANDLAB	-0.882	-0.866	0.884	-0.914	0.017
	(0.017)	(0.024)	(0.050)	(0.062)	(0.028)
Durbin Watson	0.267	0.022	0.022	0.081	0.267

Dependent variable (and sample)
Source: Author's calculations

Table 7.2 *Options for cointegration analysis*

Trend	None	None	Linear	Linear	Quadratic
Test type	No intercept No Trend	intercept No Trend	intercept No Trend	intercept Trend	intercept Trend
Trace	2	2	2	2	1
Eigenvalue	2	2	2	2	1

Source: Eviews output

When we look at the AIC and BIC values (not reported), we learn that the fifth option is preferred by both criteria. We therefore continue with imposing one cointegration relation, where the cointegration relation can have a trend and the data may have a quadratic trend. Figure 7.8 presents the cointegration relation, and it seems stationary indeed.

We now proceed with a three-equation vector error correction model. The estimation results for the first equation

$$WR_t - WR_{t-1} = \alpha_1 + \beta_{01}Cointegration\ relation_{t-1}$$
$$+\beta_{11}(WR_{t-1} - WR_{t-2}) + \beta_{21}(LANDLAB_{t-1} - LANDLAB_{t-2})$$
$$+\beta_{31}(PAPM_{t-1} - PAPM_{t-2}) + \beta_{41}Trend_t + \varepsilon_t$$

are (standard errors in parentheses)

$$a_1 = 0.458(0.213)$$
$$b_{01} = -0.021(0.009)$$

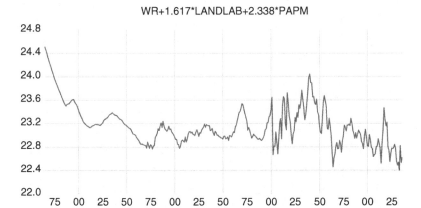

FIGURE 7.8 Cointegration relation (in case of allowing for quadratic trend).

$$b_{11} = 0.055(0.052)$$
$$b_{21} = 1.107(0.427)$$
$$b_{31} = 0.005(0.053)$$
$$b_{41} = 0.0014(0.0002)$$

The Durbin Watson value is 2.008, and the $R^2 = 0.118$. As b_{01} is significant we see that there is significant but slow error correction.

Now let us see if this first equation experiences a structural break. We apply the single-equation Quandt–Andrews unknown breakpoint test,[14] and obtain a maximum LR F test value of 7.455 (p value is 0.000) for the year 1881. The year 1881 is not the year 1828.

The second equation of the vector error correction model reads as

$$LANDLAB_t - LANDLAB_{t-1} = \alpha_2 + \beta_{02}Cointegration\ relation_{t-1}$$
$$+ \beta_{12}(WR_{t-1} - WR_{t-2}) + \beta_{22}(LANDLAB_{t-1} - LANDLAB_{t-2})$$
$$+ \beta_{32}(PAPM_{t-1} - PAPM_{t-2}) + \beta_{42}Trend_t + \varepsilon_t$$

and the OLS estimation results are

---

[14] See https://en.wikipedia.org/wiki/Structural_break for a discussion of various tests for structural breaks, in regression models.

$$a_2 = 0.098(0.018)$$
$$b_{02} = -0.004(0.001)$$
$$b_{12} = 0.004(0.004)$$
$$b_{22} = 0.680(0.036)$$
$$b_{32} = 0.008(0.005)$$
$$b_{42} = -0.0001(0.00002)$$

The Durbin Watson test value is 1.915, and the $R^2 = 0.708$. Again, there is significant error correction (look at b_{02}) for this equation. The Quandt–Andrews unknown breakpoint test results in a maximum LR F test value of 5.559 (p value is 0.000). The break date for this equation is 1674, and this is quite far from 1828.

Finally, the third equation of the vector error correction model is

$$PAPM_t - PAPM_{t-1} = \alpha_3 + \beta_{03}Cointegration\ relation_{t-1}$$
$$+ \beta_{13}(WR_{t-1} - WR_{t-2})$$
$$+ \beta_{23}(LANDLAB_{t-1} - LANDLAB_{t-2})$$
$$+ \beta_{33}(PAPM_{t-1} - PAPM_{t-2}) + \beta_{43}Trend_t + \varepsilon_t$$

$$a_3 = 0.721(0.214)$$
$$b_{03} = -0.030(0.009)$$
$$b_{13} = -0.059(0.052)$$
$$b_{23} = -0.886(0.429)$$
$$b_{33} = 0.013(0.053)$$
$$b_{43} = -0.00002(0.00003)$$

Again, the error correction term (b_{03}) is significant. The Durbin Watson test value is 2.016, and the $R^2 = 0.038$, which is small. The Quandt–Andrews unknown breakpoint test maximum LR F test is here 7.545 (p value is 0.000) for 1802, which is close to 1828.

What we have so far is that each equation has different break dates, that there is evidence of error correction, that there are two models with low R^2 values – because only for LANDLAB does the model fit the data very well; and yes, indeed, there is evidence of structural breaks, but not around 1828.

Is there any evidence of a structural break in the cointegration relation, which, for example, can amount to a regression of WR on an intercept, LANDLAB, PAPM, a trend, and a trend squared? When we assume that the breakpoint must have occurred in 1828, we can use a Chow test.[15] The F test value is 11.751, which is indeed significant at the 5 percent level. However, when we assume that the break point is 1650, the Chow breakpoint test value is 26.632, and when we assume a break point in 1750, the Chow breakpoint test value is 146.8. When we search for a break, the Quandt–Andrews test value is 148.7 for 1646. When we next estimate the model parameters from 1647 onwards, the Quandt–Andrews test value is 67.50 for 1916.

It is also possible to allow for multiple breaks using the so-called Bai–Perron test.[16] Application of this test gives evidence of breaks in 1588, 1613, 1714, 1798, and 1916. Still no 1828, or close to it.

What we learn from all this is that assuming a break data prior to any econometric modeling is not a sound strategy. It is best to create an adequate model and then, given that model, test for breaks. Upon doing so, we find evidence of various locations of breaks, and less evidence that globalization, as acclaimed, began in 1828.

7.8 SPURIOUS CORRELATION IN COHORT AND PANEL STUDIES

When we record data of individuals over time and aggregate the data across the individuals, we will have an even larger chance of finding spurious results.

Cohort and panel studies are popular in disciplines such as health, medicine, psychology, and economics. Typically, in those studies N individuals are observed over T time periods, and observations on M variables are recorded. Correlations across these variables

---

[15] Source is Christiaan Heij, Paul de Boer, Philip Hans Franses, Teun Kloek, and Herman van Dijk (2004), *Econometric Methods with Applications in Business and Economics*, Oxford: Oxford University Press, page 315.

[16] Jushan Bai and Pierre Perron (2003), Computation and analysis of multiple structural change models. *Journal of Applied Econometrics*, 18 (1), 1–22.

across individuals or groups of individuals can suggest scientifically relevant outcomes.

There are many studies that indicate that, given the wealth of data, one should be careful with the interpretation of the statistical outcomes.[17] Issues such as sample selection, attrition bias, reasoning with hindsight (harking), and multiple testing have received substantial attention in the literature. We now address yet another issue by showing that one should also be careful with the interpretation of statistically significant outcomes in case proper care is not taken of autocorrelation in the variables.

Cohort studies in medicine and epidemiology rarely if ever take account of the time series properties of the data. An example of an influential cohort study is the Generation R project,[18] which by now has resulted in over 700 academic articles. At the same time, a consultation of the PubMed database,[19] with a search for the topic "Time series autocorrelation," yielded thirty-nine hits. Furthermore, "Time series analysis * cohort" gave sixteen hits, "Autoregression * cohort" gave twelve hits, and "Autoregression * longitudinal" gave only nine hits. Hence, the topic of time series and autocorrelation is broadly absent in much of the medical literature.

In the econometrics literature it is well known that ignoring such autocorrelations leads to spurious findings. A second issue is that aggregation of observations across individuals amplifies the autocorrelations, even to such an extent that the data obtain long memory properties.[20]

[17] Cristian S. Calude and Giuseppe Longo (2017), The deluge of spurious correlations in big data, *Foundations of Science*, 22, 595–612; Marcus R. Munafo, Kate Tilling, Amy E. Taylor, David M. Evans, and George Davey Smith (2018), Collider scope: when selection bias can substantially influence observed associations, *International Journal of Epidemiology*, 47 (1), 226–235; Joseph P. Simmons, Leif D. Nelson, and Uri Simonsohn (2011), False-positive psychology: Undisclosed flexibility in data collection and analysis allows presenting anything as significant, *Psychological Science*, 22 (11), 1359–1366.

[18] https://generationr.nl/researchers/.

[19] www.ncbi.nlm.nih.gov/pubmed (consulted August 12, 2019).

[20] Clive W. J. Granger (1980), Long memory relationships and the aggregation of dynamic models, *Journal of Econometrics*, 14 (2), 227–238. Long memory implies that the autocorrelations die out only very slowly.

The following simple simulation experiment illustrates the two concerns, where we demonstrate that neglected autocorrelation means that unrelated variables can look related. Consider N individuals who are being observed for T periods and who have scores on M variables (think of blood pressure measured per month, or wage, or numbers of cigarettes smoked). The observations ($i = 1, 2, \ldots, N$, $t = 1, 2, \ldots, T$, and $m = 1, 2, \ldots, M$) are denoted as

$$x_{i,t,m}$$

Assume that the measurements are autocorrelated as follows:

$$x_{i,t,m} = \mu_{i,m} + \rho_i x_{i,t-1,m} + \varepsilon_{i,t,m}$$

where $\varepsilon_{i,t,m} \sim N\left(0, \sigma_\varepsilon^2\right)$. In the DGP, the first-order autoregressive parameter ρ_i is set at

$$\rho_i \sim N\left(\rho, \sigma^2\right)$$

Define the averages over the individuals as

$$\bar{x}_{t,m} = \frac{1}{N} \sum_{i=1}^{N} x_{i,t,m}$$

Next, consider $M \times (M-1)$ regressions (for the observations averaged over the individuals)

$$\bar{x}_{t,m} = \alpha_m + \beta_m \bar{x}_{t,n} + \varepsilon_{t,m}$$

for $m \neq n$ and $m = 1, 2, \ldots, M$ and $n = 1, 2, \ldots, M$. Finally, record the fraction of times that $\beta_m = 0$ is rejected at the 5 percent level (using the familiar two-sided t test). In the following simulations, the parameter configurations are set at

$$x_{i,0,m} = 1, \; \sigma_\varepsilon^2 = 1, \; \sigma^2 = 0.05,$$

and

$$\mu_{i,m} = 1 - \rho_i$$

which means that the data have a mean equal to 1. The interest here is in the test results for varying values of ρ and N. This simulation exercise is repeated 1,000 times.

Table 7.3 reports on the simulation results for the case that $T = 20$. When the autocorrelation is zero, that is, when $\rho = 0$, we

Table 7.3 *Simulation results for T = 20. Fraction of significant (at the 5% level) t tests for the correct null hypothesis that $\beta_m = 0$*

M	N	ρ				
		0.0	0.5	0.8	0.9	0.95
10	1	0.062	0.134	0.325	0.436	0.501
	10	0.051	0.163	0.623	0.816	0.880
	100	0.051	0.223	0.900	0.958	0.968
	1,000	0.050	0.365	0.957	0.970	0.971
	10,000	0.050	0.576	0.963	0.965	0.966
20	1	0.061	0.139	0.330	0.439	0.500
	10	0.051	0.159	0.626	0.822	0.883
	100	0.051	0.233	0.911	0.962	0.970
	1,000	0.051	0.384	0.955	0.969	0.972
	10,000	0.051	0.576	0.963	0.968	0.968
50	1	0.061	0.140	0.335	0.441	0.500
	10	0.052	0.164	0.630	0.822	0.886
	100	0.051	0.221	0.900	0.959	0.968
	1,000	0.051	0.386	0.955	0.968	0.971
	10,000	0.050	0.566	0.960	0.968	0.970

Source: Author's calculations

would expect the fraction of 0.05, which is indeed the case. For increasing values of ρ we see that the fraction of significant test results rapidly increases towards one.

The table clearly shows that when the autocorrelation gets larger, more spurious findings will be obtained. And at the same time, when aggregation is done over larger N, the situation gets worse. Unreported tables show that when T gets larger and N gets larger too, the fraction of significant outcomes converges to one. Hence, in the end, many correlations become significant.

7.9 WHAT TO DO IN PRACTICE

To alleviate the spurious results in cohort studies in practice, the remedy is remarkably simple. One can filter out the autocorrelation using time series models, which is called "pre-whitening," and then continue with the uncorrelated residuals. Otherwise, one can include lags in the model to incorporate the autocorrelation, as the initial simple regression model is not properly specified.

To illustrate, consider eleven waves of data from the US-based Health and Retirement Survey.[21] The waves concern the years 1992 to 2015. The two variables of interest here are measurements on whether an individual needed cataract surgery (a method to remove the lens of an eye), called x_1, and whether the individual belongs to a single-person household, called x_2. There are observations on 27,266 individuals. Consider the average measurements for each wave of data.

The first regression is

$$\bar{x}_{t,1} = \alpha + \beta \bar{x}_{t,2} + \varepsilon_t$$

For eleven observations, the OLS based parameter estimates are $a = -1.323(0.478)$ and $b = 9.646(2.148)$, with standard errors in parentheses. The R^2 of this regression is 0.691. Based on these results, one could conclude that living alone has a positive relation with the need for cataract surgery. It is, however, most likely that the surgery variable shows autocorrelation, and therefore one had better consider the following regression

$$\bar{x}_{t,1} = \alpha + \beta \bar{x}_{t,2} + \gamma \bar{x}_{t-1,1} + \varepsilon_t$$

For ten observations, the OLS based parameter estimates are now $a = 0.190(0.100)$, $b = 0.185(0.534)$, and $c = 0.773(0.039)$ with estimated standard errors in parentheses. The R^2 of this regression is 0.992. The one-year-lagged regressor is highly relevant, with a t statistic of 19.796, where now the variable "living alone" is not at all relevant anymore. The effect in the first regression could have been spurious.

---

[21] https://g2aging.org/?section=study&studyid=1; https://hrs.isr.umich.edu/about.

7.10   WHAT DID WE LEARN?

In this chapter we have learned that spurious relations can easily appear. Better models and properly taking care of autocorrelation can prevent obtaining spurious results.[22]

Cohort studies are particularly prone to spurious findings, at least if proper care is not taken of autocorrelation.

Low Durbin Watson values and large t values in moderately sized samples are signs of spuriousness. Hence, it is recommended to check these Durbin Watson values first before drawing inference from econometric models for time series variables.

Finally, it is interesting to mention that spurious results also happen with increasing numbers of regressors owing to data mining.[23] If each variable is included as a regressor, there will always be some coefficients that seem significant while they are zero.

7.11   EPILOGUE

Let us conclude this chapter with another fun example of a spurious relation.

In an often-cited study[24], Messerli showed for twenty-three country averages that there is positive and significant correlation between chocolate consumption and the numbers of Nobel laureates. In Messerli, and recently in Prinz (for twenty-seven

---

[22] Selective sampling can also lead to spurious results. In Stephen A. Ross (1987), Regression to the max, Working Paper Yale School of Organization and Management, the author writes: "Do economists study events because they are interesting, or do they study interesting events? If they study events because they are interesting from a theoretical perspective, then they are on safe ground. But, if they examine an event because prices or some other time series behaved in an unusual fashion at the time, then they are engaging in a much trickier exercise" (page 2). In this study, Ross (page 32) shows that "Conditional on having observed a maximum of a specific height on a sample path on [0, T], we have shown that traditional econometric analysis will reject that the path was generated by a random walk."

[23] Theory appears in Peter C. B. Phillips, Yonghui Zhang, and Ziaohu Wang (2019), HAR testing for spurious regression in trend, *Econometrics*, 7 (4), 1–28.

[24] Franz H. Messerli (2012), Chocolate consumption, cognitive function, and Nobel laureates, *The New England Journal of Medicine*, 367 (16), 1562–1564.

countries),[25] the focus is on whether such correlation could potentially associate with causation.

The positive correlation is spurious, however. The number of Nobel laureates and the consumption of a hedonistic (luxury) good correlate with countries' wealth and prosperity. Assuming that the latter can be measured by GDP per capita, the correlations for twenty-seven countries[26] are 0.690 and 0.657, for Nobel prizes and chocolate consumption, respectively. The correlation between the latter two variables is 0.607. Regressing Nobel prizes and chocolate consumption each on an intercept and on GDP, the correlation between the respective residuals reduces to 0.281. When the number of Nobel laureates is regressed on a constant, chocolate consumption *and* GDP per capita, the p value of the t test for the significance of the coefficient for chocolate consumption equals 0.164.

In short, when correcting for the impact of GDP, the initially positive and significant correlation between chocolate consumption and Nobel laurates vanishes.

---

[25] Aloys Leo Prinz (2020), Chocolate consumption and Nobel laureates, *Social Sciences & Humanities Open 2*, 100082.

[26] Thanks are due to Aloys Leo Prinz for providing me the data that he used in his article.

8 Blinded by the Data

This chapter deals with features of data that suggest a certain model or method, but this suggestion is erroneous. We will highlight a few cases where an econometrician could be directed in the wrong direction, and at the same time we show how one can prevent this from happening. These situations occur if there is no strong prior information on how the model should be specified. The data are then used to guide model construction, and this guidance can steer models in an inappropriate direction.

A key notion in this chapter is robustness: This is relevant in research practice. Models should stand basic tests, and we want our analysis to be aware of features of the data that distract us from the key features that we have to address. We do not want to be blinded by the data.

Sometimes the data give misleading signs of features, which you then erroneously think should be exploited – to create forecasts, for example. We may note a neglected structural break that may look like a trend, as in Figure 8.1.

When we apply OLS to a regression model

$$y_t = \alpha + \beta Trend_t + \varepsilon_t$$

where y_t are the data in Figure 8.1, and $Trend_t = t = 1, 2, \ldots, T$, then you can find results like (with standard errors in parentheses)

$$a = 1.504(0.243)$$
$$b = 0.028(0.004)$$

The trend seems relevant as the hypothesis $\beta = 0$ can be rejected, and you may be inclined to use this linear deterministic trend to make predictions.

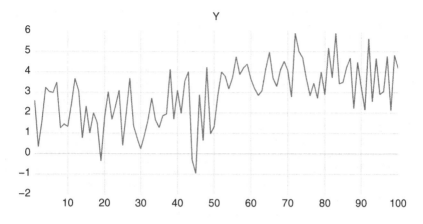

FIGURE 8.1 Data created from $y_t = 2 + 2Dummy(t > 50) + u_t, u_t \sim N(0,1)$.
Source: Author's calculations

In this chapter we review a few empirical cases where particular data features obscure a more realistic view of the data and may suggest inappropriate models. We discuss spurious cycles and the impact of additive outliers on detecting AutoRegressive Conditional Heteroskedasticity (ARCH) and nonlinearity. We also focus on a time series that may exhibit recessions and expansions, where you can also interpret the recession observations as outliers. Finally, we deal with structural breaks, trends, and unit roots, and see how data with these features can look alike.

8.1 SPURIOUS CYCLES

Let us start with an analysis of a series with the following sixteen observations: 383, 1589, 2132, 56, 137, 20, 135, 77, 479, 186, 2, 84, 62, 340, 100, and 22. Suppose it is known that these observations measure the number of months between certain events. These events can be, for example, floods or earthquakes. The data appear as a graph in Figure 8.2.

Figure 8.2 shows large fluctuations, and to reduce this variance we may take (natural) logs. Furthermore, the data have an

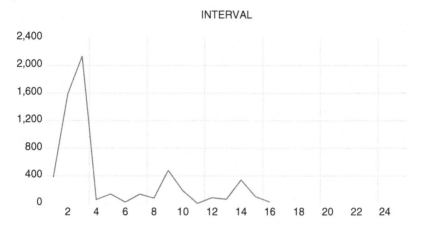

FIGURE 8.2 Intervals (measured in months) between the same events on the vertical axis and event number on the horizontal axis.

approximate cyclical pattern; that is, a series of events occurs frequently (hence small values on the vertical axis) and with a certain repetition, and with some regularity the intervals are large.

Supposing that this cyclical pattern is of interest, we may consider the model

$$\log(interval_t) = \alpha + \beta \cos\left(\frac{\pi t}{\gamma} - \delta\right) + \varepsilon_t$$

for $t = 1, 2, 3, \ldots, 16$. The application of Nonlinear Least Squares (NLS) gives

$$a = 4.633(0.361)$$
$$b = 1.651(0.516)$$
$$c = 2.912(0.165)$$
$$d = 2.636(0.594)$$

with standard errors in parentheses. The residuals and fitted values appear in Figure 8.3, and the model describes the data well.

We may now wish to make multiple-steps-ahead forecasts for the timing of the next four events. These forecasts appear in Figure 8.4, and they look reasonable.

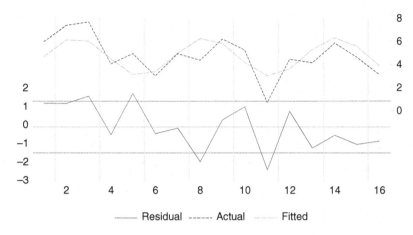

FIGURE 8.3 Actual data on time between events (in natural logs), the
fit from a nonlinear regression model, and the residuals.

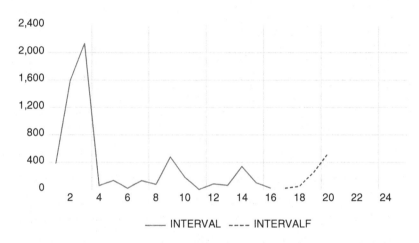

FIGURE 8.4 Forecasts for the next four events.

What events are we modeling and forecasting? The data are in
Table 8.1.

We are modeling Marian apparitions. And how about the forecasts? The next apparitions are predicted from the model to occur in
May 1985, April 1989, June 2020, and October 2064. Interestingly,
the June 2020 prediction stands out, as it is widely believed that

Table 8.1 *Marian apparitions*

	Location	Interval (months)
December 1531	Tepeyac (Mexico)	383
May 1664	Le Laus (France)	1,589
January 1842	Rome (Italy)	2,132
September 1846	La Salette-Fallavaux (France)	56
February 1858	Lourdes (France)	137
October 1859	Champion (Wisconsin, United States)	20
January 1871	Pontmain (France)	135
June 1877	Gietrzwald (Poland)	77
May 1917	Fatima (Portugal)	479
November 1932	Beauraing (Belgium)	186
January 1933	Banneux (Belgium)	2
(January) 1940	Betania (Venezuela)	84
March 1945	Amsterdam (the Netherlands)	62
July 1973	Akita (Japan)	340
November 1981	Kibeho (Rwanda)	100
September 1983	San Nicolas de los Arroyos (Argentina)	22

Source: https://en.wikipedia.org/wiki/List_of_Marian_apparitions

Mary appeared on March 27, 2020 at the Vatican,[1] which is just three months away from the prediction (Figure 8.5).

What is going on here? We have analyzed the data as if the intervals follow a deterministic cosine function. This was suggested by the graph in Figure 8.2. However, there is of course not an a priori reason to believe that there is such a strong cycle in the data. We just imposed this structure, based on a casual look at a graph. The repetitive pattern is just a coincidence.[2]

---

[1] This most recent appearance can even be found on YouTube: see www.youtube.com/watch?v=gj2YUeSFknY.

[2] On a more serious note, there is substantial research on whether anomalies in asset returns can be predicted. See, for example, Robert Novy-Marx (2014), Predicting anomaly performance with politics, the weather, global warming, sunspots, and

FIGURE 8.5 A recent Marian apparition?
Source: https://mysticpost.com/2020/03/sign-of-hope-from-the-blessed-
mother-photo-of-sky-above-saint-peters-square-during-special-urbi-et-
orbi-prayer-has-gone-viral-as-christians-look-for-hope/

But could we have somehow become suspicious about the analysis? Yes, we could have done if we had computed and presented the 95 percent confidence bounds around the forecasts. These are shown in Figure 8.6.

Figure 8.6 shows that already for the first forecast the 95 percent confidence interval includes negative values, which is impossible. Hence, these forecasts are not dependable given that the time between events cannot be negative. This confidence interval thus provides a useful robustness check.

What do we learn from this exotic example? Spurious (random) cyclical behavior suggests a model with a cosine function. The count of the event is taken as a cycle, and the chosen model is meaningless.

This reiterates statements made earlier in this book, and that is that one should always check what the data mean, where they come

the stars, *Journal of Financial Economics*, 112 (2), 137–146. To what extent such findings are robust, and whether they persist over time, is an interesting domain of research.

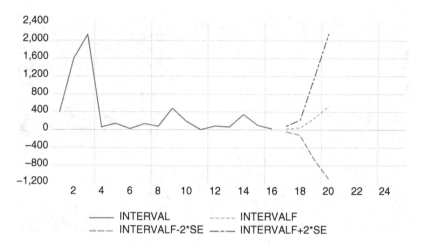

FIGURE 8.6 Forecasts of time in between events with forecast intervals.

from, how they are measured, who measured them, which features the data have, and which of these features may be spurious. And, of course, which features are really of interest for a forecasting model. In cases where they are available, are there any prior hypotheses, or is there is reliable theory?

When collecting data, one may wish to think in advance what the properties of the data could be that need to be incorporated in the subsequent analysis. Mileage data that look like draws from a uniform distribution do not make sense. Think in advance about potential trends, cycles, structural breaks, seasonality, outliers, and why these features could be present.

8.2   IGNORING ADDITIVE OUTLIERS

Outliers and structural breaks, can cause confusion, especially when they are ignored. So, if one has prior knowledge about the occurrence of these data features, it is helpful to include these in the modeling process right from the start. In fact, as we will see next, ignoring an additive outlier, which can be due to a typing error or a registration mistake, may make you believe that a suitable model for the data is an ARCH model. A first order autoregression for a time series y_t, with $t = 1, 2, \ldots, T$, is

$$y_t = \rho y_{t-1} + \varepsilon_t$$

and the ARCH model assumes that the error term can be decomposed as

$$\varepsilon_t = z_t \sqrt{h_t}$$

with, for example, $z_t \sim N(0,1)$, and where the conditional variance of ε_t given $\{y_{t-1}, y_{t-2} \ldots\}$ in an ARCH (1) model is

$$h_t = \mu + \alpha \varepsilon_{t-1}^2$$

with $|\alpha| < 1$ and $\mu > 0$. The nice property of this model is that it can predict h_{T+1} at time T, that is, the one-step-ahead conditional volatility. Depending on the ε_T, you can then have time variation in the prediction intervals. Larger absolute ε_T values (which need to be estimated) give wider intervals. This is a relevant feature in modeling asset returns, where predictability may change over time and where, for example, bear and bull markets can be reflected by variation in the h_t.

The ARCH model can be called to duty when there are neglected additive outliers.[3] To illustrate, look at Figures 8.7 and 8.8 with simulated data.

Figure 8.8 presents the same data as in Figure 8.7, now with a single additive outlier at $t = 100$. It turns out that we can fit the above AR (1)-ARCH (1) model to the data in Figure 8.8. For this simulated series, the estimation results for $y_t = \rho y_{t-1} + \varepsilon_t$ with $\varepsilon_t = z_t \sqrt{h_t}$ and $h_t = \mu + \alpha \varepsilon_{t-1}^2$, now obtained using the Maximum Likelihood method,[4] are

---

[3] Philip Hans Franses and Hendrik Ghijsels (1999), Additive outliers, GARCH and forecasting volatility, *International Journal of Forecasting*, 15 (1), 1–9; Dick van Dijk, Philip Hans Franses, and André Lucas (1999), Testing for ARCH in the presence of additive outliers, *Journal of Applied Econometrics*, 14 (5), 539–562.

[4] See Christiaan Heij, Paul de Boer, Philip Hans Franses, Teun Kloek, and Herman van Dijk (2004), *Econometric Methods with Applications in Business and Economics*, Oxford: Oxford University Press, pages 222–249.

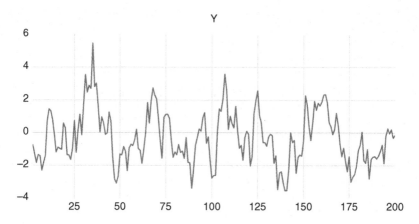

FIGURE 8.7 A first order autoregression $y_t = \rho y_{t-1} + \varepsilon_t$ with $\rho = 0.8$ and $\varepsilon_t \sim N(0,1)$.

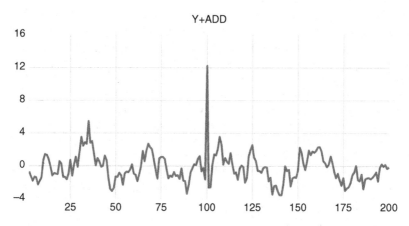

FIGURE 8.8 A first order autoregression $y_t = \rho y_{t-1} + \varepsilon_t$ with $\rho = 0.8$ and $\varepsilon_t \sim N(0,1)$ with an additive outlier of size 15 at $t = 100$.

$$r = 0.767(0.0714)$$
$$m = 0.997(0.151)$$
$$a = 0.977(0.178)$$

By ignoring, that is, not explicitly dealing with, a single outlying observation, one could be sent in the wrong direction: The part

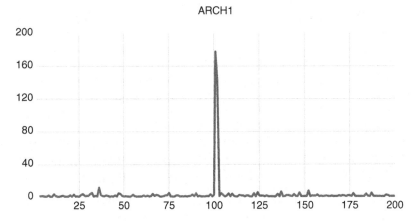

FIGURE 8.9 Estimated h_t for an AR (1)-ARCH (1) model for a true AR (1) process with just a single additive outlier ignored.

$h_t = \mu + \alpha \varepsilon_{t-1}^2$ is entirely down to a single observation. Ignoring a single additive outlier suggests the presence of ARCH. We can even estimate the h_t for this case: see Figure 8.9.

If we first estimate an AR (1) for the true AR (1) data without the outlier, then for the AR (1) with the ignored outlier, and third, for the AR (1)-ARCH (1) model, we get that the standard errors of one-step to five-steps-ahead forecasts for the AR(1)-ARCH(1) model are much larger than for the AR(1) model. This shows that the neglected additive outlier widens the prediction intervals and the relative increase in prediction intervals.

In practice, one may therefore want to correct for additive outliers when considering ARCH models,[5] to take care of additive outliers when testing for ARCH,[6] and to take care of (a potentially) misspecified conditional mean when testing for ARCH.[7]

[5] Philip Hans Franses and Hendrik Ghijsels (1999), Additive outliers, GARCH and forecasting volatility, *International Journal of Forecasting*, 15 (1), 1–9.
[6] Dick van Dijk, Philip Hans Franses, and André Lucas (1999), Testing for ARCH in the presence of additive outliers, *Journal of Applied Econometrics*, 14 (5), 539–562.
[7] Robin L. Lumsdaine and Serena Ng (1999), Testing for ARCH in the presence of a possibly misspecified conditional mean, *Journal of Econometrics*, 93 (2), 257–279.

8.3 HOW DATA FEATURES CAN LEAD TO DIFFERENT MODELS

The following case study shows how various features can be reflected in a single time series. The time series concerns annual inflation in the United States for the years 1774 up to and including 2015. The data are depicted in Figure 8.10, from which it is immediately clear that the series exhibits a few erratic patterns. Volatility does not seem to be constant over time; that is, at the beginning of the sample, inflation rates seem to move up and down quite rapidly. In that period, there are also many years with negative inflation rates.

When we consider the autocorrelations and partial autocorrelations for the full sample, we could take as a first guess model an autoregression of order 3,[8] that is,

$$y_t = \alpha + \beta_1 y_{t-1} + \beta_2 y_{t-2} + \beta_3 y_{t-3} + \varepsilon_t$$

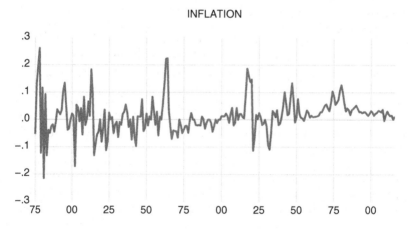

INFLATION

FIGURE 8.10 Annual inflation in the United States, 1774–2015. Source: Samuel H. Williamson (2018), The annual consumer price index for the United States, 1774–2015, MeasuringWorth 2018, www .measuringworth.com/uscpi/

[8] One could consider various subperiods of the data where these associate with war, an industrial revolution, and more. For ease of illustration, we confine the analysis to a single model.

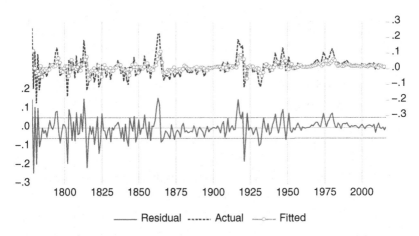

FIGURE 8.11 Residuals from an AR (3) model.

OLS gives

$$a = 0.007(0.004)$$
$$b_1 = 0.306(0.063)$$
$$b_2 = 0.242(0.067)$$
$$b_3 = -0.143(0.062)$$

It may be that the error process visualized in Figure 8.11 can best be described by an ARCH type of model, because we observe various periods with sequences of large residuals, which reflect periods with larger prediction intervals. It turns out that a useful model for the error process is a Generalized ARCH (GARCH) (1,1) model,[9] that is,

$$h_t = \mu + \alpha \varepsilon_{t-1}^2 + \beta h_{t-1}$$

It may also be that it can be described by an Integrated GARCH (IGARCH) (1,1) model, which is

$$h_t = \alpha \varepsilon_{t-1}^2 + (1-\alpha) h_{t-1}$$

This is the random walk version of a GARCH model, as the sum of α and $(1-\alpha)$ is 1, and hence the intercept term μ disappears.

---

[9] Tim Bollerslev (1986), Generalized autoregressive conditional heteroskedasticity, *Journal of Econometrics*, 31 (3), 307–327.

Maximum Likelihood estimation of an AR (3)-IGARCH (1,1) model results in

$$b_1 = 0.657(0.050)$$
$$b_2 = -0.125(0.082)$$
$$b_3 = 0.129(0.062)$$

and

$$a = 0.204(0.012)$$

in the IGARCH part. Note that the three parameters in the autoregression take quite different values than before.

The residuals suggest that there could be a structural break in the data, as the first part of the data shows much more erratic patterns. When we apply the Bai–Perron multiple breaks test for the autoregression, we find significant evidence for a break in 1862,[10] which is about halfway through the American Civil War.[11] When we look at the first sample, which is 1775 to 1862, none of the first twelve (partial) autocorrelations is significant. This emphasizes the presence of a structural break, and one may now wonder whether it is useful to create predictions from 2016 onwards taking onboard the different data in the first part of the sample. We see that this structural break makes the model change.

For the sample 1863 to 2016 we can again fit a third order autoregression, and OLS gives

$$b_1 = 0.895(0.080)$$
$$b_2 = -0.351(0.104)$$
$$b_3 = 0.112(0.079)$$

Note that these three parameters are again quite different from the earlier obtained estimates. This has an impact on out-of-sample forecasts.

The influence statistics in Figure 8.12 clearly show that something is going on for the years 1921 and beyond.

---

[10] The scaled F test statistic is 54.895 with a 5% critical value of 17.60.

[11] https://en.wikipedia.org/wiki/American_Civil_War.

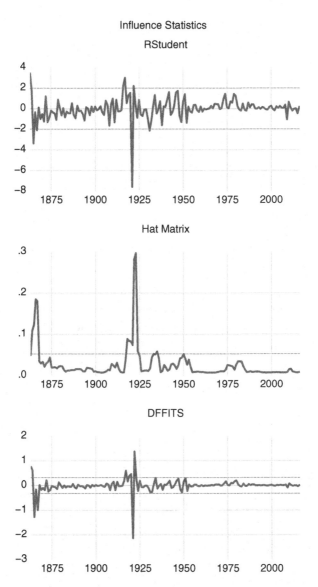

FIGURE 8.12 Influence statistics for the AR (3) model for the sample 1863–2016.

It could be that 1921 concerns an additive outlier (which may be associated with the end of World War I) but it could also be an innovation outlier or a mix of the two. To see what happens, we include

INFLATIONNEW

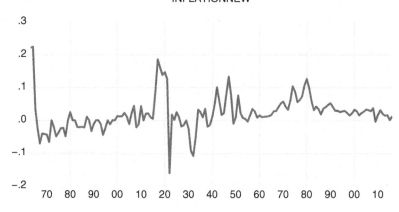

FIGURE 8.13 Inflation data when corrected for outliers in 1921 and 1922.

five 1/0 dummy variables for the years 1921, 1922, 1923, 1924, and 1925, and after estimation we delete the dummies with insignificant parameters one by one. The final model turns out to be

$$y_t = \alpha + \beta_1 y_{t-1} + \beta_2 y_{t-2} + \beta_3 y_{t-3} + \delta_1 Dummy1921_t$$
$$+ \delta_2 Dummy1922_t + \varepsilon_t$$

$$b_1 = 1.073(0.077)$$
$$b_2 = -0.504(0.096)$$
$$b_3 = 0.211(0.067)$$
$$d_1 = -0.240(0.031)$$
$$d_2 = 0.096(0.035)$$

With these estimates for the parameters for the dummy variables, we can create an "outlier-corrected" inflation series, as follows:

$$Inflationnew_t = Inflation_t + 0.240Dummy1921_t$$
$$- 0.096Dummy1922_t$$

A graph of this series appears in Figure 8.13, where the impact of World War I is now better visible.

When we now consider an AR (3)-IGARCH (1,1) model, the estimation results are

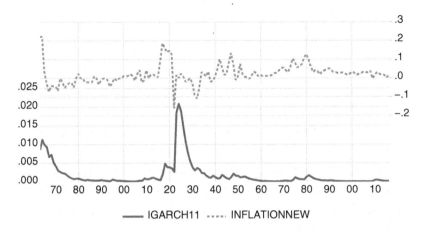

FIGURE 8.14 Estimated conditional volatility of outlier-corrected inflation.

$$b_1 = 0.817(0.053)$$
$$b_2 = -0.434(0.085)$$
$$b_3 = 0.240(0.070)$$

and

$$a = 0.289(0.035)$$

for the IGARCH part. The estimates of conditional volatility are presented in Figure 8.14.

This case study shows that a structural break may change the model and that outliers impact the volatility estimates. In turn, ignoring a structural break leads to different forecasts than when we deal with such a break explicitly. Tests and influence diagnostics guide us in the example of research practice.

8.4 NONLINEARITY?

We have looked at conditional volatility, but could it be that ignoring additive outliers also influences evidence of nonlinearity? Look again at the data presented in Figure 8.8, which represent artificial data from a first order autoregression with parameter $\rho = 0.8$ and with an additive outlier equal to 15 at $t = 50$.

Let us consider the following auxiliary regression

$$y_t = \alpha + \beta_1 y_{t-1} + \beta_2 y_{t-1}^2 + \beta_3 y_{t-1} y_{t-2} + \varepsilon_t$$

and use it as a diagnostic test for nonlinearity. Under the null hypothesis $\beta_2 = \beta_3 = 0$ the model reduces to a linear autoregression. When the null hypothesis is rejected, there is evidence of some form of nonlinearity owing to the terms y_{t-1}^2 and $y_{t-1} y_{t-2}$. For these hypothetical data, the F test for the joint null hypothesis $\beta_2 = \beta_3 = 0$ obtains a value 67.108, which is significant at the 1 percent level. Again, a single observation guides us into an incorrect direction. The use of influence statistics would have indicated that the observation at $t = 50$ is exceptional.

The next case study presents an analysis of quarterly unemployment data for the United States. Unemployment follows a business cycle; that is, there are periods with rapid increases in unemployment, typically associated with recessions, and longer periods with decreasing unemployment usually associated with expansions. As recessions often do not last long, the question is, what is a suitable way to incorporate recessions in a model that you want to use for out-of-sample forecasting?

8.5   WHAT ARE RECESSIONS?

Figures 8.15 and 8.16 depict the levels of and differences between the (seasonally adjusted) unemployment rates. Given long periods of slow mean reversion, it seems best to continue with the differenced data, here to be called $y_t = Unemployment_t - Unemployment_{t-1}$, where we continue with the creation of a univariate time series model for simplicity.

When the recession periods are viewed as data with innovation outliers, suggesting the recessions associate with a sequence of large positive ε_t values, then we can consider an autoregressive model of order 1 (more lags seem unnecessary here) with a GARCH $(1,1)$ component for the errors, that is,

$$y_t = \tau + \rho y_{t-1} + \varepsilon_t$$

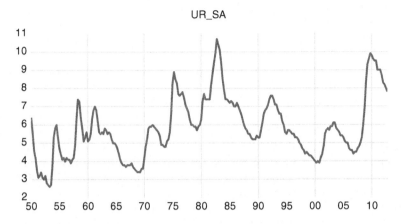

FIGURE 8.15 Quarterly unemployment rate for the United States (seasonally adjusted), 1959Q1 to 2012Q4.

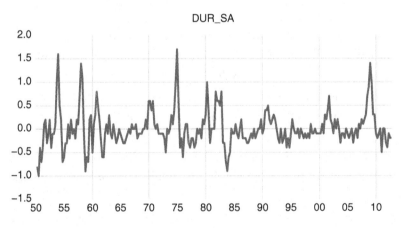

FIGURE 8.16 First differences of quarterly unemployment rate for the United States (seasonally adjusted), 1959Q2 to 2012Q4.

with

$$h_t = \mu + \alpha\varepsilon_{t-1}^2 + \beta h_{t-1}$$

The Maximum Likelihood estimates for the GARCH parameters are

$$m = 0.008\,(0.003)$$
$$a = 0.325\,(0.083)$$
$$b = 0.591\,(0.058)$$

CONDITIONAL_VARIANCE

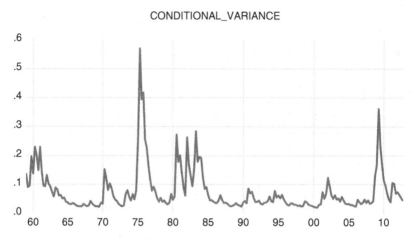

FIGURE 8.17 Estimated conditional variance from an AR (1)-GARCH (1,1) model.

while $r = 0.595(0.066)$. All parameters are significant at the 5 percent level, and this GARCH model thus leads to a forecasting model with time-variation in the predictive confidence bounds, depending on past sudden increases in ε_t. In this model, recessions are interpreted as innovation outliers, and they measure the large forecast errors due to sudden increases in unemployment. Figure 8.17 depicts the estimated conditional variance. We see that recession periods are reflected by the eruptions of the conditional variance and its aftermath.

When recession periods are viewed as periods with aberrant observations, one can also decide not to change the model, but to change the estimation method. Owing to its reliance on the squares of the errors, OLS is vulnerable to influential observations. One may now resort to alternative estimators that do not seek to minimize the sum of squared residuals but that minimize some other criterion function. This is called Robust Estimation. From the EViews helpfile we read:

> Ordinary least squares estimators are sensitive to the presence of observations that lie outside the norm for the regression model of interest. The sensitivity of conventional regression methods to

these outlier observations can result in coefficient estimates that do not accurately reflect the underlying statistical relationship. Robust least squares refer to a variety of regression methods designed to be robust, or less sensitive, to outliers.[12]

And "M-estimation: addresses dependent variable outliers where the value of the dependent variable differs markedly from the regression model norm (large residuals)."[13]

If we apply OLS to an AR (1) for the differences in unemployment, without GARCH, that is,

$$y_t = \tau + \rho y_{t-1} + \varepsilon_t$$

we get

$$r = 0.630 (0.052)$$

When we consider the EViews default version of M-estimation for the same model (the Huber method), we get

$$r = 0.552 (0.044)$$

This suggests two additional forecast models that one may wish to include in the model collection.

A third option to create forecasting models for unemployment assumes a model for recession periods and a model for expansion periods. A popular model for this purpose is the Markov-Switching model.[14] Assume that there are two states $s_t = 1$ and $s_t = 2$. Then a two-regime model can look like

$$y_t = \tau_1 + \rho_1 y_{t-1} + \varepsilon_t \quad \text{if } s_t = 1$$
$$y_t = \tau_2 + \rho_2 y_{t-1} + \varepsilon_t \quad \text{if } s_t = 2$$

This model is completed with the transition probabilities

---

[12] Helpfile manual Eviews 11.

[13] Peter J. Huber (1973), Robust regression: Asymptotics, conjectures and Monte Carlo, *Annals of Statistics*, 1 (5), 799–821.

[14] James D. Hamilton (1989), A new approach to the economics analysis of nonstationary time series subject to changes in regime, *Econometrica*, 57 (2), 357–384.

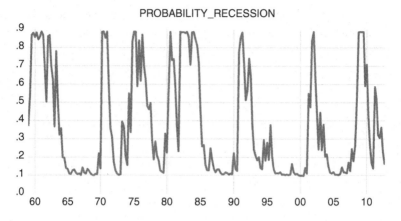

FIGURE 8.18 Estimated probabilities of recessions.

$$P\left(s_t = 1 | s_{t-1} = 1\right) = p_{11}$$
$$P\left(s_t = 2 | s_{t-1} = 1\right) = p_{12} = 1 - p_{11}$$
$$P\left(s_t = 1 | s_{t-1} = 2\right) = p_{21} = 1 - p_{22}$$
$$P\left(s_t = 2 | s_{t-1} = 2\right) = p_{22}$$

with $p_{11} + p_{12} = 1$ and $p_{21} + p_{22} = 1$. When this model is considered for the first-differenced unemployment series, we get

$$t_1 = -0.064(0.018)$$
$$\rho_1 = 0.287(0.093)$$

for the expansion regime; and for the recessions we obtain

$$t_2 = 0.075(0.048)$$
$$\rho_1 = 0.662(0.093)$$

Figure 8.18 plots the probabilities of recessions.[15]

Again, we see that the estimated probabilities are large around recession times, as they are indicated by the National Bureau of Economic Research.[16] These moments also match with locations where the AR (1)-GARCH (1,1) model indicates the presence of innovation outliers.

[15] See James D. Hamilton (1989), A new approach to the economics analysis of nonstationary time series subject to changes in regime, *Econometrica*, 57 (2), 357–384 for the computational method.
[16] www.nber.org/research/business-cycle-dating.

With this Markov-Switching model we have yet another model that can be used for out-of-sample forecasting. This case study shows that there is no single best way to describe data with potentially distinctive features, although one may have a priori preferences based on economic theory. You may interpret recessions as innovation outliers that you want to incorporate in your model, or as outliers that you want to discount when estimating parameters, or as separate periods that may require a separate model. For this example, we see that there are many choice options, and they all lead to different forecasting models. One may now decide to consider all models in a combined forecast.

8.6 STRUCTURAL BREAKS AND UNIT ROOTS

To conclude this chapter, we spend a few lines on unit roots and structural breaks.

Figure 8.19 presents hypothetical data on a first order autoregression. The data in Figure 8.20 are the same; we have just added the value of 20 to all observations from $t = 51$ onwards.

If we run the Dickey–Fuller regression

$$y_t - y_{t-1} = \alpha + \delta y_{t-1} + \varepsilon_t$$

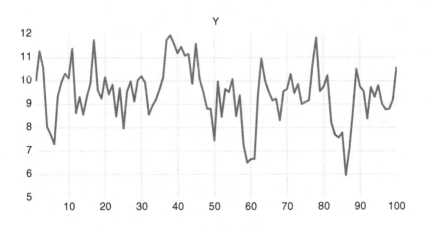

FIGURE 8.19 A (simulated) first order autoregression $y_t = 2 + 0.8y_{t-1} + \varepsilon_t$ with $\varepsilon_t \sim N(0,1)$.

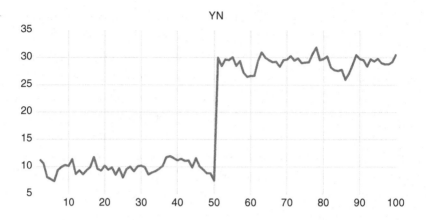

FIGURE 8.20 A (simulated) first order autoregression $y_t = 2 + 0.8y_{t-1} + \varepsilon_t$ and $\varepsilon_t \sim N(0,1)$ with a structural level shift from $t = 51$ onwards.

we get for the data in Figure 8.20

$$d = -0.413(0.083)$$

The t test value is –4.995, and this indicates the absence of a unit root. If we run the Dickey–Fuller regression

$$y_t - y_{t-1} = \alpha + \delta y_{t-1} + \gamma Trend_t + \varepsilon_t$$

for the data in Figure 8.20, we get

$$d = -0.140(0.051)$$

Here the t test value is –2.744, which does not indicate the absence of a unit root (as the relevant 5 percent critical value is –3.45). This shows that it is important when you test for a unit root that you take account of potential structural breaks.[17]

---

[17] Important studies on the interaction between breaks and unit roots are Pierre Perron (1989), The Great Crash, the oil price shock, and the unit root hypothesis, *Econometrica*, 57 (6), 1361–1401, Pierre Perron (1990), Testing for a unit root in a time series with a changing mean, *Journal of Business & Economic Statistics*, 8 (2), 153–162, and Eric Zivot and Donald W. K. Andrews (1992), Further evidence on the Great Crash, the oil-price shock, and the unit root hypothesis, *Journal of Business & Economic Statistics*, 10 (3), 251–270.

In Chapter 4 we learned that sometimes forecasts from models become robust to structural breaks, if we impose unit roots. Figure 4.6 showed that the so-called "Airline model" (LYF4 in the graph) seems to adapt quite quickly with the structural break induced by 9/11. The Airline model is

$$\Delta_1\Delta_{12}y_t = \mu + \varepsilon_t + \theta_1\varepsilon_{t-1} + \theta_{12}\varepsilon_{t-12} + \theta_{13}\varepsilon_{t-13}$$

Owing to its Δ_1 and Δ_{12} it is quite robust to changing seasonality and changing trends. It can manage changing seasonality because of Δ_{12} which assumes eleven so-called seasonal unit roots, and it can manage changing trends because of the Δ_1 and the second Δ_1 which is within Δ_{12}. This last feature can be seen from observing that

$$\Delta_{12}y_t = \Delta_1\left(y_t + y_{t-1} + y_{t-2} + \ldots + y_{t-11}\right)$$

The reason this model accommodates quickly to structural breaks, is that the estimates for the moving average parameters imply solutions that are close to the unit boundary.[18] This means that past forecast errors are taken onboard with large weights in the model.

8.7 WHAT DID WE LEARN?

In this chapter we have seen that one can easily be fooled by "obvious" patterns in the data. What looked like a cycle, can turn out to be just a random pattern. This randomness could have been learned from the forecast confidence bounds as these included nonsensical forecasts.

In other cases, matters can become complicated when there are outliers. Outliers, different regimes, and (G)ARCH can capture similar data features. This implies that one should be specific about what is the target of research. Do you want to describe different regimes? Or do you want to create a regression model where the estimation method makes those outliers have less impact on the estimation results? Do you want to allow for time-varying prediction intervals?

[18] The MA roots for this model here are $0.86 \pm 0.4i$, $0.80 \pm 0.47i$, $0.46 \pm 0.81i$, $\pm 0.93i$, $-0.47 \pm 0.80i$, $-0.81 \pm 0.46i$ and -0.93, and indeed close to the unit circle.

On the one hand, you may wish to end up with reliable and interpretable models. On the other hand, you may allow as many reasonable models as possible for which the forecasts will be combined.

All these decisions matter for the next steps. Again, if there is no target other than forecasting, one can keep all models and estimation methods and combine the forecasts with equal weights. Finally, ignoring level shifts can suggest unit roots. Yet at the same time, imposing unit roots makes forecasts robust to changes in trends or levels, although the forecast intervals will increase.

We can conclude that it is relevant to analyze data features and to conduct robustness checks on your modeling results. On the other hand, because tests always have their flaws, you may want to entertain all candidate models and take them all onboard for inference and forecasting. Obviously, inadequate models may be discarded, although they still may lead to accurate forecasts.

9   Predictability

In *Foreign Affairs* (November–December 2020), Scoblic and Tetlock write:

> Every policy is a prediction. Tax cuts will boost the economy.
> Sanctions will slow Iran's nuclear program. Travel bans
> will limit the spread of COVID-19. These claims all posit
> a causal relationship between means and ends. Regardless
> of party, ideology, or motive, no policymaker wants his or
> her recommended course of action to produce unanticipated
> consequences. This makes every policymaker a forecaster.[1]

Econometricians are often asked to provide forecasts to advisees. This chapter will argue that we should provide not only point forecasts but also prediction intervals, to allow the advisee to learn how dependable the forecasts are. Better, we should provide the limits to predictability ourselves. In some cases, this is hard, for example when we deal with long-term-ahead projections on climate or large infrastructure projects, such as the Olympic Games. Optimism may blur realism. If the mayor of a town asks to see if the organization of the Olympic Games would be a promising idea, then not everybody will be strong enough to outright say that organizing such an event can turn out to be disastrous.

This chapter starts with some quotes and insights on mega-projects. Then we turn to the construction and the use of prediction intervals in a time series context. We will see that depending on the choice of the number of unit roots (stochastic trends) or the sample

---

[1] J. Peter Scoblic and Philip E. Tetlock (2021), A better crystal ball: The right way to think about the future, Reprinted in *Foresight*, Q3 (Issue 62), 27–32.

size (when does the sample start?), we can compute a wide range of prediction intervals. Next we will see that those trends, and breaks in levels and breaks in trend, can yield a wide variety of forecasts. Again, we shall reiterate that maintaining a variety of models and outcomes is useful here, and an equal-weighted combination of results can be most appropriate. Indeed, any specific choice will lead to a different outcome. Finally, we discuss for a simple first-order autoregression how you can see what the limits to predictability are. We will see that these limits are closer than we may think from the onset.

9.1   OLYMPIC GAMES

How about the following quote?[2]

> The question then arises of why this disconnect exists and why ex-ante reports are so overly optimistic about the economic benefits that the Olympic Games will bring.
>
> The first flaw is a failure of such studies to account for the substitution effect, whereby local people spend money on going to an Olympic competition that they could have spent elsewhere in the local economy, for example at a local restaurant or theater. Thirteen percent of World Cup tickets in 2014 were sold exclusively to Brazilians [...]. These reports classify such expenditures as Olympic tourists contributing to the local economy, even though there is no money being contributed that wouldn't have been contributed otherwise. Thus, the studies are analyzing accounting profit when they should be considering economic profit.
>
> The second reason that such economic impact reports are overly optimistic is that they greatly overestimate the multiplier effect. These studies typically use input-output models that assume that when one economic sector expands, it leads to an

---

[2] From https://sites.northwestern.edu/nusportsanalytics/2017/04/01/is-it-worth-it-to-host-the-olympics/.

expansion of a second economic sector, which affects a third sector and so on. This generates a multiplier for local spending, which usually ranges between 1.7 and 3.5 in such reports but ranges between 0.7 and 1.1 in reality.[3]

The third reason why local revenues are overestimated is a leakage of money out of the local economy. The ex-ante studies operate under the assumption that one additional dollar spent within a city translates to one extra dollar added to the local economy of the city, which will be re-invested, or spent in another sector.

It is well known that organizing the Olympic Games is rarely if ever profitable. It is also not yet well understood what the benefits really are of organizing these games. Yet all bid books offered to the International Olympic Committee speak of increased income, profits, long-term impact, and the like.[4]

9.2 INFRASTRUCTURE PROJECTS

For large infrastructure projects, similar findings are obtained. Consider, for example:

> One thing's for sure: the people who predict the cost of urban mega-projects do a terrible job. Several years ago the University of Oxford scholar Bent Flyvbjerg, who's made a career researching mega-project mismanagement, analyzed 258 transportation infrastructure projects from around the world and found that nine

---

[3] Andrew Zimbalist (2016), *Circus Maximus: The Economic Gamble behind Hosting the Olympics and the World Cup*, Washington, DC: Brookings Institution Press. Kindle Edition, page 176.

[4] Interesting recent studies are Robert A. Baade and Victor A. Matheson (2016), Going for the gold: The economics of the Olympics, *Journal of Economic Perspectives*, 30 (2), 201–218, Stephen B. Billings and J. Scott Holladay (2012), Should cities go for the gold? The long-term impacts of hosting the Olympics, *Economic Inquiry*, 50 (3), 754–772, Holger Preuß, Wladimir Andreff, and Maike Weitzmann (2019), Cost and revenue overruns of the Olympic Games 2000–2018, Springer, Open Access: https://link.springer.com/book/10.1007/978-3-658-24996-0.

in ten exceeded their cost estimates. The overruns were greater on rail projects than road projects but averaged 28 percent across the board.[5]

Instead, wrote Flyvbjerg and some collaborators in 2002, it's more likely that when it comes to mega-projects, public officials engage in "strategic misrepresentation" — aka lying.

Another quote is:

This article presents results from the first statistically significant study of traffic forecasts in transportation infrastructure projects. The sample used is the largest of its kind, covering 210 projects in fourteen nations worth U.S.$59 billion. The study shows with very high statistical significance that forecasters generally do a poor job of estimating the demand for transportation infrastructure projects. For nine out of ten rail projects, passenger forecasts are overestimated; the average overestimation is 106%. For half of all road projects, the difference between actual and forecasted traffic is more than approximately 20%.[6]

Is there an issue with ethics here? We are not sure how to coin ethical issues in the context of large (infrastructure) projects, and the literature is also not yet decisive on that, but there is one potential fallacy at stake, coined by Daniel Kahneman and Amos Tversky, which is called a planning fallacy.

Wikipedia says:

The planning fallacy is a phenomenon in which predictions about how much time will be needed to complete a future task display an optimism bias and underestimate the time needed.

---

[5] www.bloomberg.com/news/articles/2013-07-30/why-mega-projects-always-end-up-costing-more-than-expected.

[6] Bent Flyvbjerg, Mette K. Skamris Holm, and Søren L. Buhl (2005), How (in)accurate are demand forecasts in public works projects?: The case of transportation, *Journal of the American Planning Association*, 71 (2), 131–146.

This phenomenon sometimes occurs regardless of the individual's knowledge that past tasks of a similar nature have taken longer to complete than generally planned.[7]

We seem to suffer from optimism bias when we create forecasts that are to be included in bid books. Well, we know for sure that if we deliver those forecasts with their associated prediction intervals, most people will doubt the projections. Who would sensibly know what will happen eight to ten years from now to a neighborhood in a city, close to the Olympic Games site. In Barcelona everything seemed to work out well, in Rio de Janeiro less so. But such projections go alongside huge prediction intervals, which in turn will be interpreted by many as, well, forecasters just don't know. And this seems true.

Let us go back to the Marian apparitions in Chapter 8. In that chapter only the point forecasts were given. These looked reasonable. We even checked the "true" data and found a date close to one of the predicted dates. This gave confidence in the models. However, if we had included the prediction intervals, as is done here, no one would have considered the forecasts:

Forecast minus 2 standard error	Forecast	Forecast plus 2 standard error
−41.5	19.7	81.0
−122.3	47.1	216.5
−663.7	256.5	1176.6
−1087.5	532.3	2152.0

Already for one step ahead, the prediction intervals contain a wide array of negative values, which would mean that the events would have already happened. Hence, these intervals show us that the model for Marian apparitions is nonsense.

---

[7] https://en.wikipedia.org/wiki/Planning_fallacy.

The main message so far is thus that reporting prediction intervals is important.[8]

The next message, however, is that prediction intervals can also be manipulated. Let us have a look at a case study.

9.3 MANIPULATING PREDICTION INTERVALS

Figure 9.1 presents the total number of motorcycles in the Netherlands for the years 1946 to 2019. Liberation by Canadians and Americans on motorcycles, made them immensely popular after World War II. The movie *Easy Rider* provided a second boost, and after the 1990s baby boomers enjoyed having a second mode of transport; hence the swings in the data.

Let us conduct an exercise in which we will create predictive models using data for 1946–2010 to make multisteps-ahead predictions for 2011–2019 for y_t, which is the level of the series, and for this out-of-sample period we compare the model forecasts. Given the

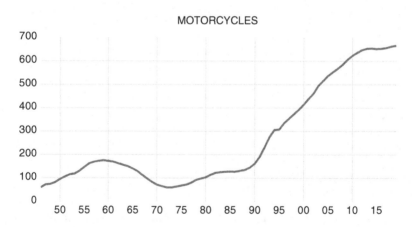

FIGURE 9.1 The total number of motorcycles in the Netherlands, 1946–2019.
Source: Statistics Netherlands

---

[8] A key reference with the same intention is Chris Chatfield (1993), Calculating interval forecasts, *Journal of Business & Economic Statistics*, 11 (2), 121–135.

fluctuations in the data, we can consider models for y_t, $\Delta_1 y_t$ and $\Delta_1^2 y_t$, thereby assuming zero, one, and two unit roots (stochastic trends), respectively.

The first model is a model for the levels, that is,

$$y_t = \alpha + \beta_1 y_{t-1} + \beta_2 y_{t-2} + \varepsilon_t$$

Application of OLS to this model gives (standard errors in parentheses)

$$a = 0.744\,(1.456)$$
$$b_1 = 1.835\,(0.079)$$
$$b_2 = -0.831\,(0.083)$$

Note that $b_1 + b_2 \approx 1$. For the nine out-of-sample observations, the Root Mean Squared Error (RMSE) of the forecasts is 73.095 and the Mean Absolute Error (MAE) is 60.366.

Next, the one unit root case is

$$\Delta_1 y_t = \alpha + \beta_1 \Delta_1 y_{t-1} + \varepsilon_t$$

for which OLS gives

$$a = 1.305\,(1.040)$$
$$b_1 = 0.859\,(0.066)$$

For 2011–2019, the RMSE of the forecasts of y_t from this model is 47.039 and the MAE is 39.341.

The second-differencing case is

$$\Delta_1 \Delta_1 y_t = \Delta_1^2 y_t = \alpha + \varepsilon_t$$

for which OLS gives

$$a = 0.079\,(0.891)$$

The RMSE of the nine forecasts is 67.792 and the MAE is 56.233.

Hence, the first-differencing model is the most accurate in terms of out-of-sample forecasting. The Dickey–Fuller test for the first differenced data would be 0.859 minus 1 divided by 0.066 is –2.136, and hence based on this unit root test value, which is not significant, one would have imposed two differencing filters. Note that this choice does not lead to the most accurate forecasts.

Table 9.1 *Standard errors for the multiple-steps-ahead forecasts, for forecasts of y_t*

		Model for	
Year	y_t	$\Delta_1 y_t$	$\Delta_1^2 y_t$
2011	7.416	6.954	7.128
2012	16.373	14.802	16.037
2013	27.017	23.649	26.995
2014	39.326	33.112	39.745
2015	52.852	42.947	54.122
2016	67.572	52.989	70.007
2017	83.415	63.122	87.314
2018	100.34	73.369	105.98
2019	118.32	83.372	126.94

Source: Author's calculations

Table 9.1 reports the standard errors for the multiple-steps-ahead forecasts for the three different models. The standard errors are quite different, and hence depending on how wide you want the prediction intervals to be, you can take your pick.[9] If you want some value not to be in the prediction interval, choose for a single unit root model as it has the narrowest intervals. If you want the widest interval, you can choose for the model that assumes two unit roots.

There is yet another angle that allows for manipulation of the prediction interval, which can also be illustrated for the motorcycles data.

9.4 PREDICTION INTERVALS AND SAMPLE SELECTION

In Figure 9.1 we presented the entire sample of the motorcycles data, but now look at Figure 9.2, which presents the final fifteen years. This looks like a time series that is easy to predict, while at the same time, the prediction intervals might be narrow.

---

[9] Note that the intervals are all too narrow as they ignore estimation uncertainty; see, for example, Peter C. B. Phillips (1979), The sampling distribution of forecasts from a first-order autoregression, *Journal of Econometrics*, 9 (3), 241–261.

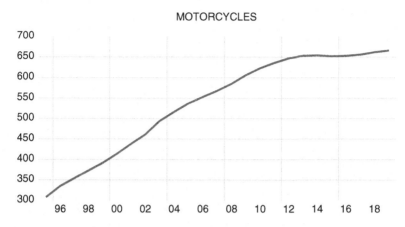

FIGURE 9.2 The total amount (stock) of motorcycles in the Netherlands, 1995–2019.

FIGURE 9.3 One-step-ahead forecast standard error, against the numbers of motorcycles.

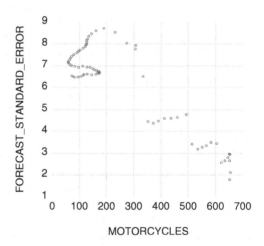

The question now is, if we want to predict from 2019 onwards, for years 2020 and further, when should our sample begin? There may be a story about Canadian soldiers or Dennis Hopper (in *Easy Rider*), but you can also run all computations and see what suits you best.

Let us consider the model $\Delta_1 y_t = \alpha + \beta_1 \Delta_1 y_{t-1} + \varepsilon_t$, and assume that we have an interest in a one-step-ahead forecast for y_t. Figure 9.3 presents the estimated model-based one-step-ahead forecast standard

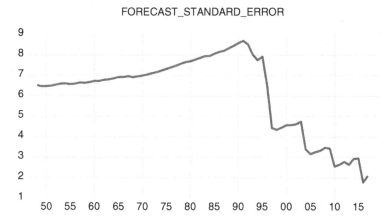

FORECAST_STANDARD_ERROR

FIGURE 9.4 One-step-ahead forecast standard error, against the starting years.

error, against the observations of motorcycles, whereas Figure 9.4 presents the same series of forecast errors but now against the starting years.

As some values of motorcycles "happen more often," we notice the peculiar pattern in the top left corner of Figure 9.3. That is, motorcycles fluctuate between 70 and 700, and hence we sometimes have (approximately) three points on the y axis for just one observation on the x axis.

Figure 9.4 shows that with more recent data, that is, the sample starting later, the prediction interval will be smaller. We can now pick any moment in time to start our sample. If we want to have very wide intervals we start our sample in 1990, and if we want small intervals we start in 2000. We may even see if there is a backup for any decision by running a test for a structural break. In fact, a Quandt–Andrews test gives a maximum LR F test statistic of 5.696 (with p value 0.067) for 1994, which suggests some evidence of a break.

So, what to choose now? You may prefer smaller standard errors if you want certain observations not to be in the forecast intervals (as the advisee may have asked you), and you may prefer larger errors if you want otherwise. You can back up your choice with a unit root test, but you may not want to do that. Hence, there are plenty of options. And indeed, the main message here is to report all choices and the reason for those choices. You should make it visible to the advisee how you arrived at your forecasts.

9.5 WHEN TO THROW AWAY OLDER DATA

It might be tempting not to consider, or to throw away, older data as they are not relevant to forecast the future. This can for example happen when recent data are collected at a higher frequency than older data. Most countries once collected only annual data for their national accounts, but nowadays in many countries we most often have quarterly data, and soon perhaps even monthly data for variables like Gross Domestic Product (GDP).

Look at Figure 9.5, which presents the quarterly and annual real GDP growth for China, starting with annual data for 1961 to 1991 and ending with quarterly data for the period 1992Q1–2009Q4. Hence, from 1992 onwards there are quarterly data, and before that there are only annual data. One may now wonder whether

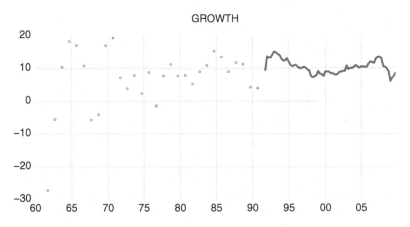

FIGURE 9.5 Quarterly and annual real GDP growth for China, starting in 1961 and ending in 1992Q1–2009Q4.
Source: Annual data https://data.worldbank.org/country/CN; Quarterly data www.stats.gov.cn/english/

it helps to include those older data for modeling, inference, and forecasting.[10]

Let us first look how China creates its GDP figures, as it turns out to be helpful to include older data. When GDP is measured, it is accumulated throughout the year $T = 1, 2, \ldots, N$ like

$$X_{1,T} = Z_{1,T}$$
$$X_{2,T} = Z_{1,T}^r + Z_{2,T}$$
$$X_{3,T} = Z_{1,T}^{rr} + Z_{2,T}^r + Z_{3,T}$$
$$X_{4,T} = Z_{1,T}^{rrr} + Z_{2,T}^{rr} + Z_{3,T}^r + Z_{4,T}$$

where $Z_{i,T}$ is the first release data of GDP in quarter Qi, $i = 1, 2, 3, 4$, and where the superscript "r" means revision. Indeed, "rrr" means third revision. It is the data on $X_{i,T}$, $i = 1, 2, 3, 4$ that are officially published. Writing X_T as total annual GDP, it is clear that

$$100\left(\log X_T - \log X_{T-1}\right) = 100\left(\log X_{4,T} - \log X_{4,T-1}\right)$$

provided there are no further revisions of $X_{4,T}$ in year $T+1$. The annual data in the years before 1992 for China match with the annual growth rates per quarter, but then only observed in the fourth quarter. In turn, this means that the annual data before 1992 can be treated as quarterly rates in Q4 with missing data for the quarters Q1, Q2, and Q3.

Assume there are quarterly real GDP growth figures, based on quarterly cumulative levels data x_t, and suppose we continue with

$$y_t = 100(\log x_t - \log x_{t-4})$$

A first order autoregression can be written as

$$y_t - \delta = \alpha_1\left(y_{t-1} - \delta\right) + \varepsilon_t$$

where δ is the mean of the variable and where ε_t is assumed to be a zero mean white noise process with variance σ^2, although the revision process shown here may introduce heteroskedasticity. When

---

[10] The example is taken from Philip Hans Franses (2021), Inclusion of older data into time series models for recent quarterly data, *Applied Economics Letters*, 28 (19), 1717–1721.

this model is fitted to the Chinese GDP data for 1992Q1 to 2009Q4, there are no signs of significant residual autocorrelation, so this autoregression seems to fit the Chinese data.

Backward substitution of the model to y_{t-4} results in

$$y_t - \delta = \alpha_1^4 \left(y_{t-4} - \delta \right) + \varepsilon_t + \alpha_1 \varepsilon_{t-1} + \alpha_1^2 \varepsilon_{t-2} + \alpha_1^3 \varepsilon_{t-3}$$

This shows that skip-sampling the data with frequency four does not introduce additional autocorrelation, because

$$\varepsilon_t + \alpha_1 \varepsilon_{t-1} + \alpha_1^2 \varepsilon_{t-2} + \alpha_1^3 \varepsilon_{t-3}$$

is uncorrelated with

$$\varepsilon_{t-4} + \alpha_1 \varepsilon_{t-5} + \alpha_1^2 \varepsilon_{t-6} + \alpha_1^3 \varepsilon_{t-7}.$$

The variance of the error term in the part of the sample that involves the annual data is, however, larger than σ^2 as it is $\sigma^2 \left(1 + \alpha_1^2 + \alpha_1^4 + \alpha_1^6 \right)$. One may now want to make use of this explicit expression, but one can also resort to the HAC estimator for the standard errors of the parameters.

Defining a variable lag_t which takes a value of 4 until 1992Q1 and of 1 afterwards, the two expressions can be combined into

$$\left(y_t - \delta \right) = \alpha_1^{lag_t} \left(y_{t-lag_t} - \delta \right) + u_t$$

where u_t is a zero mean white noise process with time-varying variance.

Fitting the model using the Generalized Method of Moments (performed in EViews version 11), the estimation results for the sample 1962Q4 to 2009Q4 (102 effective observations) are

$$d = 9.088 \left(1.279 \right)$$
$$a_1 = 0.765 \left(0.045 \right)$$

where HAC corrected standard errors are given in parentheses. The OLS-based estimate of the standard error of a_1 would have been 0.035.

When the model is fitted to the effective sample 1992Q2 to 2009Q4, the following estimation results are obtained:

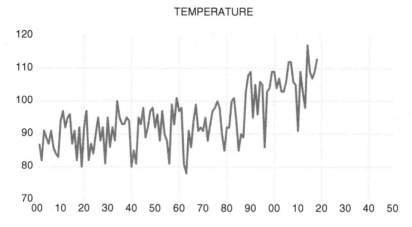

FIGURE 9.6 Average temperature (x10) in the Netherlands, 1901–2018, degrees Celsius.

$$d = 9.586\,(1.205)$$
$$a_1 = 0.918\,(0.044)$$

where now the OLS-based standard errors are reported in parentheses. Comparing the two sets of estimates, the mean growth rate is about the same across the two samples, but the estimates for the first autoregressive parameter differ substantially. In fact, a Dickey–Fuller test statistic for the shorter more recent sample is $(0.918{-}1)/0.044 = -1.864$, which when compared with the 5 percent critical value of -2.89, does not reject the presence of a unit root, while the Dickey–Fuller test statistic for the full sample is $(0.765{-}1)/0.045 = -5.222$, which suggests a clear rejection of the unit root null hypothesis.

It can matter whether to include older data or not. When the goal is to make out-of-sample forecasts, we would recommend just to use at least these two models, one with the older data included and one without such data.

9.6   CASE STUDY: TRENDS, BREAKS, AND FORECASTS

Our next case study deals with the consequences of model choice for long-term predictions. Look at the temperature data in Figure 9.6,

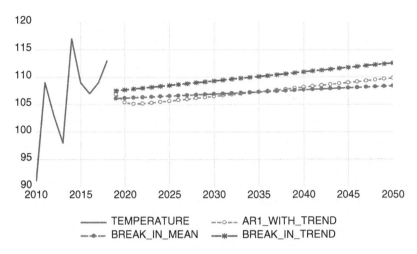

FIGURE 9.7 Forecasts until 2050 of annual temperature from three different models.

which concern annual observations for the Netherlands. What is it that we see?[11] We see mean reversion, at least in the first part of the sample, we see that there may be autocorrelation, and we see a trend in the second part of the data, and potentially a level shift, or both.

Suppose we want to make a long-term prediction for the temperature series. An agnostic univariate model could be

$$y_t = \alpha + \beta y_{t-1} + \gamma Trend_t + \varepsilon_t$$

with $Trend_t = t = 1, 2, 3, \dots$ For the full sample, OLS gives

$$a = 62.720\,(7.821)$$
$$b = 0.259\,(0.091)$$
$$c = 0.124\,(0.022)$$

and hence the parameters in this model (AR (1)_WITH_TREND in Figure 9.7) are all statistically significant at the 5 percent level. When

---

[11] Breaks are also addressed in Robert Lund and Jaxk Reeves (2002), Detection of undocumented changepoints: A revision of the two-phase regression model, *Journal of Climate*, 15 (17), 2547–2554.

we consider a Quandt–Andrews test this gives a maximum LR F test statistic of 7.566 (with p value 0.002) for 1988. Hence, there could be a break in the time series data.

When we take this evidence seriously, we should aim to modify this model. For the moment, we assume that the break happens instantaneously, and we create a dummy variable $Dummy1988_t$ which is 1 in 1988 and otherwise 0. And we create a dummy variable $Break1989_t$ which is 0 until and including 1988 and 1 for 1989, 1990 and further.

The next regression we consider is

$$y_t = \alpha + \beta y_{t-1} + \gamma Trend_t + \delta_1 Dummy1988_t + \delta_2 Break1989_t + \delta_3 Break1989_t \times Trend_t + \varepsilon_t$$

The application of OLS gives

$$a = 80.746\,(8.487)$$
$$b = 0.087\,(0.095)$$
$$c = 0.054\,(0.026)$$
$$d_1 = 9.723\,(5.897)$$
$$d_2 = -6.980\,(12.774)$$
$$d_3 = 0.158\,(0.124)$$

Various parameters are now not significant (anymore). This more general model can be reduced (stepwise backwards) to this one, that is (BREAK_IN_TREND)

$$y_t = \alpha + \gamma Trend_t + \delta_3 Break1989_t \times Trend_t + \varepsilon_t$$

for which OLS gives

$$a = 88.055\,(1.248)$$
$$c = 0.069\,(0.024)$$
$$d_3 = 0.093\,(0.018)$$

Alternatively, the model

$$y_t = \alpha + \gamma Trend_t + \delta_2 Break1989_t + \varepsilon_t$$

can also be maintained (BREAK_IN_MEAN), for which OLS gives

$$a = 87.845\,(1.243)$$
$$c = 0.074\,(0.024)$$
$$d_2 = 9.406\,(1.858)$$

You may want to choose between these two models, but before doing that it is informative to see what the long-term projections from these models look like. Point forecasts are given in Figure 9.8, and we see that there is an increase in the temperature from 9.5 degrees (which is the unconditional mean until 2009, where for the moment the break is ignored) to a range from 10.8 to 11.3 degrees in 2050.

We thus see that just a simple model with one variable gives different long-run projections. We see a difference of half a degree Celsius in 2050, just because of the option of two models. Of course, the prediction intervals would substantially overlap, and then the differences between the forecasts disappear. There is no reason not to use such models anymore, but it is good to be aware of substantial differences when it comes to long-term forecasts. And again, reporting prediction intervals is relevant.

9.7   LIMITS TO PREDICTABILITY, THEORY

To provide some more detailed insights into how far ahead you can predict with some degree of confidence, consider for simplicity the following first order autoregression:

$$y_t = \rho y_{t-1} + \varepsilon_t$$

with $|\rho| < 1$. The ε_t is a white noise process with $E(\varepsilon_t) = 0$ and $E(\varepsilon_t^2) = \sigma^2$, $t = 1, 2, \ldots, T$. The observation at time $T+1$ is

$$y_{T+1} = \rho y_T + \varepsilon_{T+1}$$

As $E(\varepsilon_{T+1} \,|\, \text{the past}) = 0$, we have the one-step-ahead forecast from origin T

$$\hat{y}_{T+1|T} = \rho y_T$$

The one-step-ahead forecast error is (assuming knowledge of ρ)

$$e_{T+1|T} = y_{T+1} - \hat{y}_{T+1|T} = \rho y_T + \varepsilon_{T+1} - \rho y_T = \varepsilon_{T+1}$$

The variance of the one-step-ahead forecast error $e_{T+1|T}$ is

$$V\left(e_{T+1|T}\right) = V\left(\varepsilon_{T+1}\right) = \sigma^2$$

At time $T + 2$ we have

$$y_{T+2} = \rho y_{T+1} + \varepsilon_{T+2} = \rho^2 y_T + \rho \varepsilon_{T+1} + \varepsilon_{T+2}$$

Hence, the two-steps-ahead forecast from time T is

$$\hat{y}_{T+2|T} = \rho^2 y_T$$

The two-steps-ahead forecast error is

$$e_{T+2|T} = \rho \varepsilon_{T+1} + \varepsilon_{T+2}$$

The variance of the two-steps-ahead forecast error is

$$V\left(e_{T+2|T}\right) = \left(1 + \rho^2\right)\sigma^2$$

Let us take it one step further. For three steps ahead the true observation is

$$y_{T+3} = \rho^3 y_T + \rho^2 \varepsilon_{T+1} + \rho \varepsilon_{T+2} + \varepsilon_{T+3}$$

The associated forecast made at time T is

$$\hat{y}_{T+3|T} = \rho^3 y_T$$

The variance of the three-steps-ahead forecast error is

$$V\left(e_{T+3|T}\right) = \left(1 + \rho^2 + \rho^4\right)\sigma^2$$

In general, for h steps ahead, we have

$$V\left(e_{T+h|T}\right) = \left(1 + \rho^2 + \rho^4 + \ldots + \rho^{2(h-1)}\right)\sigma^2$$

When $h \to \infty$, while of course $|\rho| < 1$, we have that

$$V\left(e_{T+h|T}\right) \to \frac{\sigma^2}{1 - \rho^2} = \gamma_0$$

With increasing h, the forecast error variance approaches the unconditional variance. This helps to give an insight in how well and how far ahead a time series variable can be predicted. When

$$\frac{V\left(e_{T+h|T}\right)}{V\left(e_{T+\infty|T}\right)}$$

gets close to 1, there is not much in the model that can help to predict. Note that for a first order autoregression, things are easy to

FIGURE 9.8 Ratio of two-steps-ahead forecast standard error against unconditional variance.

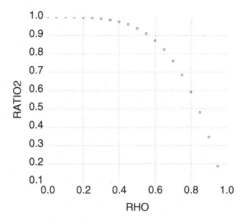

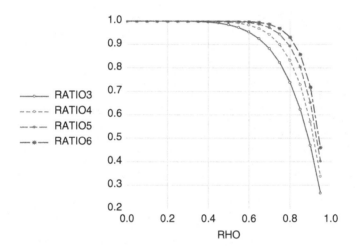

FIGURE 9.9 Ratio of multiple-steps-ahead forecast standard error against unconditional variance, $h = 3, 4, 5$ and 6.

derive analytically, whereas for other models, one must just create forecast intervals.

Figure 9.8 plots $\dfrac{V\left(e_{T+h|T}\right)}{V\left(e_{T+\infty|T}\right)}$ against ρ for $h = 2$. We see that when $\rho < 0.4$, the two-steps-ahead predictability is about 0. Figure 9.9 shows, among others, that only when $\rho > 0.8$, six-steps-ahead forecasting is meaningful.

9.8 MAJOR EARTHQUAKES, 1900–2005

To illustrate this, consider again the earthquakes data in Figure 9.10. Figure 9.11 plots the forecasts and prediction intervals from 2005 onwards using an AutoRegressive Moving Average (ARMA) (1,1) model. Quite quickly the prediction interval covers the (spread in

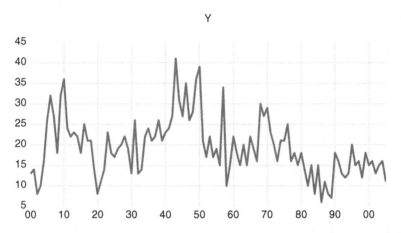

FIGURE 9.10 Major earthquakes in the world, Magnitude ≥ 7, 1900–2005.

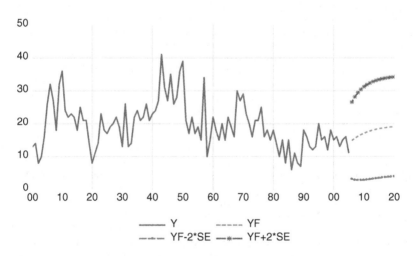

FIGURE 9.11 Multiple-steps-ahead forecasts for major earthquakes in the world, $M > 7$, 2005–2020, and the 95 percent confidence intervals.

the) data, and hence it seems fair to say that we can predict these data with this model with some confidence only one year ahead, at a maximum.

9.9 WHAT DID WE LEARN?

The major lesson that we have learned in this chapter is that not reporting forecasting intervals can be (or, better, is) misleading. This is also what we learned from the case of Marian apparitions in Chapter 8. Moreover, imposing (or not) imposing unit roots after the use of unit root tests matters for forecasting. Next, selective sampling can help to increase or to reduce forecast uncertainty. And, allowing (or not) for trends and shifts can give different forecasts, especially for the longer term. From the case studies on infrastructure projects and the like, we can conclude that confidence in predictability can be grossly high, on purpose so it seems.

9.10 WHAT TO DO?

Some guidelines seem obvious now. One should report prediction intervals. Next, one could report forecasts from models with and without imposing unit roots and continue with a combined forecast with equal weights. One should show forecasts for a range of samples and provide compelling arguments why a choice is made for a particular sample. Next, one should present forecasts for models with a trend and breaks, if there is evidence of these phenomena.

In sum, one should be honest about the limits to predictability; that is, how far ahead we can predict with reasonable confidence. Perhaps it is good to be aware that professional forecasters in macroeconomics often forecast only one year ahead.[12]

---

[12] See for example www.consensuseconomics.com/.

10 Adjustment of Forecasts

In practice it often happens that forecasts from econometric models are manually adjusted. There can be good reasons to do this. Foreseeable structural changes can be incorporated. Recent changes in data, in measurement, or in the relevance of particular factors can be addressed.

A main issue with manual adjustment is of course that the end user of a forecast needs to know why someone modified a forecast and, next, how that forecast was changed. Indeed, following the main theme of this book, only when everything, or at least as much as possible, is documented can we learn about the choices made, and here about the quality of the forecast. With an example we show that one needs to know specific details of econometric models, here growth curves, to understand that even a seemingly harmless adjustment leads to any result that you would like to have.

In this chapter we will discuss some reasons why people manually adjust forecasts. We discuss the optimal situation of adjustment and what the experience with manual adjustment is so far. A plea will be made to consider model-based adjustment of model forecasts, which allows for a clear understanding of how and why adjustment was done.

10.1 THE OPTIMAL SITUATION

There are various good reasons for experts to manually adjust model-based forecasts. These reasons can be data-based, can be based on foreseeable structural changes, and can be motivated by delayed updates of parameter estimates, among various other reasons. When properly done, one can also expect that expert-adjusted forecasts provide higher forecast accuracy than purely model-based forecasts. It is for example found from an analysis of the forecasts of the Netherlands Bureau for Economic Policy Analysis (CPB) that

> our key findings [...] are that (i) experts adjust upwards more often; (ii) expert adjustments are not autocorrelated, but their sizes do depend on the value of the model forecast; (iii) the CPB model forecasts are biased for a range of variables, but (iv) at the same time, the associated expert forecasts are more often unbiased; and that (v) expert forecasts are far more accurate than the model forecasts, particularly when the forecast horizon is short.[1]

An expert-adjusted forecast would look like

$$\text{Expert-adjusted Forecast} = \text{Model Forecast} + \text{Adjustment}$$

Preferably, the adjustment should be unpredictable from its own past, but it can be that the adjustment depends on variables other than those already included in the model. Adjustment preferably has mean zero, on average per variable. Moreover, adjustment may be dependent on the model forecast in cases where model forecasts are extremely out of range, but adjustment must not depend on the model forecasts such that it pleases the advisee.[2]

10.2 WHAT DO WE SEE IN PRACTICE?

The empirical evidence is scattered throughout the literature, and it shows that there can be substantial differences between optimal behavior and the observed behavior of experts adjusting model-based forecasts. There is variation across the types of variables that are

---

[1] Philip Hans Franses, Henk C. Kranendonk, and Debby Lanser (2011), One model and various experts: Evaluating Dutch macroeconomic forecasts, *International Journal of Forecasting*, 27 (2), 482–495.

[2] Part of the material in this chapter draws upon the summary of results in Philip Hans Franses (2014), *Expert Adjustment of Model Forecasts*, Cambridge: Cambridge University Press.

being predicted, such as Stock Keeping Unit level sales for companies, airline revenues, or key macroeconomic variables, but it is possible to draw a few conclusions.

Often it is found that adjustment is correlated with the model forecast. In that case, adjustment involves content that one would preferably have included in the model. This may happen when the individual who adjusts the forecasts is not the one who built the model.

The deviation between an expert-adjusted forecast and a model forecast can be predicted by past adjustment behavior and by past accuracy of expert-adjusted forecasts and model forecasts. Hence, the behavior of the adjuster can be predicted to some extent. This can also be viewed as a sign that the model is not well specified. This can happen, of course, but then we would think that the first step for the modeler would be to readdress the model, instead of adjusting the forecasts. It seems pointless to modify inappropriate econometric model forecasts.

Experts seem quite persistent in modifying model forecasts, and their behavior might be predicted by the Law of Small Numbers,[3] as discussed in the decision-making literature. That is, experts see patterns in a small number of data when those patterns are not there. This is the fallacy to erroneously recognize winning strikes in a casino, such as a range of hits on red in a roulette game.

Experts also have a preference to adjust upwards. This behavior could be a sign that they misunderstand how econometric models or forecast algorithms work. Indeed, econometric models are geared towards creating unbiased forecasts. Alternative reasons to modify in a particular direction are an optimism bias or the reliance on an alternative loss function. This loss function is usually not known or available. And, as we will see, it may also be rational to appease a manager or superior.

Experts may also find it difficult to disentangle their forecasting task from their task, for example, of managing shipments and

---

[3] Matthew Rabin (2002), Inference by believers in the Law of Small Numbers, *Quarterly Journal of Economics*, 117 (3), 775–816.

stock. If you dislike out-of-stock situations in your supermarket, you may be tempted to lift the forecast upwards. There is, however, no need to do so, as you can always stick to the forecast but then simply order more. So the role of the forecast in the decisions process matters.

Macroeconomic forecasters often deal with variables that get updated values as time proceeds. In many countries, GDP is revised five to seven times in subsequent years, and often such revisions are upwards. When forecasting GDP, one can take these upwards revisions into account, which may then look optimistic.

10.3 WHY WOULD EXPERT ADJUSTMENT BE OPTIMISTIC?

The following quotes can be found in the literature:

> Rational analysts intentionally bias earnings forecasts upward in order to gain management's favor and improve access to company management

and

> Analysts exhibit greater optimism as the forecast's importance to management increases

and

> our results suggest that analysts rationally trade-off forecast bias to improve management access and forecast accuracy.[4]

Forecasters can benefit from delivering optimistic forecasts. Indeed, it seems rational to say to the mayor of your city that organizing the Olympic Games could lead to some benefits, instead of saying from the beginning that such an event will be a disaster. Hence,

---

[4] Terence Lim (2001), Rationality and analysts' forecast bias, *Journal of Finance*, 56 (1), 369–385, as referred to in David P. Mest and Elizabeth Plummer (2003), Analysts' rationality and forecast bias: Evidence from sales forecasts, *Review of Quantitative Finance and Accounting*, 21 (2), 103–122, pages 103, 104, and 105.

being optimistic can make sense. It all depends on what you think the mayor wants to hear and whether you might want to be hired again for future advice.

Moreover, from the management side there is evidence that management penalizes forecasters who provide unfavorable forecasts, by sharing less information with them.[5] This is less likely to occur for macroeconomic forecasts, although some evidence exists. A relevant quote here is:

> This paper investigates strategic motives of macroeconomic forecasters and the effect of their professional affiliations. The "wishful expectations hypothesis" suggests that a forecaster predicts what his employer wishes. The "publicity hypothesis" argues that forecasters are evaluated by both accuracy and ability to generate publicity, and that forecasters in industries that emphasize publicity most will make most extreme and least accurate predictions. The "signaling hypothesis" asserts that an extreme forecast signals confidence in own ability, because incompetent forecasters would mimic others to avoid public notice.[6]

If you want to hit the media as a forecaster, then it seems better to stand out instead of admitting that you fully agree with all the other forecasters. This also happens when you are considered an expert. You will be unlikely to be seen as an expert if you never adjust a model forecast.

To conclude this section on intentional forecasts biases, it is written that forecasts can be subject to managerial pressure, they can be intentionally flawed, or even be the "result of deliberate and rational decision-making behavior on the part of the forecasters."[7]

---

[5] Kent L. Womack (1996), Do brokerage analysts' recommendations have investment value? *Journal of Finance*, 51 (1), 137–167.

[6] Masahiro Ashiya (2009), Strategic bias and professional affiliations of macroeconomic forecasters, *Journal of Forecasting*, 28 (2), 120–130.

[7] Clint L. P. Pennings, Jan van Dalen, and Laurens Rook (2019), Coordinating judgmental forecasting: Coping with intentional biases, *Omega*, 87 (C), 46–56.

So there are plenty of reasons why forecasters may adjust econometric model forecasts. This can also happen without it explicitly being known, as the next example will show.

10.4 WHEN A HARMLESS MI ADJUSTMENT DOMINATES THE INFERENCE

Consider the following setting. Your company has launched a new product. You receive the first four weeks of cumulative sales figures. Suppose these are 1, 2, 4, and 8. So things look good. You go to the responsible product manager and ask when she thinks peak sales will happen, in which week. Based on her experience, she will say, for example, peak sales will happen in week ten. We will now see that this fully dominates subsequent forecasts.

Suppose you use either one of the following familiar growth curves discussed in Chapter 4, that is, a logistic model, a Gompertz model or a Bass model to model the trajectory of cumulative sales. For cumulative sales y_t these models have the following format, that is,

$$y_t = f(m, \beta, t^*),$$

where $f(.)$ is some nonlinear function, and m is the maturity level or final sales, β describes the shape of the S curve, and t^* is the point of inflection and equal to the moment of peak sales. If you fix the value of t^* as $t^* = \tau$, and you apply NLS to

$$y_t = f(m, \beta, t^* = \tau) + \varepsilon_t$$

where ε_t is an error term, then you get estimates for m and β.

Table 10.1 shows what kinds of results for m can be obtained. The reason that this happens is that the inflection point is the key parameter for a growth curve,. Once its location is known, the rest of the curve can be drawn easily. This means that when you are not aware of this, while your product manager is, she can deliver you any total final sales figure that makes you happy by just quoting some number for the week of the potential inflection point. Hence, you had better be aware of results such as those in Table 10.1.

Table 10.1 *Nonlinear Least Squares estimation results for a sample of just four observations given the first four observations and when the moment of peak sales is fixed when estimating m and β*

	Logistic		Gompertz		Bass	
	m	$β$	m	$β$	m	$β$
First four observations:	1, 2, 4, 8					
$t^* = 10$	539	0.699	172	0.187	280	0.570
$t^* = 15$	16,427	0.693	689	0.136	4,008	0.555
$t^* = 20$	500k	0.693	2,424	0.109	63,086	0.554
First four observations:	1, 2, 5, 11					
$t^* = 10$	1502	0.818	318	0.202	910	0.724
$t^* = 15$	85,926	0.815	1,532	0.145	31,233	0.718
$t^* = 20$	5m	0.815	6,376	0.116	1m	0.717
First four observations:	1, 2, 6, 14					
$t^* = 10$	3078	0.897	491	0.212	2,024	0.821
$t^* = 15$	200k	0.895	2,665	0.151	100k	0.817
$t^* = 20$	23m	0.895	12,366	0.120	7m	0.817

Source: Author's calculations

Now what to do in practice? One strategy is that you estimate parameters in the growth curve, models once the actual inflection point has already happened, assuming there is just one inflection point. But you do not want to wait for that long. An alternative strategy is to plug in a range of projected peak sales moments, and as such obtain a range of estimates for m and $β$. As the $β$ parameters have a different functionality across the three models they are difficult to compare, but the estimates for m all associate with the same number, the total final sales, and hence one can create empirical distributions of their values. Table 10.2 shows some results for a Bass curve and some values for inflection point $τ$. The mean value of estimated m is 562 and the median value is 225. A first guess value of 225 is now the safest bet, after the first four data points have come in.

In sum, a seemingly harmless quote based on the inflection point can lead to a range of estimates of total sales given the variation in these

Table 10.2 *Estimation results given the first four observations 1, 2, 4, and 8 and when the moment of peak sales is fixed when estimating m and β, in the case of the Bass model and with different imposed inflection points (standard errors in parentheses)*

Inflection point	m	β
5	26.00 (1.602)	0.751 (0.071)
6	41.12 (3.975)	0.671 (0.059)
7	65.13 (9.068)	0.625 (0.054)
8	104.3 (19.59)	0.598 (0.053)
9	169.5 (40.90)	0.581 (0.052)
10	279.7 (83.44)	0.570 (0.053)
11	468.0 (167.2)	0.564 (0.054)
12	791.9 (330.3)	0.560 (0.054)
13	1352 (644.5)	0.557 (0.055)
14	2323 (1245)	0.556 (0.055)

figures. This illustration shows that we must be aware of the properties of econometric models, in this case growth curves with inflection points.

10.5 CASE STUDY: MANUAL ADJUSTMENT AND FORECAST UPDATES

To illustrate the consequences of manual adjustment of forecasts, consider the forecasts in Figure 10.1 for monthly airline revenues (KLM Royal Dutch Airlines) for the Asia region for the period 2004M04 to 2008M12. The forecasts are the one-step-, two-steps-, and three-steps-ahead forecasts, each for the same month. In a more formal notation, these are $F_{t|t-h}$ for $h = 1, 2, 3$, where $t \mid t - h$ concerns a prediction for time t made at time $t - h$.

The forecasts are tight together in the first part of the sample, but once the economic crisis of 2008/2009 comes closer, we see that the forecasts start to diverge. The three-steps-ahead forecasts are still optimistic, but the last part the forecast updates are downwards.

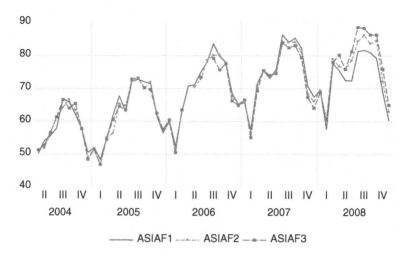

FIGURE 10.1 Forecasts for monthly airline revenues (millions of euros) for the Asia region for 2004M04 to 2008M12. The forecasts are the one-step-, two-steps-, and three-steps-ahead forecasts, each for the same month. Source: KLM Royal Dutch Airlines

A relevant quote concerning these forecast updates is

In sum, when the KLM experts would have included econometric model-based forecasts, then their adjustment has been most often upwards. Anecdotal evidence obtained when discussing the above findings with the two senior staff members of KLM confirms the noticed tendency to adjust upwards. In 2008 when the market went down quickly, it was considered better to inform top management about this downturn when spread out over a few months. Hence, instead of a forecast with say a 12% downturn, a range of subsequent forecasts were tuned down each with, say, 4%.[8]

This so-called forecasting smoothing,[9] or partial adjustment of expectations, implies that forecast updates or adjustments are positively

[8] Philip Hans Franses (2014), *Expert Adjustment of Model Forecasts*, Cambridge: Cambridge University Press, page 46.

[9] Prakash Loungani (2001), How accurate are private sector forecasts? Cross-country evidence from consensus forecasts of output growth, *International Journal of Forecasting*, 17 (3), 419–432.

correlated. To see whether this holds for the forecasts in Figure 10.1, consider the regression model

$$F_{t|t-1} - F_{t|t-2} = \alpha + \beta \left(F_{t|t-2} - F_{t|t-3} \right) + \varepsilon_t$$

An application of OLS for the full sample gives (OLS-based standard errors in parentheses)

$$a = -0.198 \, (0.294)$$
$$b = 0.359 \, (0.172)$$

The t test for $\beta = 0$ is 2.082 with a p value of 0.042. When we deliberately only look at the last two years of the data, closer to the recession period, then OLS leads to

$$a = -0.744 \, (0.351)$$
$$b = 0.932 \, (0.184)$$

The t test for $\beta = 0$ is now 5.073 with a p value of 0.000. Note that this result is obtained by selective sampling with hindsight. So, indeed, and bearing in mind the anecdotal evidence, some smoothing of forecasts is going on here.

A first order forecast update (revision) is written as

$$F_{t|t-h} - F_{t|t-(h+1)}$$

An often-used auxiliary test regression to examine how forecast updates proceed over time is

$$F_{t|t-h} - F_{t|t-(h+1)} = \alpha + \beta \left(F_{t|t-(h+1)} - F_{t|t-(h+2)} \right) + \varepsilon_{t,h}$$

When $\beta = 0$ we have what is called "weak-form model forecast efficiency."[10] When this test regression is applied in practice, it often happens that the hypothesis $\beta = 0$ is rejected. In fact, it is often found that $\beta < 0$, but sometimes $\beta > 0$. This latter case is of interest here, given the results presented here, with positive-valued estimates b.

[10] William Nordhaus (1987), Forecasting efficiency: Concepts and applications, *The Review of Economics and Statistics*, 69 (4), 667–674.

Now, which values for β can appear under which circumstances?[11] It may help to start with considering a manually adjusted forecast such as

$$F_{t|t-h} = M_{t|t-h} + v_{t|t-h}$$

where $M_{t|t-h}$ is a forecast from an econometric model and where $v_{t|t-h}$ is "intuition" (or the adjustment made by an expert). The standard case in the literature with no adjustment is that

$$F_{t|t-h} = M_{t|t-h}$$

In this case, $\beta = 0$ is plausible. When the completely opposite case occurs,

$$F_{t|t-h} = v_{t|t-h}$$

that is, no econometric model is considered, and the forecast is thus fully based on intuition, we need to know more about the time series properties of $v_{t|t-h}$. When intuition (or expertise) can be described by a first order autoregression, then it can be derived[12] that

$$\beta = \frac{-1 + 2\rho_1 - \rho_2}{2 - 2\rho_1}$$

with ρ_1 and ρ_2 the first two autocorrelations of the time series process for intuition. Suppose the relevant autoregression for $v_{t|t-h}$ is a first order autoregression, with parameter δ, then

$$\beta = \frac{\delta - 1}{2}$$

So, when $|\delta| < 1$, then $-1 < \beta < 0$. Hence, the finding of negative values of β in practice could be a sign that forecasters do not take onboard an econometric model. To arrive at $\beta > 0$ values, it can be derived that this happens when there is a negative correlation between current news (on the variable of interest) and current intuition, and at the same time that there is a positive correlation between past news

---

[11] The next few results are based on Chia-Lin Chang, Bert de Bruijn, Philip Hans Franses, and Michael McAleer (2013), Analyzing fixed event forecast revisions, *International Journal of Forecasting*, 29 (4), 622–627.

[12] See Chang et al., Analyzing fixed event forecast revisions.

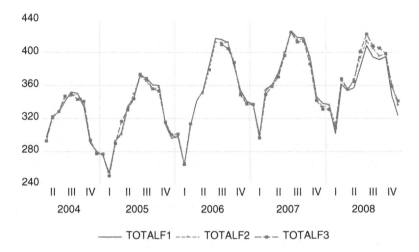

FIGURE 10.2 Forecasts for total monthly airline revenues (millions of euros) for 2004M04–2008M12. The forecasts are the one-step-, two-steps-, and three-steps-ahead forecasts, each for the same month.

and current intuition. This matches the situation here, and hence, in other words, forecast smoothing or piecewise adjusting forecasts gives a positive β.

To provide another illustration, consider the forecasts for the total revenues in Figure 10.2. It is less prominent than in Figure 10.1, but again we see a divergence between the forecasts towards the end of the sample. OLS applied to

$$F_{t|t-1} - F_{t|t-2} = \alpha + \beta \left(F_{t|t-2} - F_{t|t-3} \right) + \varepsilon_t$$

for these data gives

$$a = -0.875\,(0.660)$$
$$b = 0.222\,(0.163)$$

for the full sample, and

$$a = -2.857\,(1.023)$$
$$b = 0.665\,(0.270)$$

for the last two years of monthly observations, where the t test for $\beta = 0$ in the latter regression obtains the value 2.390, with a p value of 0.026.

10.6   WHAT TO DO?

Econometric model builders and others who use statistical algorithms to create model-based forecasts should provide information
on how the model forecasts were created: which variables were
included, which variables were excluded (if known) and why, how
the parameters were estimated, how the forecasts were created, and
what available information were they based on.

Model builders usually aim to create unbiased forecasts, and
when these model forecasts are biased, they should inform the
experts what the origins of those biases are. At the same time, when
forecasts are unbiased, model builders should inform the experts
about the absence of intentional bias.

Finally, if the past adjustment of experts has turned out to be
a useful addition to econometric models, it is wise that information
from experts should be explicitly incorporated in the econometric
models.

We have seen that experts often, perhaps too often, modify
model-based forecasts wherever these model forecasts come from.
Experts should therefore pay more attention to understanding where
the model forecasts originated and how they were created. They
should learn that persistent adjustment cannot be the best strategy.
Experts should provide documentation of why and how they decided
to modify model forecasts.

At the same time, experts should be aware that forecasts and
managerial decisions are two different things. If management so
requires, one can always do something different than the forecasts
would entail, and there is no reason to modify the forecasts.

An analyst who needs to evaluate the final forecasts should
pay more attention to how the experts created their forecasts. More
knowledge about this will facilitate the analysis of the accuracy of
the forecasts and can also suggest future modifications to the model
forecasts.

A strategy to create more transparency in the adjustment process can be the following.

10.7 MODEL-BASED FORECAST ADJUSTMENTS

It is possible to make adjustments to model-based forecasts using other models, thereby making the adjustment process more transparent. That is, adjustment becomes model based.

One line of thought can be based on a random coefficient model.[13] A basic version first order random coefficient model reads as

$$y_t = (\alpha + \delta_{t-1}) y_{t-1} + \varepsilon_t$$

One may now consider, for example,

$$\delta_t = X_t \beta \text{ if } X_t \beta \geq \tau$$
$$\delta_t = 0 \text{ if } X_t \beta < \tau$$

where τ is a scalar threshold and where X_t is a vector with some explanatory variables. One may, for example, use Factor Analysis on the X_t variables to determine the weights collected in the vector β. The threshold can be set at a multiple of the standard deviation of $X_t \beta$. The one-step-ahead forecasts are then

$$y_{T+1|T} = \alpha y_T \text{ if } X_T \beta < \tau$$

and

$$y_{T+1|T} = (\alpha + X_T \beta) y_T \text{ if } X_T \beta \geq \tau$$

Of course, all kinds of variants and extensions of this idea can be considered.[14]

10.8 WHAT TO DO WHEN IT IS NOT KNOWN HOW THE FORECASTS ARE CREATED

What can you do if it is not known how the forecasts were created.[15] Well, the only thing you can do is to combine the

---

[13] Des F. Nicholls and Barry G. Quinn (1982), *Random Coefficient Autoregressive Models: An Introduction*, Berlin: Springer-Verlag.

[14] A model version of this idea could include an additional error term μ_t, such as $\delta_t = X_t \beta + \mu_t$ if $X_t \beta + \mu_t \geq 0$ and $\delta_t = 0$ if $X_t \beta + \mu_t < 0$; see Philip Hans Franses, Richard Paap, and Björn Vroomen (2004), Forecasting unemployment using an autoregression with censored latent effects parameters, *International Journal of Forecasting*, 20 (2), 255–271.

[15] This is the situation when you consider the forecasts presented in www .consensuseconomics.com/. There are many forecasts made by many forecasters for

forecasts.[16] This is in any case a good thing to do when the forecasts are all unbiased, as will be shown next. But it can also be shown that this is a good thing to do when experts have manually modified model-based forecasts, even if they have done so in the wrong direction.[17]

To illustrate, assume you have two one-step-ahead unbiased forecasts F_1 and F_2 for a variable y. The variance of $y - F_1$ is σ_1^2 and that of $y - F_2$ is σ_2^2, and the covariance between the forecast errors $y - F_1$ and $y - F_2$ is σ_{12}. The combined forecast is

$$F_c = wF_1 + (1-w)F_2$$

with $0 < w < 1$. The variance of the combined forecast is

$$w^2\sigma_1^2 + (1-w)^2\sigma_2^2 + 2w(1-w)\sigma_{12}$$

The optimal value of w can be found as

$$w^* = \frac{\sigma_2^2 - \sigma_{12}}{\sigma_1^2 + \sigma_2^2 - 2\sigma_{12}}$$

Substituting this optimal value in the expression for the variance of the forecast error of the combined model forecast results in

$$\sigma_c^2(w^*) = \frac{\sigma_1^2\sigma_2^2 - \sigma_{12}^2}{\sigma_1^2 + \sigma_2^2 - 2\sigma_{12}}$$

It can be derived that $\sigma_c^2(w^*) < \sigma_1^2, \sigma_2^2$.[18] As a specific case, when the variances of the forecast errors are equal, and the forecast errors are uncorrelated, then

$$w^* = \frac{\sigma_1^2}{\sigma_1^2 + \sigma_1^2} = \frac{1}{2}$$

many countries, but it is unclear how the forecasters arrived at their predictions. Empirical research tries to address this issue through the use of approximative models.

[16] John J. Bates and Clive W. J. Granger (1969), The combination of forecasts, *Operations Research Quarterly*, 20 (4), 451–468; Robert T. Clemen (1989), Combining forecasts: A review and annotated bibliography, *International Journal of Forecasting*, 5 (4), 559–581. See also Daniel Kahneman, Olivier Sibony, and Cass R. Sunstein (2021), *Noise: A Flaw in Human Judgment*, London: William Collins.

[17] See Dick van Dijk and Philip Hans Franses (2019), Combining expert-adjusted forecasts, *Journal of Forecasting*, 38 (5), 415–421.

[18] Bates and Granger, The combination of forecasts.

and

$$\sigma_c^2 \left(w^* \right) = \frac{\sigma_1^4}{2\sigma_1^2} = \frac{1}{2}\sigma_1^2$$

Other weights are of course also possible, although in practice one often uses an equally weighted forecast combination, which is quite simple and convenient.[19]

10.9 WHAT DID WE LEARN?

We have learned that one should make any manual adjustment of model-based forecasts explicit and give a motivation for the adjustment. Not saying what you did is a form of misconduct. If you follow this route, it is impossible to say why and how a forecast is accurate or not, and nobody will know why your forecast was wrong or approximately right. As a forecaster, you can also not build a reputation, as others may be tempted to believe that you were just lucky when you quoted an accurate forecast. Hence, there is no proof of your abilities. We have also argued here that model-based adjustment of forecasts may have a way to go, but at present little is known how this should be done best.

Finally, we have learned that combining forecasts can be especially useful and lead to more accurate forecasts.[20]

---

[19] It is frequently found that a simple arithmetic average of the forecasts is hard to beat: see Gerda Claeskens, Jan R. Magnus, Andrey L. Vasnev, and Wendung Wang (2016), The forecasting combination puzzle: A simple theoretical explanation, *International Journal of Forecasting*, 32 (3), 754–762; and Jeremy P. Smith and Kenneth F. Wallis (2009), A simple explanation of the forecast combination puzzle, *Oxford Bulletin of Economics and Statistics*, 71 (3), 331–355, for explanations.

[20] This is also one of the main findings of the so-called M5 competition: see Spyros Makridakis, Evangelos Spiliotis, and Vassilios Assimakopoulos (2022), M5 accuracy competition: Results, findings and conclusions, *International Journal of Forecasting*, 38 (4), 1346–1364.

11 Big Data

The running thread throughout this book is that the application of econometric methods and techniques requires us to make choices, and that ethics in econometrics involves that these choices are well articulated and well documented. So far, we have considered basic econometric models, such as regression models or time series models, as these are often considered in practice. However, currently we can have access to large databases, sometimes known as Big Data,[1] and for those large datasets simple econometric models will not do. When you have a million people in your database, as insurance firms or telephone providers or charities have, and you have collected information on these individuals for many years, you simply cannot summarize these data using a small-sized econometric model with just a few regressors. Even making a scatterplot with millions of data points is unlikely to be informative, in the sense that any patterns will be difficult to discern.

In this chapter,[2] we will address diverse options for handling Big Data. We will kick off with a discussion about what Big Data is, and why it is special. Next, we will discuss a few options such as selective sampling, aggregation, nonlinear models, and variable reduction. Methods such as ridge regression, lasso, elastic net, and artificial neural networks will also be addressed, and these latter

---

[1] A historical overview of where the term Big Data comes from is given in Francis X. Diebold (2012), On the origin(s) and development of the term "Big Data," PIER Working Paper No. 12-037, Available at http://dx.doi.org/10.2139/ssrn.2152421.

[2] Parts of this chapter benefited from comments made by participants at the IETI conference in Hong Kong (2017), a workshop at the Banque de France (2017), the New CFO training (2017, 2018 and 2019), a seminar at the Anton de Kom University, Paramaribo (2016), and a workshop at the Royal Netherlands Academy of Arts and Sciences (2017), as well as the attendees at a seminar at the Royal Maas Yacht Club (2020).

concepts are nowadays captured as so-called machine learning methods. We will see that with these methods the number of choices rapidly increases, and that as such, reproducibility can reduce. So, the analysis of Big Data comes at a cost of more analysis and of more choices to make and to report.

II.I HOW NEW IS BIG DATA?

Large data sets, particularly in business disciplines such as marketing and finance, have been around for a while.[3] Already in 1983, marketing scholars were the first to analyze scanner data based on the bar codes that were introduced on so-called Stock Keeping Units in retail stores.[4] Bar codes look like as in Figure 11.1.

Originally, bar codes were introduced for transactions management and distribution purposes, but it was quickly recognized that they provide information that can be used to model consumer behavior at a detailed level, for example. Using loyalty cards, customers can receive tailor-made offers: "Hi, how about purchasing our brand-X chocolate cookies today, which you bought earlier?"

In finance, large databases appeared in the early 1990s, and these databases contained tick-by-tick information on stock market transactions and exchange rates. Forecasts could be made for minute-by-minute volatility, and one could analyze market spillovers across the globe at a high-frequency level. This data availability paved the

FIGURE 11.1 An example of a barcode. Source: Internet

---

[3] Philip Hans Franses (1998, editor), Large data sets in business economics, *Statistica Neerlandica*, 52 (3), 255–385.
[4] Peter M. Guadagni and John D. C. Little (1983), A logit model of brand choice calibrated on scanner data, *Marketing Science*, 2 (3), 203–238.

way for new econometric methods and techniques,[5] and it also motivated research on the optimal sampling frequency. Indeed, it was
soon recognized that detailed data could contain noise and irrelevant
information. Hence, much research has been dedicated to find the
optimal frequency.[6]

About halfway through the 1990s, organizations such as
insurance firms, energy providers, telephone providers, and charities started to rely on a concept called Customer Relationship
Management, where they often used call centers. Customers could
be contacted when they showed an inclination to leave a company
as a customer (called "churn"), while current customers could
receive offers for additional products (called "cross selling") and
new customers could be acquired. This was made possible by large
databases with customer information relating to all transactions
and contacts.

11.2   WHAT IS THE NEW PART OF BIG DATA?

Large databases have been around for a while, and hence the question
is what the novelty of Big Data is. There are all kinds of definitions of
the term, but for econometrics the key difference from long-available
large databases is simply the size of Big Data. While we might have
had financial data per minute, with hundreds of columns with information in spreadsheets on customers, nowadays Big Data provides
data per second, on every tweet, every Facebook post, on any energy
aspect of a dwelling, on any word in newspapers, in many countries
and at any time. We can therefore have all data available on a particular phenomenon.

Altogether, this is an overwhelming amount of data. However,
Big Data does not necessarily mean more useful information. In other

---

[5] Robert F. Engle (2000), The econometrics of ultra-high frequency data, *Econometrica*, 68 (1), 1–22.

[6] Yacine Aït-Sahalia, Per A. Mykland, and Lau Zhang (2005), How often to sample a continuous-time process in the presence of market microstructure noise, *Review of Financial Studies*, 18 (2), 351–416.

words, with the advent of Big Data has also come more noise or non-sense (think of tweets with emojis or words with unclear meaning).

11.3 WHAT DOES BIG DATA ALLOW US TO DO?

In principle, with so much more data one can create better forecasts of individual behavior because econometric models benefit from more variation in the data. That is, often with the increased size also comes more variation and more detail.[7] It may also be possible to obtain timely information on the current state-of-affairs in an economy.[8] This can be achieved by searching for words posted on the internet, words such as "inflation," "unemployment," "jobs," and with these one can create a current indicator of the economy. This is particularly useful in developing countries, where newspapers and websites exist with information but a central statistical office may take much more time to create a GDP figure. One can also create subtler links between variables, where the standard regression model is replaced by models with much more flexible forms, such as, for example, artificial neural networks, as we will discuss in Section 11.6. Big Data raises questions about which data are relevant and which relationships hold in parts of the data that could be considered as homogeneous.

With more data, econometric models can allow for more latent variables such as attitudes, beliefs, and awareness. With more data, we can create clusters of similarly behaving individuals, which makes it possible to make accurate forecasts about the behavior of other individuals who are not yet in the database. Somewhere in the world, there are people with the same spending behavior as you have. If so,

---

[7] Liran Einav and Jonathan Levin (2014), Economics in the age of big data, *Science* 346 (6210) 1243089; Serena Ng (2017), Opportunities and challenges: Lessons from analyzing terabytes of scanner data, in *Advances in Econometrics and Economics, Eleventh World Congress* (Bo Honoré, Ariel Pakes, Monika Piazzesi and Larry Samuelson, editors), Cambridge: Cambridge University Press, pages 1–34; Hal R. Varian (2014), Big Data: New tricks for econometrics, *Journal of Economic Perspectives*, 28 (2), 3–28.

[8] Dario Buono, George Kapetanios, Massimiliano Marcellino, Gianluigi Mazzi, and Fotis Papailias (2018), Big Data econometrics: Now casting and early estimates, BAFFI CAREFIN Working Papers 1882, Centre for Applied Research on International Markets Banking Finance and Regulation, Universita' Bocconi, Milan, Italy.

internet companies can make you the same offer: "Others who bought this product were also interested in this one. Perhaps you are too."

When we think of Big Data, we can think along at least three dimensions of more observations. We can think of individuals $i = 1, 2, ..., I$, in which I can be all past and current customers of an internet firm. This can therefore be millions of individuals. We can think of a time series dimension, in which $t = 1, 2, ..., T$, and the data can be of ultra-high frequency. And we can think of variables $k = 1, 2, ..., K$, in which K refers to, for example, all products in a retail store.

11.4   WHAT CAN BE DONE?

How can we approach the econometric analysis of Big Data? It is convenient to think of two general strategies. The first is to extend the standard (regression or time series) models to make suitable models for large databases. We can think of panel models in which the parameters are functions of variables in a second level of a model, and we can think of various nonlinear relations between variables, among which an artificial neural network is quite popular. The second approach is to somehow reduce, summarize, or classify the data and the variables prior or while doing the analysis. We can think of aggregation, clustering, and selective sampling, or of variable reduction methods such as Principal Components Analysis, ridge regression, lasso, and elastic net, among the currently popular methods.

An important consequence of the econometric analysis of large datasets is that models and methods become more complicated. The analysis involves (many) more choices, the effects of which are not always known. The interpretation of results becomes less easy, and hence one tends to look only at whether the forecasts are accurate. At the same time, computation time increases, and reproducibility can become difficult if not all (and there can be many) choices have been recorded. Finally, comparison between methods or models is not easy as it becomes difficult to measure success.

We will now proceed with a review of a few of the possible approaches to model large datasets.

11.5 MULTIPLE-LEVEL MODELS

Consider a panel with individuals $i = 1, 2, ..., I$, with variables observed over time, $t = 1, 2, ..., T$. Suppose that I is large and that T is large enough to fit for every individual a regression model like

$$y_{i,t} = \alpha_i + \beta_i x_{i,t} + \varepsilon_{i,t}$$

where we consider just a single explanatory variable for notational convenience. If $I = 1,000,000$, this means one million OLS-based estimates of α_i and of β_i. Now, what to do next with all these estimates?

In the applied econometrics literature, we see that diverse options are considered. A first, and simple,[9] one is that you assume that, for example,

$$\beta_i \sim NID(\beta, \sigma_\beta^2)$$

where *NID* means normally and independently distributed. This reduces one million β_i parameters to just two, that is, β and σ_β^2. You may also allow not for just one distribution,[10] but for more distributions in a mixture, such as S different distributions (latent classes) as

$$\beta_{i,s} \sim NID(\beta_s, \sigma_{\beta_s}^2)$$

with latent probabilities $p_1, p_2, ..., p_S$ of being assigned to one of the S classes.

An alternative elegant and informative way to have a second level in the model, now for the parameters, is, for example,

$$\beta_i = \beta_0 + \beta_1 z_i + v_i$$

with the unknown error term $v_i \sim NID(0, \sigma_v^2)$ and a time-constant variable z_i. Think, for example, of z_i as household size for a certain period and β_i as a price elasticity. Note that this multilevel model has two unknown error terms, and that in the second model for β_i the

---

[9] An early contribution to random coefficient models is Paravastu Ananta Venkata Bhattanatha Swamy (1970), Efficient inference in a random coefficient regression model, *Econometrica*, 38 (92), 311–323.

[10] Michel Wedel and Wagner A. Kamakura (1999), *Market Segmentation: Conceptual and Methodological Foundations*, Boston, MA: Kluwer Academic Publishers.

left-hand variable is unobserved. This means that we need to resort to alternative estimation methods as we cannot use a least squares estimation method anymore. In practice one does sometimes see the application of a two-step OLS method; that is, first obtain the b_i and then adopt these estimates as an "observed" variable in the second model. OLS-based standard errors are then not correct. A more appropriate estimation method is the Hierarchical Bayes method.[11]

11.6 ARTIFICIAL NEURAL NETWORKS

Another popular method for large data sets is a so-called artificial neural network (ANN).[12] Such a network amounts to specific nonlinear links between input variables and an output variable. To illustrate, consider a variable y_i and a single explanatory variable x_i, and suppose that a linear regression will not do and that there is a preference for

$$y_i = f(x_i; \theta) + \varepsilon_i$$

where the function $f(.)$ is an unknown function, where θ are unknown parameters, and where the data are instrumental in establishing the function. You can think of $f(.)$ being a sine or a cosine function, or a power raise of x_i, but those choices can be viewed as restrictive. Moreover, there are too many options for such nonlinear functions. Instead, one may now opt for a function that can come arbitrarily close to a perfect fit of y_i.[13] As will be illustrated next, such a function can be created by a sequence of, for example, logistic functions.

---

[11] Greg M. Allenby and Peter E. Rossi (1998), Marketing models of consumer heterogeneity, *Journal of Econometrics*, 89 (1–2), 57–78.

[12] A very readable first general account is Christopher M. Bishop (1995), *Neural Networks for Pattern Recognition*, Oxford: Oxford University Press.

[13] Kurt Hornik, Maxwell Stinchcombe, and Halbert White (1989), Multilayer feedforward networks are universal approximators, *Neural Networks*, 2 (5), 359–366; Kurt Hornik, Maxwell Stinchcombe, and Halbert White (1990), Universal approximation of an unknown mapping and its derivatives using multilayer feedforward networks, *Neural Networks*, 3 (5), 551–560.

Consider the logistic function

$$G(x_i) = \frac{1}{1 + \exp\left[-\gamma_1(x_i - \gamma_0)\right]}$$

where $\gamma_1 > 0$, and the model

$$y_i = \alpha + \beta_1 G(x_i) + \varepsilon_i$$

where ε_i is some independent and identically distributed (IID) error term. The logistic function $G(.)$ maps the x_i to a number in between 0 and 1. When $x_i \gg \gamma_0$, the function $G(x_i)$ approaches 1, and when $x_i \ll \gamma_0$, the function $G(x_i)$ approaches 0. Next, the output of this $G(x_i)$ is scaled by β_1. The $G(x_i)$ is called a knot, and hence here there is a single knot. The $G(x_i)$ part in the model is called a hidden layer.

You can also have two knots:

$$G_1(x_i) = \frac{1}{1 + \exp\left[-\gamma_{11}(x_i - \gamma_{10})\right]}$$

$$G_2(x_i) = \frac{1}{1 + \exp\left[-\gamma_{21}(x_i - \gamma_{20})\right]}$$

with $\gamma_{11} > 0$ and $\gamma_{21} > 0$, and have the model

$$y_i = \alpha + \beta_1 G_1(x_i) + \beta_2 G_2(x_i) + \varepsilon_i$$

To see what kind of patterns can be described by this still rudimentary ANN model, consider generating 300 observations as follows:

$$u_i \sim N(0,1)$$
$$v_i \sim N(0,1)$$
$$x_i = 10 + Trend_t + 4u_i$$
$$y_i = \frac{3}{1 + \exp\left[-0.1(x_i - 100)\right]} + \frac{-1}{1 + \exp\left[-0.2(x_i - 200)\right]} + 0.5v_i$$

with $Trend_t = 1, 2, 3, \ldots, 300$. A scatter plot of these y_i and x_i appears in Figure 11.2. Quite a special link between the two variables y_i and x_i can appear. Note that when we reduce the error term from $0.5v_i$ to say $0.005v_i$, a smooth line will appear. Furthermore, note that in terms of a nonlinear regression model, the model contains

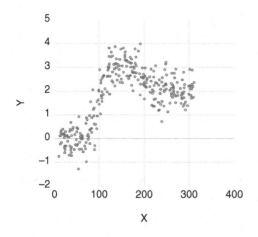

FIGURE 11.2 Artificial data from an artificial neural network.
Source: Author's calculations

just a single explanatory variable, that is, x_i, and that the model contains six unknown parameters (abstaining from the variances of the random terms). This already tells us that least squares methods will not work here and alternative estimation methods are needed. A technique that is often used to obtain parameter estimates is called backpropagation.[14]

When we move from a single explanatory variable to, for example, two explanatory variables, such as x_i and z_i, we can have an ANN like

$$y_i = \sum_{j=1}^{q} \frac{\beta_j}{1 + \exp\left[-\gamma_j\left(x_i + \alpha_j z_i - \gamma_{0,j}\right)\right]} + \varepsilon_i$$

When we add to the above data generating process

$$w_i \sim N(0,1)$$
$$z_i = 100 - Trend_t + 4w_i$$

and we create data from

$$y_i = \frac{3}{1 + \exp\left[-0.1\left(0.5x_i + z_i - 100\right)\right]}$$
$$+ \frac{-2}{1 + \exp\left[-0.2\left(x_i - 2z_i - 200\right)\right]} + 0.5v_i$$

[14] https://en.wikipedia.org/wiki/Backpropagation.

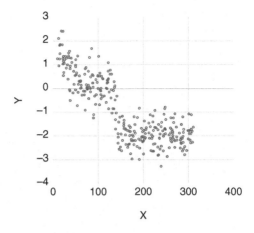

FIGURE 11.3 More artificial data from an artificial neural network, now with two variables, scatter plot of y_i against x_i.

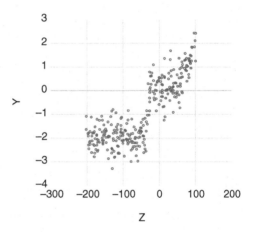

FIGURE 11.4 More artificial data from an artificial neural network, now with two variables, scatter plot of y_i against z_i.

then we can get the scatter plots of y_i against x_i as in Figure 11.3, of y_i against z_i as in Figure 11.4, while the overall data on y_i are presented in Figure 11.5.

We see that even from these simple data generating processes, we can appreciate that a wide range of patterns in the data is possible. The more of those $G(.)$ functions come into play, and the more variables can be considered, the closer can an ANN approximate the data to be explained.

This is also the major pitfall of an ANN. We can arrive at a fit, in terms of an R^2, that is close to 1 for the in-sample data. This

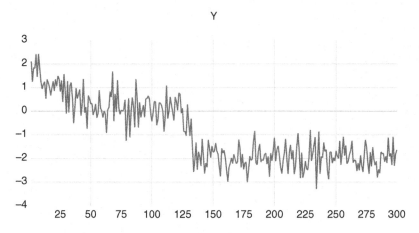

FIGURE 11.5   More artificial data from an artificial neural network, now with two variables, arranged from $i = 1, 2, ..., I = 300$.

implies overfitting. Therefore, ANN models are usually "trained" on one part of the data and "tested" on hold-out samples.

When it comes to incorporating an artificial neural network into your modeling and forecasting toolbox, there are many choices to make. First, we must think of estimating the parameters, and there are various methods.[15] We must also decide on the number of hidden layers, where the illustrative cases here involved a single hidden layer. An ANN with two hidden layers looks like, for example,

$$y_i = \alpha + \beta_2 F\big(\beta_1 G(x_i)\big) + \varepsilon_i$$

where $F(.)$ can be a logistic function too. And we must decide on how many knots q to incorporate.

A prominent issue with an ANN is that there are typically many more parameters than input variables. This implies that the parameters themselves become difficult to interpret,[16] and that we also cannot

---

[15] https://en.wikipedia.org/wiki/Artificial_neural_network.

[16] To see which variables contribute the most to the fit of the accuracy of the forecasts, one can also consider Shapley values; see, for example, Kjersti Aas, Martin Jullum, and Anders Løland (2021), Explaining individual prediction when features are dependent: More accurate approximations to Shapley values, *Artificial Intelligence*, 298, 103502.

resort to t values, p values, an R^2, and the like. So, statistical inference is cumbersome and usually absent. Often, one uses an ANN for out-of-sample prediction or for pattern recognition. Once you have fitted an ANN you can visualize the various functions, make scatters, and try to assign meaning to the observed patterns.[17] Overfitting remains a fundamental problem with these nonlinear and very flexible models, and hence cross-validation is also often considered in practice.

We have seen two reasonably frequently used methods to describe enormously large datasets: These are random coefficient models and ANNs. Of course, these are just two examples of methods that can be considered.

A second approach to large datasets is the reduction of the data. This can be achieved by selective sampling, by aggregation or by variables reduction.

11.7 SAMPLE SELECTION

We discussed in Chapter 6 on missing observations that selective sampling can benefit data analysis.[18] We can think of reducing the number of zeroes in a logit model if there are many more zeroes than ones. Knowing how to accommodate the model when there is sample selection can help to make choices here. Not all data have to be analyzed if the sampling process is incorporated in the modeling stage. Such a new model can then contain a model part to describe how you choose

---

[17] In early work we tried to interpret the outcomes of an artificial neural network: see Philip Hans Franses and Gerrit Draisma (1997), Recognizing changing seasonal patterns using artificial neural networks, *Journal of Econometrics* 81 (1), 273–280. We wrote:

> In this paper we propose a graphical method based on an artificial neural network model to investigate how and when seasonal patterns in macroeconomic time series change over time. Neural networks are useful since the hidden layer units may become activated only in certain seasons or periods, and since this activity can be stepwise or smooth. The graphical method is based on the partial contribution of the hidden layer units to the overall fit. We apply our method to quarterly Industrial Production in France and Netherlands.

[18] James J. Heckman (1976), The common structure of statistical models of truncation, sample selection and limited dependent variables and a simple estimator for such models, *Annals of Economic and Social Measurement*, 5 (4), 475–492.

which observations to include in the modeling process, and a next step is then a model for the data given that they have been observed.

It should be mentioned here that if the type of sample selection is unknown, matters can become difficult. If someone else, not you, has decided to "clean" the data and cannot tell you how they did it, then the resulting analysis can be dominated by this cleaning, without knowing how. In practice it is therefore recommended always to ask for the raw original data. For example, if someone has decided to delete all the high-income individuals beyond a certain but unknown income threshold, then your model with income as an explanatory variable can become quite unreliable.

11.8 AGGREGATION

The aggregation of data is often done, for example when it comes to privacy matters. People may know the average number of dogs owned by households in your street, but rarely would they know who exactly owns a dog. One should be aware though that such an average is not informative about individuals. If the average number of dogs is one and there are ten households, it may be that a single household owns all these dogs. As another example, the average score on an intelligence test per state is not informative about individual scores. A low scoring state may contain the highest scoring individuals. This illustrates a phenomenon that is called ecological fallacy.[19]

Wikipedia says:

> An ecological fallacy is a formal fallacy in the interpretation of statistical data that occurs when inferences about the nature of individuals are deduced from inferences about the group to which those individuals belong.
>
> Example: if a particular group of people is measured to have a lower mean IQ than the general population, it is an error to conclude that a randomly-selected member of the group is more

---

[19] Gary King (1997), *A Solution to the Ecological Inference Problem: Reconstructing Individual Behavior from Aggregate Data*, Princeton: Princeton University Press.

likely than not to have a lower IQ than the mean IQ of the general population.[20]

When data are aggregated over time, that is, they are temporally aggregated, then we should be aware that usually the model changes, as we saw in Chapter 6. That is, we shall not have the same time series model for the higher frequency and for the lower frequency. For example, we have already seen that temporal aggregation of a random walk process leads to an Integrated Moving Average (1,1) process.

11.9 PRINCIPAL COMPONENTS, FACTOR ANALYSIS

A common approach in macroeconomic forecasting involves the application of a so-called dynamic factor model (DFM). A representation of a DFM is

$$y_{t+1} = \mu + W_t \beta_W + F_t \beta_F + \varepsilon_{t+1}$$

$t = 1, 2, \ldots, T$, where y_{t+1} is the variable to be predicted. Usually, one takes for W_t the first p lags of y_t. The factors F_t are unobservable factors collecting variables. There are N predictors $x_{i,t}$ where $i = 1, 2, \ldots, N$, where N can be large. Next, the predictors are associated with the factors as follows

$$x_{i,t} = F_t \lambda_i + \eta_{i,t}$$

where F_t is a $T \times k$ matrix with k factors, and λ_i is a $k \times 1$ vector with factor loadings, and $k \ll N$. These factors must be estimated from the data, and one often resorts to factor analysis (FA),[21] or PCA.[22] It may sometimes be wise to a priori restrict the number of variables to be included in FA or PCA.[23]

Two issues about PCA are worth mentioning. One of the choices that one must make is the number of factors k to be included. This can

---

[20] https://en.wikipedia.org/wiki/Ecological_fallacy.

[21] https://en.wikipedia.org/wiki/Factor_analysis.

[22] https://en.wikipedia.org/wiki/Principal_component_analysis.

[23] A review of various preselection methods is given in Hyun Hak Kim and Norman R. Swanson (2018), Mining big data using parsimonious factor, machine learning, variable selection and shrinkage methods, *International Journal of Forecasting*, 34 (2), 339–354.

Scree Plot (Ordered Eigenvalues)

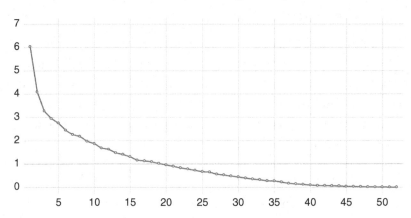

FIGURE 11.6 The fifty-two estimated eigenvalues from a PCA on real GDP growth rates for fifty-two African countries, 1963–2006 (see Chapter 4).

be done using cross-validation methods, but sometimes one looks at a so-called scree plot, which gives the sequence of eigenvalues of the sample covariance matrix of the N predictors $x_{i,t}$ (from high to low), and which should indicate an "elbow" in the sequence. When there are many variables, however, it shall become more difficult to visually fix k. Look, for example, at the ordered eigenvalues in Figure 11.6, which are obtained when incorporating real GDP growth rates for all fifty-two African countries. It is not easy to spot the location of k here.

One other issue with PCA and time series variables is related to the topic of Chapter 7; it deals with spurious relations. When one does not take proper care of any autocorrelation in the variables, one may find too many relevant principal components.

Consider, for example, the following DGP:

$$x_t = \alpha x_{t-1} + \varepsilon_t^x, \varepsilon_t^x \sim NID(0,1)$$
$$y_t = \alpha y_{t-1} + \varepsilon_t^y, \; \varepsilon_t^y \sim NID(0,1)$$
$$z_t = \alpha z_{t-1} + \varepsilon_t^z, \; \varepsilon_t^z \sim NID(0,1)$$

The cells in the first panel in Table 11.1 present the average value of the first eigenvalue in a PCA and the standard deviation across these first eigenvalues, across 10,000 replications. In the second panel, we

Table 11.1 *The top panel gives the estimated first eigen-value in a PCA involving x_t, y_t and z_t, and the bottom panel gives the frequency that the hypothesis $\beta = 0$ can be rejected in the PCR using a 5 percent significance level*

	Sample size		
	50	100	500
α			
0.5	1.288 (0.127)	1.205 (0.090)	1.091 (0.041)
0.8	1.448 (0.196)	1.328 (0.147)	1.150 (0.067)
0.9	1.567 (0.242)	1.448 (0.194)	1.219 (0.097)
0.95	1.656 (0.275)	1.568 (0.247)	1.305 (0.135)
0.99	1.786 (0.325)	1.738 (0.306)	1.572 (0.245)
α			
0.5	6.8%	5.9%	5.6%
0.8	9.5%	6.8%	5.4%
0.9	13.4%	9.7%	5.9%
0.95	17.1%	13.5%	6.7%
0.99	19.6%	18.7%	13.0%

Source: Philip Hans Franses and Eva Janssens (2019), Spurious principal components, *Applied Economics Letters*, 26 (1), 37–39.

report the frequency of significant parameters (5 percent level) associated with the first principal component in the PCR,[24] where the first estimated component is included as a variable in a regression model. There, we additionally have that the DGP is

$$w_t = \alpha w_{t-1} + \varepsilon_t^w, \varepsilon_t^w \sim N(0,1)$$

whereas the PCR is $w_t = \mu + \rho w_{t-1} + \beta pc_{t-1} + \varepsilon_t$, with pc_{t-1} denoting the first lag of the first principal component.

The results in Table 11.1 show that with larger values of α, the value of the first eigenvalue increases and that the fraction of spuriously significant principal components (because $\beta = 0$ gets rejected) in a PCR increases too. As before, the solution is simply to first fit

---

[24] https://en.wikipedia.org/wiki/Principal_component_regression.

univariate time series models to the variables, and then continue with PCA with the white noise residuals.

11.10 RIDGE REGRESSION

In Chapter 4, we discussed model selection and the various strategies one may follow. These approaches were all based on (sequences of) statistical tests. One may, however, also consider methods that do not involve statistical tests but address the size of the estimated parameters.

A popular technique that goes back a long way is ridge regression.[25] Recently it received revived attention for the practical cases where we wish to include many regressors in our model. This method seeks to estimate parameters and to select variables in one go.

Consider the regression model for y_i with explanatory variables $x_{i,j}$, that is,

$$y_i = \alpha + \sum_{j=1}^{k} \beta_j x_{i,j} + \varepsilon_i$$

OLS seeks to minimize

$$\sum_{i=1}^{n} \left(y_i - a - \sum_{j=1}^{k} b_j x_{i,j} \right)^2$$

In ridge regression we seek to minimize

$$\sum_{i=1}^{n} \left(y_i - a - \sum_{j=1}^{k} b_j x_{i,j} \right)^2 + \lambda \sum_{j=1}^{k} b_j^2$$

There is a penalty on the size of the parameters β_j. The parameter to be selected is $\lambda > 0$.

11.11 LASSO

A more recent updated version of ridge regression with the name lasso,[26] which is an acronym for Least Absolute Shrinkage and Selection Operator, seeks to minimize

[25] Arthur E. Hoerl and Robert W. Kennard (1970), Ridge regression: Biased estimation for nonorthogonal problems, *Technometrics*, 12 (1), 55–67.

[26] Robert Tibshirani (1996), Regression shrinkage and selection via the lasso, *Journal of the Royal Statistical Society Series B (methodological)*, 58 (1), 267–288.

$$\sum_{i=1}^{n} \left(y_i - a - \sum_{j=1}^{k} b_j x_{i,j} \right)^2 + \lambda \sum_{j=1}^{k} |b_j|$$

Here not the squares of the parameters, but their absolute values are at stake. There is no evidence that one method, ridge, or lasso, is better than the other. Lasso seems to work well when there is a small number of large parameters, and the remaining parameters are indeed close to zero. Ridge regression appears to work well with many large parameters (of about the same size). For both methods, we often use cross-validation to see which method is best in a practical setting.

11.12 ELASTIC NET

Yet another method is elastic net.[27] This is proposed as a weighted combination of the two. With the elastic net method we seek to minimize

$$\sum_{i=1}^{n} \left(y_i - a - \sum_{j=1}^{k} b_j x_{i,j} \right)^2 + \lambda \left(\alpha \sum_{j=1}^{k} |b_j| + (1-\alpha) \sum_{j=1}^{k} b_j^2 \right)$$

Note that this involves another "tuning" parameter α.

With more data come more choice options. It is important that all these choices are reported. And sometimes the empirical results depend crucially on the chosen configurations. It is then useful to repeat the analysis and average or combine the outcomes.[28]

To give an impression of the kind of choices one needs to make, have a look at Figure 11.7. It contains the diverse options in EViews (version 12), when you want to use ridge, lasso, or elastic net.

Let us see how things can matter in practice. Let us go back to the annual real GDP growth rates in Africa, as these were depicted in Figure 4.1. And suppose we are interested in predicting the growth

---

[27] Hui Zou, and Trevor Hastie (2005), Regularization and variable selection via the elastic net, *Journal of the Royal Statistical Society Series B*, 67 (2), 301–320.

[28] In weather forecasting, people often rely on so-called ensemble methods, where various forecasts are included. See, for example, Tim N. Palmer (2002), The economic value of ensemble forecasts as a tool for risk management: From days to decades, *Quarterly Journal of the Royal Meteorological Society*, 128 (581), 747–774.

penalty=arg (default="el")	Type of threshold estimation: "el" (elastic net), "ridge" (ridge), "lasso" (LASSO).
alpha=arg (default=".5")	Value of the mixing parameter. Must be a value between zero and one.
lambda=arg	Value of the penalty parameter. Can be a single number, list of space-delimited numbers, a workfile series object, or left blank for an EViews-supplied list (default). Values must be zero or greater.
xtrans=arg (default="none")	Transformation of the regressor variables: "none" (none), "L1" (L1), "L2" (L2), "stdsmpl" (sample standard deviation), "stdpop" (population standard deviation), "minmax" (min-max).
lambdaratio=arg (default=0.0001)	Ratio of minimum to maximum lambda for EViews-supplied list.
nlambdas=arg (default=100)	Number of lambas for EViews-supplied list.
maxit=integer	Maximum number of iterations.
conv=scalar	Set convergence criterion. The criterion is based upon the maximum of the percentage changes in the scaled estimates. The criterion will be set to the nearest value between 1e-24 and 0.2.
showopts / −showopts	[Do / do not] display the starting coefficient values and estimation options in the rotation output.
prompt	Force the dialog to appear from within a program.
p	Print basic estimation results.
cvmathod=arg (default="kfold_cv")	Cross-validation method: "kfold" (k-fold), "shuffle" (shuffle), "leavepout" (leave p out), "leave1out" (leave one out).
cvmeasure=arg (default="mse")	Error measurement from cross-validation: "mse" (mean-squared error), "mae" (mean absolute error), "r2" (r-squared).
training=arg (default=0.8)	Proportion of data or number of data points in training set for shuffle method.
test=arg (default="mse")	Proportion of data or number of data points in test set for shuffle method.
nreps=arg (default=1)	Number of shuffle method repetitions.
nfolds=arg (default=5)	Number of folds for k-fold method.
leaveout=arg (default=2)	Number of data points left out for leave p out method.
seed=positive_ integer from 0 to 2,147,483,647	Seed the random number generator. If not specified, EViews will seed random number generator with a single integer draw from the default global random number generator.
rnd=arg (default="kn" or method previously set using rndseed	Type of random number generator: improved Knuth generator ("kn"), improved Mersenne Twister ("mt"), Knuth's (1997) lagged Fibonacci generator used in EViews 4 ("kn4") L'Ecuyer's (1999) combined multiple recursive generator ("le"), Matsumoto and Nishimura's (1998) Mersenne Twister used in EViews 4 ("mt4").[29]

FIGURE 11.7 Options in Eviews for Lasso, Ridge and Elastic Net.
Source: Eviews, version 11

[29] See the manual of the program Eviews.

Table 11.2 *Outcome of Elastic Net analysis*

Dependent Variable: KENYAP1
Method: Elastic Net Regularization
Date: 11/18/21 Time: 11:40
Sample (adjusted): 1963 2015
Included observations: 53 after adjustments
Penalty type: Ridge (alpha = 0) *analytic
Lambda at minimum error: 1.363e+04
Regressor transformation: None
Cross-validation method: K-Fold (number of folds = 5), rng = kn, seed = 728325470
Selection measure: Mean Squared Error

Source: Author's calculations

Table 11.3 *Outcome of Elastic Net analysis, a few seconds later*

Dependent Variable: KENYAP1
Method: Elastic Net Regularization
Date: 11/18/21 Time: 11:40
Sample (adjusted): 1963 2015
Included observations: 53 after adjustments
Penalty type: Ridge (alpha = 0) *analytic
Lambda at minimum error: 1.496e+04
Regressor transformation: None
Cross-validation method: K-Fold (number of folds = 5), rng = kn, seed = 1886255342
Selection measure: Mean Squared Error

Source: Author's calculations

rate in Kenya, using the one-year lagged growth rates of all fifty-two countries. It is shown that cross-validation methods can work for time series if proper care is taken of any autocorrelation.[30]

Now, have a look at the following two prints of the output in Tables 11.2 and 11.3, obtained in the very same minute.

---

[30] Christophe Bergmeir, Rob J. Hyndman, and Bonsoo Koo (2018), A note on the validity of cross-validation for evaluating autoregressive time series prediction, *Computational Statistics and Data Analysis*, 120 (issue C), 70–83.

The chosen value of λ is different, owing to a different seed value. The output (not reported here) also delivers different values of the b_j parameters, and hence different forecasts will be made. It is therefore a promising idea to run these methods 1,000 times and average the estimated parameters. The practical use of ridge, lasso, and elastic net methods will benefit from combining inference results if you are interested in the β_j parameters, and from combining the forecasts if you are interested in out-of-sample forecasts. Just relying on a single run of the computations does not seem wise. And such a single run also does not allow someone else to reproduce your results.

11.13 WHAT DID WE LEARN?

For Big Data it holds even more that it is important to document all steps taken. Do not take available software and computer code for granted. Run simulations to check how they work. Create artificial data and try to recreate the DGP. Be aware of autocorrelation and of course other features of the data. Do not blindly adopt default options in programs, and combine the outcomes from various runs. And, of course, report every choice.

12 Algorithms

With Big Data comes algorithms to run many and involved computations. We cannot oversee all these data ourselves, so we need the help of algorithms that can make computations for us. We might label them under the header of Artificial Intelligence (AI), but this might give a suggestion that these algorithms can do things on their own. They can run massive computations, but they still need to be fed with data. And this feeding is usually done by us, humans – and we also choose the algorithms.

Often the algorithms are used to make predictions.[1] They can do that fast, and they can incorporate substantial amounts of observations. Many companies use algorithms to target current and potentially future customers with product offers: holidays, books, anything. As sending emails is cheap, any purchase of such a product means turnover and profit.

Accurate predictions from a sample do not necessarily mean that we also learn more about human behavior.[2] In fact, prediction via machine learning methods has similar caveats to what is called "null hypothesis significance testing." Good predictions do not automatically involve good explanations.[3] Moreover, there is a

---

[1] A readable overview is given in Ajay Agrawal, Joshua Gans, and Avi Goldfarb (2018), *Prediction Machines*, Boston, MA: Harvard Business School Publishing. A more technical but highly informative book is Bradley Efron and Trevor Hastie (2016), *Computer Age Statistical Inference*, Cambridge: Cambridge University Press.

[2] See Jessica Hullman, Sayash Kapoor, Priyanka Nanayakkara, Andrew Gelman, and Arvind Narayanan (2022), The worst of both worlds: A comparative analysis of errors in learning from data in psychology and machine learning, arXiv:2203.06498v8.

[3] See Jake M. Hofman, Duncan J. Watts, Susan Athey, Filiz Garip, Thomas L. Griffiths, Jon Kleinberg, Helen Margetts, Sendhil Mullainathan, Matthew J. Salganik, Simine Vazire, Alessandro Vespignani, and Tal Yarkoni (2021), Integrating explanation and prediction in computational social science, *Nature* 595 (July 8, 2021), 181–188.

phenomenon called "leakage," which means that information that is not available at the time when predictions are finally made is used to train (create) algorithms.[4]

People make algorithms.[5] So, we should bear in mind that

> The rise of misinformation and disinformation keeps us up at night. No law or fancy new AI is going to solve the problem.[6]

And

> We just need to be reminded: Big data is not better; it's just bigger. And it certainly doesn't speak for itself.[7]

Yet also,

> The key is to learn what the machines are looking for.[8]

12.1   OUTLINE

This chapter will use a range of quotes and findings from the internet and the literature. The key premises, which will be illustrated with examples, are the following: Big Data requires the use of algorithms;[9] algorithms can create misleading information; algorithms can lead to destructive outcomes. But we should not forget that humans program algorithms.

What is it that Big Data allows us to do? Basically, we might create better forecasts of individual behavior because statistical models

---

[4] See, for an overview of its consequences, Sayash Kapoor and Arvind Narayanan (2022), Leakage and the reproducibility crisis in ML-based science, arXiv: 2207.07048v1.

[5] Nada R. Sanders and John D. Wood (2019), *The Humachine: Humankind, Machines, and the Future of Enterprise*, London: Routledge.

[6] Carl T. Bergstrom and Jevin D. West (2020), *Calling Bullshit*, New York: Random House, page 286.

[7] Bergstrom and West, *Calling Bullshit*, page 205, footnote 6.

[8] Cathy O'Neil (2017), *Weapons of Math Destruction*, London: Penguin Random House, page 115, footnote 8.

[9] Thomas Davenport, Abhijit Guha, Dhruv Grewal, and Timna Bressgott (2020), How artificial intelligence will change the future of marketing, *Journal of the Academy of Marketing Science*, 48 (1), 24–42.

benefit from more variation in the data, from the design of subtler links between variables (forget about linear regression and move to very flexible forms such as an artificial neural network, as we saw in Chapter 11), and from the possibility that latent variables in models (attitudes, beliefs, awareness) can be included. We do not need to observe you personally: We can match your behavior with people who did similar things, and then we make you an offer. Somewhere in the world there are individuals who behave like you. Therefore, you get offers for books, travel, music, hotels, whatever, if we just apply a marketing perspective.

Can we easily manage Big Data? No, quite often we cannot. Running a regression on various variables is easy, but finding structures in millions of trips made by train passengers, to see if there are some clusters of people behaving similarly, is difficult to do by hand. What we need are fast, fast algorithms, and clever data storage and retrieval procedures.

That everything seems to go fast: Is that science fiction? Not really, as we can see from the following:

Wikipedia says

> The May 6, 2010 Flash Crash also known as The Crash of 2:45, the 2010 Flash Crash, or simply the Flash Crash, was a United States stock market crash on Thursday May 6, 2010 in which the Dow Jones Industrial Average plunged about 1000 points (about 9%) only to recover those losses within minutes. It was the second largest point swing, 1,010.14 points, and the biggest one-day point decline, 998.5 points, on an intraday basis in Dow Jones Industrial Average history.[10]

The key number in this short text is 2:45. This means that a financial crash can last for just a single minute. In 1987 we had Black Monday, a full day with a financial crash. Little over two decades later, a financial crash takes only a minute. One reason for this is

---

[10] https://en.wikipedia.org/wiki/2010_flash_crash.

that many financial transactions on stock markets are not made by people, but by algorithms.

Of course, we have not yet gone as far as the following – to quote from the movie *Terminator 2* (1991):

> In three years, Cyberdyne will become the largest supplier of military computer systems. All stealth bombers are upgraded with Cyberdyne computers, becoming fully unmanned. Afterwards, they fly with a perfect operational record. The Skynet Funding Bill is passed. The system goes online August 4th, 1997. Human decisions are removed from strategic defence. Skynet begins to learn at a geometric rate. It becomes self-aware at 2:14 a.m. Eastern time, August 29th. *In a panic, they try to pull the plug* [emphasis added].

The suggestion here is that in the future humans will be too late to halt the machines. Things have not progressed so far just yet.

To understand a bit more about how algorithms work, consider the following clustering technique, called K means clustering, which is very often used.[11] Suppose there are N data points, and you want to put them in K clusters. Let us start with $N = 6$ and $K = 2$. Consider the six points

$$1 \quad 2 \quad 3 \qquad\qquad\qquad 6 \quad 7 \quad 8$$

which are already arranged such that we immediately see two clusters of numbers. A first cluster is 1, 2, and 3 and a second cluster is 6, 7, and 8. The means of the numbers in the two clusters are 2 and 7. The distances to the mean in the first cluster are $(1-2)^2 + (3-2)^2$ is 2 and for the second cluster $(6-7)^2 + (8-7)^2$ is also 2. The total sum of the distances is $2 + 2 = 4$. It is easy to see that any other set of clusters with each three observations other than cluster 1, 2, and 3 and cluster 6, 7, and 8 would have given a larger total sum of distances.

---

[11] Google Scholar gives millions of hits for "K means clustering."

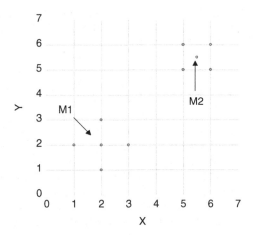

Let us move towards two dimensions and look at $N = 8$ points in a two-dimensional space, as they are depicted in Figure 12.1. There are two midpoints M1 and M2.

The distances to M1 in cluster 1 are all 1, whereas the distances for the second cluster points to M2 are $\frac{1}{2}\sqrt{2}$. The total sum of distances is $4 + 2\sqrt{2}$. Shorter distances in case of other clusters with each four data points cannot be obtained.

These computations are of course quite simple and can be done by hand. In the case of real data, we need an algorithm to quickly run all computations to find the midpoints via nonlinear optimization, for $K = 2$, $K = 3$ or any value of K, and for any number of observations N. Using cross-validation, one can seek an optimal (in terms of a preset criterion) value of K. One can also randomize the starting point, that is, choose which variable we start with.

K means clustering can be done for many more dimensions. Note, however, from the two illustrations that the numbers and the points in Figure 12.1 were given. We ourselves gave the relevant information to the clustering method. Now think of a database of an insurance firm, a bank, a travel agency, or a tax office. And think of the availability of data such as

ID	Age	Gender	Education	Income	....	Tax paid last time
1						
2						
3						
4						
5						
:						
N						

When N becomes large and the number of dimensions, which are the M variables observed, or the number of columns in your database too, then the method of K means clustering becomes time consuming, but is still doable when we make some intermediate choices, for example the minimum size of the clusters. There are also stopping rules for the number of clusters K. Research in this area in part concerns the design of fast algorithms to detect the clusters.

But, most importantly for the discussion in this chapter, is that the columns with the data are provided by a company or a tax office. Consider, for example, the variable "Tax paid last time." If an algorithm does not get fed with this variable, it is not going to ask for it. In other words, a key feature here is that data are provided to the algorithm by a person. The algorithm will classify people into categories related to the paid tax. If that variable is not in the database, the algorithm cannot use it.

This notion is important in what follows. Here is a quote from a report by Amnesty International, which deals with the Netherlands Tax Office, and the use of a model to classify individuals and their risk scores:

> The risk classification model was developed by comparing historic examples of correct and incorrect applications. In practice, this meant that the more an incoming application resembled an application that had previously been classified as inaccurate, the higher the risk score assigned to that incoming

application. The system selected applications with the highest risk scores for manual review by a civil servant. The civil servant in turn had the power to label an application as fraudulent. The civil servant, however, was given no information as to why the system had given the application a high-risk score for inaccuracy.

And:

The nationality of the applicant was used to determine whether that person was a Dutch citizen. "Dutch citizenship: yes/no" was used as a parameter in the risk classification model for assessing the risk of inaccurate applications.

Note, this parameter was not added by an algorithm, as a person provided it.

The Amnesty International report continues:

For example, after suspicions of irregularities and fraud committed by some people with roots or links to a particular country, civil servants searched for other people who had those nationalities by querying their databases, and subsequently retrieved additional information regarding *all* applicants with that nationality. For example, a fraud alert concerning 120 to 150 individuals with Ghanaian nationality resulted in an investigation of *all* 6047 applicants with Ghanaian nationality.[12]

In Chapter 1 we see what this means. This is an example of harking, that is, hypothesizing after the results are known. If one finds an overrepresentation of a certain nationality, one could perhaps draw another random sample to see if such an overrepresentation occurs again. And if so, one can design a new study into the possible reasons for such an overrepresentation. Is it a different language? Or did the individuals have the same tax advisor?

---

[12] Amnesty International (2021), *Xenophobic machines*, London: Amnesty International PTD, all quotes taken from page 16.

The next example is also an example of something machines do not do by themselves.

The following quote is translated from Dutch.[13]

> In practice, the model came down to lower incomes, according to documents released earlier. Of the one thousand highest risk scores, no less than 82.3 percent had a household income of less than 20,000 euros per year. That is more than eleven times the average: of all applications, only 7.3 percent had a household income of less than 20,000 euros.
>
> Also striking is the remarkably high proportion of single parents selected for control: almost 90 percent.

Note that in part this could be due to various subsidies that lower income households receive.

Problematic outcomes from algorithms cannot fully be attributed to the algorithms. If we feed algorithms with inappropriate data, the algorithms work with these data, and they may end up with inappropriate results.

Here is an example of an AI tool created by Amazon that discriminates against women.

> In 2015, the team realized that its creation was biased in favor of men when it came to hiring technical talent, like software developers. The problem was that they trained their machine learning algorithms to look for prospects by recognizing terms that had popped up on the resumes of past job applicants—and because of the tech world's well-known gender imbalance, those past hopefuls tended to be men.
>
> In effect, Amazon's system taught itself that male candidates were preferable. It penalized resumes that included the word "women's," as in "women's chess club captain." And it

---

[13] RTL Nieuws Belastingdienst controleerde extra bij lage inkomens in jacht op fraude, November 22, 2021, 22:59. www.rtlnieuws.nl/nieuws/nederland/artikel/5268918/toeslagenaffaire-inkomen-van-huffelen-risicoselectie.

downgraded graduates of two all-women's colleges, Reuters reported.[14]

The key phrase here is "that they trained their machine learning algorithms .... those past hopefuls tended to be men." If you hired men in the past, then this can become a decisive criterion in the future.

If the data available on the internet are biased, and if you feed your algorithms with these data, the algorithms automatically become biased too. Look here:

> We find that state-of-the-art unsupervised models trained on ImageNet, a popular benchmark image dataset curated from internet images, automatically learn racial, gender, and intersectional biases. We replicate 8 previously documented human biases from social psychology, from the innocuous, as with insects and flowers, to the potentially harmful, as with race and gender. Our results closely match three hypotheses about intersectional bias from social psychology. For the first time in unsupervised computer vision, we also quantify implicit human biases about weight, disabilities, and several ethnicities. When compared with statistical patterns in online image datasets, our findings suggest that machine learning models can automatically learn bias from the way people are stereotypically portrayed on the web.[15]

Now, you may have heard of a person called Lombroso. Wikipedia says that "Lombroso's theory of anthropological criminology essentially stated that criminality was inherited, and that someone 'born criminal' could be identified by physical (congenital) defects, which

---

[14] https://slate.com/business/2018/10/amazon-artificial-intelligence-hiring-discrimination-women.html.

[15] Ryan Steed and Aylin Caliskan (2021), Image representations learned with unsupervised pre-training contain human-like biases, FAccT '21: Proceedings of the 2021 ACM Conference on Fairness, Accountability, and Transparency, March 2021, Pages 701–713, https://doi.org/10.1145/3442188.3445932, www.theguardian.com/commentisfree/2021/feb/03/what-a-picture-of-alexandria-ocasio-cortez-in-a-bikini-tells-us-about-the-disturbing-future-of-ai.

confirmed a criminal as savage or atavistic."[16] In other words, you can recognize a criminal from his or her face. This was at the end of the nineteenth century, but how about the following abstract of a very recent study?

> We show that faces contain much more information about sexual orientation than can be perceived or interpreted by the human brain. We used deep neural networks to extract features from 35,326 facial images. These features were entered into a logistic regression aimed at classifying sexual orientation. Given a single facial image, a classifier could correctly distinguish between gay and heterosexual men in 81% of cases, and in 71% of cases for women. Human judges achieved much lower accuracy: 61% for men and 54% for women. The accuracy of the algorithm increased to 91% and 83%, respectively, given five facial images per person. Facial features employed by the classifier included both fixed (e.g., nose shape) and transient facial features (e.g., grooming style). Consistent with the prenatal hormone theory of sexual orientation, gay men and women tended to have gender-atypical facial morphology, expression, and grooming styles. Prediction models aimed at gender alone allowed for detecting gay males with 57% accuracy and gay females with 58% accuracy. Those findings advance our understanding of the origins of sexual orientation and the limits of human perception. Additionally, given that companies and governments are increasingly using computer vision algorithms to detect people's intimate traits, our findings expose a threat to the privacy and safety of gay men and women.[17]

This article was published in a journal with a remarkably high Article Influence Score: 4.542.

---

[16] https://en.wikipedia.org/wiki/Cesare_Lombroso.

[17] Yilun Wang and Michal Kosinski (2018), Deep neural networks are more accurate than humans at detecting sexual orientation from facial images, *Journal of Personality and Social Psychology*, 114 (2), 246–257.

12.2 WHAT TO DO?

We need to develop ethical guidelines for AI. Some attempts are already around,[18] but perhaps more is needed to arrive at a well-established list, which could be a list such as that addressed in Chapter 1 with reference to ethical guidelines. And there are also recommendations by the World Economic Forum (These were taken from their website in 2022):

1. **Active Inclusion:** the development and design of machine learning applications must actively seek a diversity of input, especially of the norms and values of specific populations affected by the output of AI systems
2. **Fairness:** People involved in conceptualizing, developing, and implementing machine learning systems should consider which definition of fairness best applies to their context and application, and prioritize it in the architecture of the machine learning system and its evaluation metrics
3. **Right to Understanding:** Involvement of machine learning systems in decision-making that affects individual rights must be disclosed, and the systems must be able to provide an explanation of their decision-making that is understandable to end users and reviewable by a competent human authority. Where this is impossible and rights are at stake, leaders in the design, deployment, and regulation of machine learning technology must question whether or not it should be used
4. **Access to Redress:** Leaders, designers, and developers of machine learning systems are responsible for identifying the potential negative human rights impacts of their systems. They must make visible avenues for redress for those affected by disparate impacts and establish processes for the timely redress of any discriminatory outputs.[19]

12.3 WHAT DID WE LEARN?

For us, econometricians, the most important lesson is well put as follows: "How do we start to regulate the mathematical models that

---

[18] Thilo Hagendorff (2020), The ethics of AI ethics: An evaluation of guidelines, *Minds and Machines*, 30, 99–120.
[19] www.weforum.org/whitepapers/how-to-prevent-discriminatory-outcomes-in-machine-learning/, https://en.wikipedia.org/wiki/Machine_ethics.

run more and more of our lives? I would suggest that the process begin [*sic*] with the modelers themselves."[20]

12.4 EPILOGUE

You may find the following an interesting story to read.

> In December 2020, her employment with Google as technical co-lead of the Ethical Artificial Intelligence Team ended after higher Google managers asked her to either withdraw an as-yet-unpublished paper, or remove the names of all the Google employees from that paper (that is, five of the six coauthors, leaving Emily M. Bender). She requested to know the names and reasons of everyone who made that decision and said she would work with Google on an employment end date after an appropriate amount of time if not provided with that information. Google did not meet her request and terminated her employment immediately, saying they accepted her resignation. Google stated that the paper in question, titled "On the Dangers of Stochastic Parrots: Can Language Models Be Too Big?,"[21] ignored recent research that showed methods of mitigating the bias in those systems. Her departure caused public controversy.[22]

---

[20] O'Neil, *Weapons of Math Destruction*, page 205.

[21] https://dl.acm.org/doi/10.1145/3442188.3445922. FAccT '21: Proceedings of the 2021 ACM Conference on Fairness, Accountability, and Transparency, March 2021, Pages 610–623, https://doi.org/10.1145/3442188.3445922.

[22] https://en.wikipedia.org/wiki/Timnit_Gebru.

Conclusion

This last chapter summarizes most of the material in this book in a range of concluding statements. It provides a summary of the lessons learned. These can be viewed as guidelines for research practice.

We start with the recommendation to try to replicate earlier studies. Contact the authors, ask for the data, or retrieve the data from a publicly available database, use the same methods of analysis, and use the same estimation methods. You may also want to collect experimental data again and use the same methods. This is now often done in some disciplines such as social psychology and economics.[1] You, as a researcher, should also allow people to replicate your studies.

Detected scientific misconduct sometimes shows that people "overdo it" when they misbehave. Knowledge of statistical methods and techniques is useful when detecting scientific misconduct.

WHEN CERTAIN DATAPOINTS ARE INFLUENTIAL

Anyone can make mistakes. And mistakes must be admitted and resolved. We have learned that influential observations can happen, do happen, and can happen quite frequently. Influential observations are not always visually obvious. For a two-variable model, it can be visualized, but when the number of regressors increases, graphs will

---

[1] Interesting recent research shows that handing out the same database and the same research question to different teams results in different outcomes: see Albert J. Menkveld, Anna Dreber, Felix Holzmeister, Juergen Huber, Magnus Johannesson, Michael Kirchler, Sebastian Neusüss, Michael Razen, Utz Weitzel, and many others (2021), Non-standard errors, Tinbergen Institute Discussion Paper, TI 2021-102/IV, https://papers.ssrn.com/sol3/papers.cfm?abstract_id=3981597, "Our working definition of nonstandard errors is the standard deviation across researchers for the results they report when independently testing the same hypotheses on the same sample".

not help much. Diagnostic tests are needed, and these are easy to compute and easy to interpret.

It is best to perform analysis on influential observations based on model estimation results. That implies that you do not remove data prior to model building.

Once you have found such influential observations, make explicit how you dealt with them. You can replace the observations by others, new-to-compute, values, in your analysis (not in the raw database) or you can delete them.

WHEN THERE ARE MORE MODELS TO CHOOSE FROM

Trying to end up with one single final model has all kinds of drawbacks. You need various diagnostic tests, and sometimes these tests do not have much power (such as tests for unit roots). Moreover, sequential strategies to arrive at a single final model can lead to quite different final models. Data mining has its downsides. Multiple testing has consequences for the reliability of the last round t values and p values.

Hence, it seems better to maintain various models, for inference and for forecasting. We could, for example, estimate the average loss in airline revenues owing to 9/11 based on forecasts from three distinct models. Forecasts can also be based on the combination of forecasts.

ON DATA COLLECTION

Measurement errors happen, and like other features of the data such as simultaneity, such errors can require alternative estimation methods, alternative to simple OLS. This does not have to be dramatic, but if data collection makes modeling more complicated, one may want to spend more effort in collecting better data. A plea for better research designs is well made,[2] and exactly laying out how the data were collected is important.

---

[2] A recent example of meticulous and accurate data collection is given in Michael Peters (2022), Market size and spatial growth – Evidence from Germany's post-war population expulsions, *Econometrica*, 90 (5), 2357–2396, https://doi.org/10.3982/ECTA18002.

WHEN DATA ARE MISSING

Data can be missing, and there are several reasons for that. We should be aware that interpolation has consequences and that we should record how interpolation took place.

We should report on how missing data were managed either by using an adapted estimation method or by constructing another model, after aggregation.

Note also that missing data can occur on purpose, to facilitate data collection and data analysis. There is no need to collect a few $y_i = 1$ observations and contrast these with millions of $y_i = 0$ observations. Furthermore, models for temporally aggregated data can still be informative about parameters in a higher frequency process. The consequence of aggregation is that models and estimation methods can (and must) be adapted.

WHEN SPURIOUS RESULTS MAY APPEAR

Spurious relations can easily appear. Better models and, for example, properly taking care of autocorrelation can prevent spurious results. We have seen that cohort studies are particularly prone to spurious findings (when autocorrelation is neglected).

For time series data it holds that low Durbin Watson values and exceptionally large t values are signs of spuriousness.

Anyway, with increasing numbers of regressors spurious results can also appear (owing to data mining). This is the downside of including lots of regressors on the right-hand side of your model to explain or predict a dependent variable.

WHEN DATA TELL DIFFERENT STORIES

We have seen for key macroeconomic variables such as inflation and unemployment that outliers, different regimes, and ARCH can capture similar data features. This implies that we must be specific what the target of our research is. Do we want to describe different regimes? Do we want to make outliers less influential in our forecasting model? Do we want to allow for time-varying prediction intervals? Or do we want to propose a model that most accurately describes the data?

We have learned that ignoring level shifts suggests the presence of unit roots. On the other hand, imposing various unit roots makes forecasts robust to changes in trends. And we have learned that ignoring additive outliers points us in the wrong direction in subsequent modeling.

HONESTY ABOUT FORECASTS

A key message when it comes to out-of-sample forecasting is that we should report prediction intervals. This allows us and our advisees to understand the limits to predictability. It is best to report forecasts from models with and without imposing unit roots. And, again, it is commendable to work with combined forecasts.

We could show forecasts for a range of samples where each time the sample starts at another moment in time. We should better present forecasts for models with trends and breaks, as we have seen that longer-term point forecasts can be quite different.

In sum, we should be honest about the limits to predictability.

WHEN THERE ARE MORE FORECASTS

Combined forecasts are useful and often successful. It is not the way in which experts agree in their judgment, but it is the way in which they do not agree that can make the average forecast work well.

WHEN THERE ARE (TOO) MANY DATA

For Big Data it holds even more that we should document all steps taken and all choices made. We should not take available software or the outcomes of machine learning methods for granted. With available data, we can always run simulations to check how these tools work. To examine what certain methods do, prior to incorporating these in analysis, we can create artificial data and then try to recreate the data generating process.

We should not blindly adopt default options in programs, and should rather try variants. If computations are based on seed starting values, then we should run the computations many times and take an average of the outcomes. Without the seed, we cannot definitively replicate outcomes. If we run 100 trials and take averages, someone else's results can come closer to our results.

WHEN IT BECOMES (TOO) MUCH FOR HUMANS

We have learned that algorithms can create misleading information, and that they can lead to destructive outcomes. We should not forget, though, that humans program those algorithms, and that they feed information to algorithms. So yes, algorithms discriminate, for example by allocating people into clusters, but the variables that are used to cluster are delivered by humans.

FINALLY

When we give advice as an econometrician, we must report all choices that we have made (if at all possible). And these choices concern the data, the sample, the method, and more.

In fact, we should quite literally report everything. And this constitutes ethics in econometrics.

EPILOGUE: THIS IS WHAT YOU DO NOT WANT!

This article retracts the following:
Adriano A. Rampini, S. Viswanathan, Guillaume Vuillemey, "Risk Management in Financial Institutions"

https://doi.org/10.1111/jofi.12868
First published: December 12, 2019
The authors hereby retract the above article, published in print in the April 2020 issue of *The Journal of Finance*. A replication study finds that the replication code provided in

the supplementary information section of the article does not reproduce some of the central findings reported in the article. Upon reexamination of the work, the authors confirmed that the replication code does not fully reproduce the published results and were unable to provide revised code that does. Therefore, the authors conclude that the published results are not reliable and that the responsible course of action is to retract the article and return the *Brattle Group Distinguished Paper Prize* that the article received. The authors deeply regret the damage this caused to the journal and the scholarly community. The specific contributions of the authors to the article were as follows: the first and second author provided the theoretical hypothesis; all three authors jointly designed the empirical approach and identification strategy; the third author constructed and handled the data, implemented the empirical analysis, and provided the empirical results as well as the replication data and code. The third author states that the original data and code that produced the published results were lost. The first and second author were not notified of the loss of the original data and code at the time it occurred and had no prior knowledge of the issues with the replication data and code provided to the journal.[3]

---

[3] https://onlinelibrary.wiley.com/doi/10.1111/jofi.13064.

Index

additive outlier, 59–60, 80–81, 187, 192–195, 199, 201, 284
advice, xvii, 1, 3–5, 15, 32, 71, 90, 236, 285
advisor, 275
aggregation, 121, 124, 144, 154, 157–159, 180, 182, 248, 252, 259–260, 283
Anscombe's quartet, 61
ARCH, 187, 193, 195, 197, 209, 283
attrition, 140, 142, 150, 180
autocorrelation, 104, 113, 131, 144–148, 157, 163, 180–184, 223, 225, 262, 267–268, 283

Bayesian forecast combination, 107
Benford's law, 38–39

causality, 27, 30, 162
choices, xvii, 2–3, 5, 7, 12, 23, 32, 88–89, 113, 158–159, 170, 221, 232, 248–249, 252, 254, 258–259, 261, 265, 274, 284–285
cohort studies, 6, 182, 283
cointegration, 60, 90, 97–98, 100–101, 103, 174, 176, 179
configurations, 3, 7, 90, 101, 165, 181, 265
consequences, 1–2, 5, 12, 23, 32, 67, 83, 121, 140, 144, 154–155, 159, 163, 211, 224, 239, 270, 282–283
correlation, 27, 30, 56–57, 86, 91–92, 114, 116, 124, 128, 133–134, 138, 144, 151, 157, 161–162, 164, 167–168, 179, 184–185, 242
counterfactual exercise, 102
cross-validation, 96, 259, 262, 265, 267, 273

data mining, 89–92, 132, 184, 283
detection of influential observations, 54, 57, 61, 64, 68–70, 73, 82
diagnostic tests, 82, 89, 92, 104, 112, 114, 122, 124, 130–131, 282
Durbin Watson test, 166, 168–169, 171–172, 178

error correction model, 74, 76–77, 98, 170, 176–178
ethical guidelines for statistical practice, 11, 14, 31, 279

fake data, 4, 51
forecast intervals, 7, 192, 210, 220, 229

good research practice, 4, 11
growth curves, 109, 232, 237–239

harking, 11, 15, 24–25, 91, 129, 275

influence statistics, 73, 78, 84, 135, 198, 202
infrastructure projects, 211, 213–214, 231
instrumental variables, 5, 115–116
interpolation, 6, 140, 144–147, 159, 167–169, 172, 283

Koyck model, 155–156, 158

limits to predictability, 6, 211–212, 231, 284

measurement error, xvii, 5, 113–115, 118, 120, 126
measuring persistence, 147–148
MIDAS model, 158–159
missing at random, 143
missing completely at random, 143
missing not at random, 143
misspecification, 114, 163–164
model selection, 5, 88, 97, 110, 264
multicollinearity, 5, 71, 113, 124–129, 132, 138
multiple testing, 15, 26, 31, 180

nonlinearity, 6, 187, 201–202

Olympic Games, 16, 211–213, 215, 235
outlier at forecast origin, 61, 78, 80–81
outlier diagnostics, 68, 70

Printed in the United States
by Baker & Taylor Publisher Services